Resonances against Fascism

SUNY series, Humanities to the Rescue
—————
David R. Castillo, editor

Resonances against Fascism

Modernist and Avant-Garde Sounds
from Kurt Weill to Black Lives Matter

Edited by

LAURA CHIESA

Cover design by Julian Montague

Published by State University of New York Press, Albany

© 2024 State University of New York

All rights reserved

Printed in the United States of America

No part of this book may be used or reproduced in any manner whatsoever without written permission. No part of this book may be stored in a retrieval system or transmitted in any form or by any means including electronic, electrostatic, magnetic tape, mechanical, photocopying, recording, or otherwise without the prior permission in writing of the publisher.

For information, contact State University of New York Press, Albany, NY
www.sunypress.edu

Library of Congress Cataloging-in-Publication Data

Name: Chiesa, Laura, [date], editor.
Title: Resonances against fascism : modernist and avant-garde sounds from Kurt Weill to Black Lives Matter / edited by Laura Chiesa.
Description: Albany : State University of New York Press, [2024]. | Series: Humanities to the rescue | Includes bibliographical references and index.
Identifiers: LCCN 2023019235 | ISBN 9781438496290 (hardcover : alk. paper) | ISBN 9781438496313 (ebook) | ISBN 9781438496306 (pbk. : alk. paper)
Subjects: LCSH: Fascism and music. | Sound—Political aspects. | Sound (Philosophy) | Weill, Kurt, 1900–1950—Criticism and interpretation. | Music—20th century—History and criticism. | Modernism (Music) | Avant-garde (Aesthetics)
Classification: LCC ML3916 .R468 2024 | DDC 306.4/842—dc23/eng/20230523
LC record available at https://lccn.loc.gov/2023019235

10 9 8 7 6 5 4 3 2 1

Contents

Acknowledgments   vii

Introduction
Resonant Listening: Sound and Music to the Rescue   1
    Laura Chiesa

Chapter 1
Political (Effort/Exhaustion)   15
    James Currie

Chapter 2
"[C]ounting Your Heads / As I'm Making the Beds":
Piratesthetics, Weill-Brecht to Simone   35
    Jacques Lezra

Chapter 3
Sonic Ordeals: Music, Torture, and *The New Orpheus*   51
    Peter Szendy

Chapter 4
What Makes Weill Weill?   65
    Kim H. Kowalke

Chapter 5
A Walk on the Weill Side: Musical Theater and Rock Music
in the 1960s   85
    William Solomon

Chapter 6
Marguerite Duras's Musical Return of the Real 113
    Fernanda Negrete

Chapter 7
Outside In: Chorus and Clearing in the Time of Pandemic
and Protest 143
    Julie Beth Napolin

Afterword
Sounding Silence, Sounding Thought 167
    Krzysztof Ziarek

Contributors 177

Index 181

Acknowledgments

During its second year, Humanities to the Rescue—an ongoing public humanities project sponsored by the Humanities Institute at the University at Buffalo, State University of New York—joined in a yearlong series of events catalyzed by "Kurt Weill Festival: A Story of Immigration." This festival was a creative partnership that united the University at Buffalo's College of Arts and Sciences and the Buffalo Philharmonic Orchestra in a celebration of Weill's legacy; it included cabaret performances, exhibits, lectures, master classes, and concerts in which other colleges and universities in the city participated.

The Humanities Institute's Modernisms Research Workshop, which Damien Keane and I lead, connected to the festival by designating "Sounds" as its theme for the 2018–2019 academic year. In addition, I organized a one-day Modernisms symposium, "Sounds: Avant-Garde, Modernism, and Fascism," that dovetailed perfectly both with the Kurt Weill Festival and with other Humanities to the Rescue events, such as the keynote address by the artist, journalist, and writer Molly Crabapple. In this volume with a slightly modified title are collected most of the papers delivered at the symposium by invited speakers and faculty from the University at Buffalo, who intervened through a multiplicity of perspectives, as cultural critics rather than as historians of fascism(s), and opened anew a dialogue that, starting from modernism and Kurt Weill's life and work, aimed at reading times closer to us if not simply the urgencies of today.

The yearlong series of events devoted to Weill was taken as the hinge for the one-day symposium, where the critical voices showcased exactly because of the multiplicity of their pitches—if the analogy doesn't seem too dissonant—a kaleidoscopic critical-auditory realm, in tune with what is termed "long modernism," as Krzysztof Ziarek later remarked to me.

Presented before a large audience in the Baird Recital Hall, a multipurpose performance space with excellent acoustics, the symposium, in the spirit of the festival, derived its multidimensional tempo and rhythms as much from the speakers' talks as from the live performances, the musical intermezzi that punctuated the day.

I want to thank the chair of the Department of Music at that time, professor, composer, and performer Jonathan Golove, who was a critical contact between the University at Buffalo's College of Arts and Sciences and the Buffalo Philharmonic Orchestra during the planning of the festival. Professor Golove not only made the Baird Recital Hall available but also organized the excellent program of intermezzi, working with faculty and students of the Department of Music. I am grateful not only for his own cello performance, but also for those of pianists Eric Huebner and Michael Serio, soprano Tiffany Du Mouchelle, violinist Shannon Reilly, cellist Conor Sullivan, and clarinetist Michael Tumiel. Other members of the faculty who contributed to the symposium also deserve our gratitude: Damien Keane, who along with me co-organized the Modernisms Research Workshop, Carine Mardorossian, Noam Pines, and Justin Read, and also Krzysztof Ziarek, who enthusiastically agreed to participate in the final roundtable and to write an afterword for this volume. The numerous and lively audience drawn from the university community deserves a round of applause too: I greatly appreciate the interest that University at Buffalo undergraduate and graduate students demonstrated in the symposium's topic and format.

Finally, I want to thank the Department of Romance Languages and Literatures, the Melodia Jones Chair, the College of Arts and Sciences, and Dean Robin Schulze for supporting the Humanities Institute, Professor David Castillo (director of the Humanities Institute at the time of the symposium) for supporting the symposium, and the Office of the Vice President for Research, which generously sponsors the Humanities to the Rescue book series.

Introduction

Resonant Listening: Sound and Music to the Rescue

LAURA CHIESA

res•o•nance |ˈrɛzənəns| ▸n. the quality in a sound of being deep, full, and reverberating: *the resonance of his voice.*

—Figurative the ability to evoke or suggest images, memories, and emotions: *the concepts lose their emotional resonance.*

—Physics the reinforcement or prolongation of sound by reflection from a surface or by the synchronous vibration of a neighboring object.

—From the New Oxford American Dictionary (2001)

At 5:32 p.m. on June 9, 2022, I checked news feeds on the online version of the *New York Times*, and I read one of the first of a long series of live updates about the presumed outcome of public hearings that were then just beginning: "Jan. 6 Hearings Will Put Trump at the Center of Plot that Resulted in Capitol Riot, Aides Say."[1] I was also drafting notes for this introduction to papers from a symposium—"Sounds: Avant-Garde, Modernism, and Fascism"—that considered the threshold between democracy and fascistic regimes and explored the relations between sound and music, in an expanded field of scholarship that points also at the tension between "hearing" and "listening," so the start of the "hearings" caught my attention and confronted me with a puzzle. The update from the *Times* preceded the live broadcast of the first of eight hearings planned by a United States House select committee whose aim was to investigate the attack on democracy at the United States Capitol and the Trump administration's inaction, misconduct, manipulation, and attempted overturning of election results that culminated in white supremacist violence. Hearings, in the plural, that show the extreme and complex ramifications of the more or less direct participation in criminal acts or at least certainly in the sick ideology and misinformation that subtends all that fueled the January 6 insurrection. Hearings, in the plural, brought forth by the committee's commendable work that I hope will have an effective and durable impact on the people and on the Department of Justice, so that the multiplicities of hearings will be followed, so to speak, by as many (if not more) acts of listening(s). And—to linger for just one more line in the auditory realm—it suffices, in order to measure the gravity of the time we live in, just to be silent to the silence that a part of the complex machine of the media-political-scape is maintaining and upholding in relation to the committee's findings.

When I first proposed the idea of the symposium four years ago, the wide spectrum indicated by the quite generic title was meant to allow for a critical dialogue between modernist and sound studies and the Kurt Weill Festival taking place in Buffalo (as mentioned in the acknowledgments), and one of the encouraged trajectories was to consider or compare the German composer-artist's production and time period with times closer to today. And, four years ago, alarming, self-interested interference in politics, and a demagogic, aggressive, toxic and intoxicated, racist, antidemocratic, and autocratic—if not simply fascistic—general political atmosphere had become a new daily concern for many, with not only resonances and consequences but also a network of alliances beyond the United States. The proposal for the symposium therefore aimed to resonate in dialogue with the uncountable alarmed voices arising from the general public, as well as from cultural critics and philosophers who were not necessarily experts in the history of fascism who were solicited to employ and think back at the term "fascism," and it is along this meridian of thought that the notion of fascism appears here. Philosophers such as Judith Butler responded with nonviolent modes of resistance to "the dangerous current trends of authoritarian, neo-Fascist rule,"[2] while Jean-Luc Nancy affirmed plainly that the "nature of fascism can be characterized as the inverse of democracy."[3] The historian Enzo Traverso opened his 2017 *The New Faces of Fascism* by affirming that "the world has not experienced a similar growth of the radical right since the 1930s,"[4] then aimed to detect how, in what he defines as a new regime of historicity that we have entered with the new century, the inheritance of classical fascism has been tinted with new elements not belonging to its tradition. Hence, Traverso's notion of *post-fascism* and his remark that "Trump is not threatening to make an army of black shirts (or brown shirts) march on Washington, for the simple reason that he does not have organised troops behind him" (24–25) seemed to urge vigilance, if not immediately when the book was published, then just a couple of years later. Cultural critic Alberto Toscano took another route that also intersects with some of the essays in this volume, intentionally avoiding a plain analogy with the 1930s to underscore "how viewing fascism through the prism of the Black radical tradition can redirect our contemporary debate in fruitful and important ways."[5]

Sound, for its part, as Veit Erlmann and Michael Bull affirmed in 2015 in the editorial for first issue of the *Journal of Sound Studies*, has emerged in the last two decades as a rich field of inquiry able to the provide potential relationalities among many established disciplines, and the editors pointed to the fact that literary scholars were also "beginning to examine the representation of sound in literature and, perhaps more importantly, how a new awareness of sound may alter our sense of literature as a whole."[6] In this respect, several recent single-authored monographs and volumes are, so to speak, auscultating literature, and modernist studies give a specific access to amplified auditory dimensions. Helen Groth, Julian Murphet, and Penelope Hone inquire, as they map out a synthetic constellation relating the scholarship of sound studies and modernist studies in their introduction to *Sounding Modernism*, "what it means to attend to the dynamics and aesthetics of sonic mediation in modern writing, acoustic and cinematic forms produced from the 1880s through the mid-twentieth century"; they direct attention to "literature's historically complex relationship to extra-literary sounds, and the identification of parallels and divergences with other modern media, such as the phonograph, radio and cinema."[7] Nevertheless, these editors access and direct the question through the filter of multiple recent scholarships that avoid positing the possibility of a clear-cut divide between premodern and modern soundscapes.

The essays collected here are interventions that, far from aligning with sound studies as a "problematic interdiscipline,"[8] critically break down silos of specialization and disciplinary fields, listening and manifesting the force of expansion as well as the force of interruption of music—and of sound more generally—for the humanities, in sync with the Humanities to the Rescue book series that aims—as imagined by the editor, David Castillo—to be a public humanities project dedicated to discussing the role of the arts and the humanities today.

To get back to Kurt Weill, the Italian composer Luciano Berio wrote a short, and hence intense, text on Weill that he titled in Italian "Kurt Weill il rivoluzionario" and in its original dispatch in English "Liebeslied for Weill." Berio considers Weill's musical theater a revolution. For Berio, Weill's modernity resides in "his constant search for the 'other' and 'elsewhere'—due not only to his conception of epic theater but also to the way in which he defines and puts to use his specific musical ingredients. Song is only one of these, but one of the most significant. . . . Songs can be instruments of revolution. And Weill's songs are indeed revolutionary, because they aimed above all at the listener rather than the consumer wanting to purchase escape."[9] Such a musical notion of revolution, so to speak, communicates with what Kim Kowalke—renowned scholar of the exiled German composer—affirms in this volume: in the attempt to rescue opera from its "splendid isolation," Weill was expanding its reach in "adapting popular idioms and song forms for serious dramatic purposes." Kurt Weill's itinerary and works, merging and crossing over several fields of intellectual endeavor (literature, theater, film, and music), his collaboration with Bertolt Brecht amid the musical and theatrical avant-gardes of the interwar period, his escape from Nazism in 1933 that set him on a transatlantic itinerary to the United States, and his legacy or analogous modernist or later musical practices, all partly propelled—to use a verb of avant-gardist tone, the symposium. Indeed, in "Political (Effort/Exhaustion)"—the first essay of this volume—James Currie reflects, in a preamble mimicking a soliloquy performed on a stage of our time, upon the term "fascism": if for several decades past it has seemed too broad a term, with the arrival of the Trump administration, two quite straightforward and simple ways of defining fascism—on the one hand, as an autocratic and dictatorial government, nationalist and racist, and, on the other, as a vague distaste for authority—seem to be losing their line of separation. It is from this development, Currie reflects, that his scholarly essay takes its tone and, marked by engagement, becomes "distracted by the past and irked by the present." The first three essays articulate their critical interdisciplinary crossing-over of the conceptual lexicon of sound through particular keywords that, being by no means celebratory in their access to music and sound, perform acts of comparative aesthetics.[10] Currie's keywords are "Effort/Exhaustion," and they give access to rethinking "work" and "labor" when the political and the aesthetic come into close proximity, reconceptualizing the audience-performance relationality. Currie establishes a trajectory that from modernist and avant-garde attempts to politicize artistic practices—in this case by Kurt Weill and Bertolt Brecht—arrives at a more forceful effort and effect by Nina Simone and her politicized performance practice during the civil rights era. Currie locates and interprets Simone's performance of "Mississippi Goddam" and her political strategies as part of a vast constellation of transhistorical modernist practices—autonomous but analogous—exactly to bypass the very idea that European historical avant-gardes have influenced the African American performances of the 1960s. If in such a constellation Currie explores the stylistic features of bebop music, it is exactly because, in a Marxian way, they transform and dislocate sounds enacting alternate positions of hearing, and with Simone's performance such a potential is radicalized. Jacques Lezra—in "'[C]ounting Your Heads / As I'm Making the Beds': Piratesthetics, Weill-Brecht to Simone"—draws a further trajectory navigating critical-aesthetical sea-changing routes that move, drifting among currents from Weill-Brecht's ballad "Seeräuber Jenny" to Simone's performance and on to Chico Buarque's Brazilian rewriting. Lezra's keywords, "pirate," "piracy," and "pirating," become affirmative idiomatic and singular critical-aesthetical hinges, whose portmanteau notion is that of piratesthetics; such singular aesthetics are found or, better, are active in the ballad itself, soliciting another key notion of Lezra's pirating performative interpretative lexicon: aesthetics outrage (of the self-commodifying figure of pirating). Lezra's interpretative tour de force, his piratesthetics, navigates while keeping in sight different critical currents, among them a rereading of critical theory, exemplary of Walter Benjamin's writing on Fascism and the Futurist avant-garde in which the aesthetic outrage pirates or, if you like, interrupts the symmetric circuitry of *fiat ars-pereat mundus* into *pereat ars-fiat mundus*, relaunching thereby a potential or possible radical force of the avant-gardes and of modernisms; it is by listening to and reading in translation the versions and transpositions of such a ballad starting from the 1728 *Beggar's Opera* that Lezra affirms that "Brecht, Weill, Hauptmann, Blitzstein, Simone, and Buarque's undoing of the aesthetic object makes it untranslatable too." It is through such a drifting, sovereign *untranslatability* as well as through Jenny's or Polly's revenge song that "piratically" Lezra proposes his ending note; this note is one though that still leaves open the question of the always-already-present arrival of political or eventually revolutionary subjectivity.

For his part, Peter Szendy opens "Sonic Ordeals: Music, Torture, and *The New Orpheus*" with a hypothesis gathered from *The New Orpheus*, an early Weill cantata inspired by a poem of the avant-garde French-German writer Iwan Goll: the cantata becomes a metonymy for the conditions of music today. In sketching a genealogy not of music but "of sound as a means of torture in the age of technological reproducibility," the essay clearly exceeds or diverts the reach of one of the main notions of the symposium's title—sound—and indeed Szendy's keywords are "torture" and "ordeal." Without touching the cantata but only pointing at how this New Orpheus succumbs to the new conditions for music-making with mechanical instruments, Szendy draws our attention to the bonds between interrogation techniques and technological means of composing, recording, and reproduction. Atrocious tortures enhanced by means of music and sound—as in Guantánamo and Abu Ghraib—are part, Szendy advances, of a long-term genealogy for which the non-touch torture objective is "confession"; that is how music or sound is bound by what remains of an old practice, the ordeal. In scenes from film noir—*The Big Combo* up to Roman Polanski's *Death and the Maiden*, from Alfred Hitchcock's *Foreign Correspondent* and Billy Wilder's *One, Two, Three* up to Kathryn Bigelow's *Zero Dark Thirty*—Szendy detects continuity between the two practices. Although film is the main medium through which Szendy advances toward the end, the essay steps back in time to consider the literary fictions of Auguste Villiers de l'Isle-Adam's *Tomorrow's Eve* and—indulging in Edison's laments about the not-yet-invented audio-visual recording devices—ends up articulating an unexpected link to Jean-Luc Godard's film *Le petit soldat*, making us sense how the immemorial power of phonordeal of sound is released in the age of technological reproducibility. While Szendy's "In the Footsteps of Orpheus" section of *All Ears* invited his readers to take their time to embark upon a singular audiovisual adventure, unpacking "the tale of listening,"[11] now, with what is only apparently a non-touch approach to *"The" New Orpheus*, he gives us an oblique alternative access, as if expanding the criticism toward the condition of music-making and listening of *"A" New Orpheus*,[12] to quote the title of the seminal collection of essays that opened the path toward an open-ended and multidimensional scholarship on Weill edited some time ago by musicologist Kim Kowalke. Placed in the middle of this volume, Kowalke's contribution—"What Makes Weill Weill?"—reorients Weill's modernist mid-century scholarship, which with criticism springing from both sides of the Atlantic in their opposite directions persists in defining two Weills. Directing our ears to the twisted and therefore puzzling pronunciation of the composer's last name, which differs in German and in American English, and anchoring his study in the last twelve months of Weill's life in order to answer the titular question, which was posed to Weill himself, Kowalke causes us to time-travel as we read his essay. The Weill scholar deconstructs dismissive criticisms, starting with a consideration of the year before Weill's death, when he had already been living in the United States fifteen years and was restlessly working on several compositions that were not only seen on stage but also reached a broader audience via radio and television broadcasts: *Love Life* (recognized much later as the first nonlinear "concept musical"), another musical titled *Lost in the Stars* (which Weill with Maxwell Anderson adapted from Alan Paton's anti-apartheid novel *Cry, the Beloved Country*), and the opera *Down in the Valley* (televised by NBC). Reviewing comments on Weill's works in obituaries, journalistic in their format yet authoritative, Kowalke demonstrates not only that these were already marked by a dichotomic reception but also that they then propagated in scholarship during the Cold War era until after the fall of the Berlin Wall. Interestingly enough, it is Milan Kundera's essays on modernism and his notion of "itinerary" (demarcating itself from notions such as "identity") that break down exhausted dichotomies and facilitate a renewed reading of the extremely hybrid (and hence modernist) musical language of the composer; sketching crucial musical details of works from *Diegroschenoper* to *Lady in the Dark*, Kowalke then answers the question "What Makes Weill Weill?" by insisting on Weill's focus on musical theater, on the subtle or at times "subversive relationships among words, notes, rhythms, and instrumentation" entangled with a constitutive incorporation of contemporary political and social issues or, as Weill himself affirmed, "the music score itself becom[ing] its own form of storytelling," expanding beyond any plain intratextual technique.

After Kowalke's contribution comes William Solomon's—"A Walk on the Weill Side: Musical Theater and Rock Music in the 1960s"—proposing an extension from Weill/Brecht and modernism into rock music; substituting Weill for wild, the sounding title recalls indelibly Lou Reed's voice from 1972 and later, almost inviting us to participate in the "Doo do doo do doo do doo . . ." chorus. Solomon adventures where musicologist Stephen Hinton merely mentioned at the end of his study on Weill's musical theater the "inspiration Weill has provided to rock musicians such as Dylan or The Doors"[13] and to other artists such as the contributors to the 1985 tribute CD, *Lost in the Stars*. To this collection with tracks by Lou Reed, Tom Waits, Marianne Faithfull, Sting, and Bob Dylan, Solomon adds consideration of a later project of similar scope from 1997, *September Songs* (with P. J. Harvey and Elvis Costello among the contributors). After outlining that David Bowie's debt to Brecht-Weill is to be found even before *The Rise and Fall of Ziggy Stardust and the Spiders from Mars* (indubitably inspired by Brecht-Weill's opera *The Rise and Fall of the City of Mahagonny*), Solomon posits that the theatrical model, with its drama and artifice, is crucial to defining the egoless and soulless public image of rock celebrities, as opposed to communicative subjectivity. Hence, to determine the impact of Weill on rock music, the essay focuses on a somewhat earlier era: on the 1960s and on a certain strain of rock performance—a minor modernist one. The essay distills from Jim Morrison's performances of "Alabama Song (Whisky Bar)" influences of Lotte Lenya or of a ventriloquized Howlin' Wolf producing a distancing effect in relation to the bluesman model; redirecting our ears to listen to Eric Clapton and to a Bob Dylan who in a theater backstage was captured forever by the "outrageous power" of "Pirate Jenny," the essay affirms a potential opening for the questioning of interracial interplay. Dylan and Patti Smith listened to and read Lenya, Weill, and Brecht, and finally Lou Reed—who wanted to be the Kurt Weill of rock and roll. Solomon argues that Kowalke's alternative to the "two-Weills" is effective for Reed too. In inviting the reader for a walk on the wild side and concluding with "Let's Dance"—in unleashing glances at puzzling iconic covers and sonic cascades of music—this contribution seems almost like a preview, imagined by a scholar yet still rock and roll, for a new addition to the long list of stellar documentaries about popular music that have recently been released.

The last two essays of the volume leave Weill's works, exploring interrelations between reading and listening and among fictional, experiential, and personal modes to delve into further intersections of modernism and its resonances in other times and spaces. Fernanda Negrete focuses on Marguerite Duras's 1977 play *L'Éden Cinéma* to study how music, the mother figure, and her piano recur as themes of the late modernist writer. In "Marguerite Duras's Musical Return of the Real," digging into specific scenes and moments when music surges, Negrete brings to the fore a distinct musical time that is present in Duras's play. To critically address such a question, Negrete makes the Lacanian understanding of the return of the real (and repetition) communicate with Gilles Deleuze and Felix Guattari's idea of "another opening" and the concept of the refrain that permits the fabrication of time decentering fascistic regimes; the essay returns to, reiterates, and auscultates Duras's tempo, timbre, and specific *waltz* time in the play. The return of the real as it articulates Negrete's interpretation is not a reproduction of events, but instead resonance plays out impossible irruptions of the real into reality. Moreover, the essay's tempo in exploring nonchronological time resonates between Duras's autobiographical writings and Negrete's personal notes, merging soundly with her own interpretation.

In Julie Beth Napolin's *The Fact of Resonance*, a study that crosses modernist narrativity, media, and sound, resonance is a keyword, which as a matter of fact defines her book better than sound for its "fundamental relational"[14] aspect. In Napolin's contribution to this volume, "Outside In: Chorus and Clearing in the Time of Pandemic and Protest," resonance returns as one of the critical tools through which she documents her distinct experience in New York City in the spring of 2020—a quieting of the city due to the COVID-19 pandemic, which was shattered a few months later by an outbreak of voices and sounds during the Black Lives Matter protests—capturing anew, affirms Napolin, the sensorial, transformative tone suggested in Virginia Woolf's reflection on listening. Commenting on her own personal notes taken in a journal during the first months of the pandemic and shortly before the protests against innumerable instances of racial violence, the essay proposes a particular political approach to listening in light of what it can mean and perform. To the expression "I hear you," emptied out and unbearably uttered in a "listening session" with survivors of the Florida school shooting of February 2018 by the president at the time, Donald Trump, Napolin contraposes listening exactly when a gesture of withdrawing allows room for another; during Black Lives Matter marches, the chants repeating as a chorus *I can't breathe* meant also *I am listening*. As Napolin reflects, "For me to chant *I can't breathe* is . . . to listen to people who have said these words." Napolin's attention to the interspersion of the mediascape and soundscape captures an extremely suggestive threshold when she affirms having "understood later that, in documenting the experience of quieting, I had been unwittingly recording the sound of uprising, a sound about to rise up." This last essay, the only one not a part of the original symposium but invited shortly afterward, participates utterly in the sounding fabric of the volume. Indeed, it is exactly for the fact of pulsating and breathing through listening to vulnerable voices that—needless to say, as a resonance—invites me or commands me to quote her transcription of what a young person said whose words ends her essay: "So right now, what I would like everyone to do, we can just close our eyes for a few moments and take a few collective breaths for those that cannot breathe anymore, to be grateful to our planet as a source of life that connects us all."

If I started with a wide and only superficial look or hint at what was happening in relation to the white supremacist attack at the US Capitol when I was drafting these introductory notes, I have been silent about the massacre that had just happened in my area and that left all silent. The symposium took place in the city where I work and reside, Buffalo, whose name has grievously resounded in so many parts of the world after the racially motivated act of extreme violence on May 14, 2022, once again another mass murder dictated by a white supremacist ideology. The massacre happened just ten minutes away by car from where I live, in a neighborhood, one of the poorest of the country, segregated by a highway where many don't own a private means of transportation. It is the neighborhood that India Walton, the person who was elected by Buffalonians in the Democratic primary in 2021 to run for mayor, planned in her political program to give a new start to by ending the separation from other parts of the city its inhabitants suffer from. Walton was selected by the citizens, but the defeated incumbent mayor, supported by several special interests and seemingly going against a democratic vote, ran against her as a write-in candidate in the general election for mayor and won. Again so many questions resonate, populating my mind in the silence of my room while drafting these notes—such as but not only: How can democracy circulate as a force in public or shared spaces? How can it be audible and how are we to listen to it? How can we send Humanities to the Rescue? This book is dedicated to the victims of the massacre, their families and friends, and to all the inhabitants of Buffalo's East Side neighborhoods.

In "Sounding Silence, Sounding Thought," Krzysztof Ziarek ponders over what an "afterword" written almost after the pandemic may mean, suggesting that there is no response without listening resonance and no sound without attentive silence. The afterword establishes a potential relatedness of three separate elements: Ziarek waiting to hear Clara Iannotta's premiere of her new work "where the dark earth bends," the suggestive title of the RAGE Thormbones work "zero said in a low voice" that was performed instead because Iannotta had contracted COVID-19, and a crystal-clear yet transformative take on the German term *Stimmung*. Ziarek suggests to attentive readers and listeners—in a low, almost inaudible voice—potential links to many glittering critical moments that constellate the collection of essays as if performing inventive echoes and resonances in relation to them. Ziarek writes through and on a modality of thinking that is musically poetic, one that "enfolds silence and sound, voice and noise" and that remains enchanted by the avant-gardes and their aftermath, even if only at the threshold of "zero said." In accord with a meditative disposition or tonality of "poietic thinking," Ziarek closes the volume with a reflection that addresses an additional, non-facile—yet extremely necessary—question of what may keep politics and the arts together in today's epoch of digital technical systems.

Buffalo and Paris, May–July 2022

Notes

1. "In First Jan. 6 Hearing, Graphic Footage and Stark Testimony Show Depth of Attack," *New York Times*, June 9, 2022, accessed June 9, 2022, https://www.nytimes.com/live/2022/06/09/us/jan-6-hearings.

2. Masha Gessen, "Judith Butler Wants Us to Reshape Our Rage," *New Yorker*, February 9, 2020, accessed June 16, 2022, https://www.newyorker.com/culture/the-new-yorker-interview/judith-butler-wants-us-to-reshape-our-rage.

3. Jean-Luc Nancy, "Populism, Democracy, and Neofascism: Two Essays," *Los Angeles Review of Books*, February 19, 2019, accessed June 16, 2022, https://lareviewofbooks.org/article/populism-democracy-and-neofascism-two-essays. Nancy expands the concise sentence in this way:

> The nature of fascism can be characterized as the inverse of democracy. On both sides, it is a matter of the power of the people. But whereas in democracy the people itself is postulated, in fascism it is incarnated. I mean "postulated" here in a Kantian sense: a reality of the people must be thought, or represented, in order to serve as a rule in the conception of politics. And I mean "incarnated" in a phantasmatic way since neither an individual nor any other alleged entity (race or nation, for instance) would be able to incorporate a people.

> In this sense, fascism is premised upon a rejection of the democratic postulate: it rejects democracy's will to regulate itself in accordance with an idea of the people that itself responds to the visionary or ideal character of this idea and, in its place, substitutes its own decision to affirm the tangible reality of the people.

> It is clear that the democratic postulate involves a fragility that is constitutive: in one sense, democracy itself declares that, in order to have a functional democracy, what it names is not, and must not, be made present. Conversely,

fascism involves a force that is constitutive: it affirms itself as the only real, almost immediate, expression (be it in the immediacy of a figure or symbol).

4. Enzo Traverso, *The New Faces of Fascism: Populism and the Far Right*, interview by Régis Meyran, trans. David Broder (London: Verso, 2019), 3. Other lines of research exploring our time in relation to historical precedents have been brought forth recently by Ruth Ben-Ghiat, *Strongmen: Mussolini to the Present* (New York: Norton, 2021) and Theo Horesh, *The Fascism This Time: And the Global Future of Democracy* (Boulder: CO: Cosmopolis Press, 2020).

5. Alberto Toscano, "Incipient Fascism: Black Radical Perspectives," *CLCWeb: Comparative Literature and Culture* 23, no. 1 (2021), doi:10.7771/1481-4374.4015.

6. Veit Erlmann and Michael Bull, "Editorial," *Sound Studies* 1, no. 1 (2015), doi:10.1080/20551940.2015.1079059.

7. Helen Groth, Julian Murphet, and Penelope Hone, "Introduction: Sounding Modernism 1890–1950," in Julian Murphet, Helen Groth, and Penelope Hone, eds., *Sounding Modernism: Rhythm and Sonic Mediation in Modern Literature and Film* (Edinburgh: Edinburgh University Press, 2017), 4.

8. I am importing the notion from music historian Suzanne Cusick. Whatever musicology's new "Other" might be called, by its attention to the whole spectrum of acoustic experience in which musical behaviors nestle, the new field promises to be intellectually exciting because, unlike the musicologies, it tries to theorize the myriad relationships among acoustical energy, human agency, technologies, power that characterize contemporary acoustical experience—whether that experience be called musical or not. Yet until quite recently "sound studies"/acoustemology has also proven to be a problematic interdiscipline. Curiously detached from critical thinking about race, gender, sexuality, or class, it is more celebratory than critical about the new regimes of listening enabled by twenty first-century technology. Almost exclusively a practice of white men, too, it is often oblivious to questions of performance and performativity, even when, as in the case of hip-hop deejaying, the performance of relationships to technology, commerce, history, and power are obviously inseparable from the production of a characteristic set of sounds. See Susanne G. Cusick, "Musicology, Performativity, Acoustemology," in Deborah A. Kapchan, ed., *Theorizing Sound Studies* (Middletown, CT: Wesleyan University Press, 2017), 5–26.

9. Luciano Berio, "Foreword: Liebeslied for Weill," in David Farneth, Elmar Juchem, and Dave Stein, eds., *Kurt Weill: A Life in Pictures and Documents* (Woodstock: Overlook Press, 2000), vii.

10. See David Novak and Matt Sakakeeny, eds., *Keywords in Sound* (Durham, NC: Duke University Press, 2015).

11. Peter Szendy, *All Ears: The Aesthetics of Espionage* (New York: Fordham University Press, 2017), 70.

12. Kim H. Kowalke, ed., *A New Orpheus: Essays on Kurt Weill* (New Haven, CT: Yale University Press, 1986).

13. Stephen Hinton, *Weill's Musical Theatre: Stages of Reform* (Berkeley: University of California Press, 2012), 122.

14. The author explains her project in her introduction, as follows: "Resonance, rather than 'sound' more generally, provides the form, content, and method of this book because it is fundamentally relational or, as W. E. B. Du Bois would say, split into two. While resonance is defined by relating, it is also defined by a spaciotemporal delay. A sound is a wavelength, and it takes time to travel to a wall, for example, off which it reflects." Julie Beth Napolin, *The Fact of Resonance: Modernist Acoustics and Narrative Form* (New York: Fordham University Press, 2020), 5.

References

Ben-Ghiat, Ruth. *Strongmen: Mussolini to the Present*. New York: Norton, 2021.

Berio, Luciano. "Foreword: Liebeslied for Weill." In *Kurt Weill: A Life in Pictures and Documents*, edited by David Farneth, Elmar Juchem, and Dave Stein, vii. Woodstock, NY: Overlook Press, 2000.

Cusick, Susanne G. "Musicology, Performativity, Acoustemology." In *Theorizing Sound Studies*, edited by Deborah A. Kapchan, 25–45. Middletown, CT: Wesleyan University Press, 2017.

Erlmann, Veit, and Michael Bull. "Editorial." *Sound Studies* 1, no. 1 (2015). doi: 10.1080/20551940.2015.1079059.

Gessen, Masha. "Judith Butler Wants Us to Reshape Our Rage." *New Yorker*, February 9, 2020. Accessed June 16, 2022. https://www.newyorker.com/culture/the-new-yorker-interview/judith-butler-wants-us-to-reshape-our-rage.

Groth, Helen, Julian Murphet, and Penelope Hone. "Introduction: Sounding Modernism 1890–1950." In *Sounding Modernism: Rhythm and Sonic Mediation in Modern Literature and Film*, edited by Julian Murphet, Helen Groth, and Penelope Hone, 1–15. Edinburgh: Edinburgh University Press, 2017.

Hinton, Stephen. *Weill's Musical Theatre: Stages of Reform*. Berkeley: University of California Press, 2012.

Horesh, Theo. *The Fascism This Time: And the Global Future of Democracy*. Boulder, CO: Cosmopolis Press, 2020.

"In First Jan. 6 Hearing, Graphic Footage and Stark Testimony Show Depth of Attack." *New York Times*, June 9, 2022. Accessed June 9, 2022. https://www.nytimes.com/live/2022/06/09/us/jan-6-hearings.

Kowalke, Kim H., ed. *A New Orpheus: Essays on Kurt Weill*. New Haven, CT: Yale University Press, 1986.

Nancy, Jean-Luc. "Populism, Democracy, and Neofascism: Two Essays." *Los Angeles Review of Books*, February 19, 2019. Accessed June 16, 2022.

https://lareviewofbooks.org/article/populism-democracy-and-neofascism-two-essays.

Napolin, Julie Beth. *The Fact of Resonance: Modernist Acoustics and Narrative Form*. New York: Fordham University Press, 2020.

Novak, David, and Matt Sakakeeny, eds. *Keywords in Sound*. Durham, NC: Duke University Press, 2015.

Szendy, Peter. *All Ears: The Aesthetics of Espionage*. New York: Fordham University Press, 2017.

Toscano, Alberto. "Incipient Fascism: Black Radical Perspectives." *CLCWeb: Comparative Literature and Culture* 23, no. 1 (2021). doi.10.7771/1481-4374.4015.

Traverso, Enzo. *The New Faces of Fascism: Populism and the Far Right*. Interview by Régis Meyran. Translated by David Broder. London: Verso, 2019.

Chapter 1

Political (Effort/Exhaustion)

James Currie

1

In the months leading up to the writing of this essay the relationship of left-wing academics in the humanities to the word "fascism" underwent a certain transformation. Fascism is one of those words that for many decades until relatively recently had seemed broadly to circulate on two levels. On the one hand, the term had functioned in a relatively strict sense, as denoting for the purposes of say political theory, or history, or serious intellectual journalism "a political philosophy, movement, or regime that exalts nation and race above the individual and that stands for a centralized autocratic government headed by a dictatorial leader, severe economic and social regimentation, and forcible suppression of opposition."[1] On the other hand, the term had functioned in a looser, more colloquial fashion, and in its less impressive examples has sometimes been redolent of teenagers rejecting their parents. Here fascism has been more the means of rhetorically upping the ante of a rejection of something because of distaste at how it imposes some kind of restriction, or conservative attitude, or that it stands for authority. So, for example, it has been easier to say of our governments in the past that they were fascist even when, in a strict sense, that was not always true. In many instances, it was perfectly forgivable to act in such a fashion rhetorically since the actions of said governments were often pretty appalling anyway. But over the course of the four years of the Trump administration, the distinction between these two uses of the term started increasingly to disappear. Events such as the unambiguously alarming actions of federal agents in Portland, Oregon, for example, made possible a sober minded, and precisely informed "Yes" in answer to a question that continues to haunt political commentary: are we yet living in a condition of fascism?[2] As a word, fascism started to burn with a significantly more brutal, neon effulgence, because it increasingly was charged with the horror of the thing itself, rather than being the means by which the thing's presence is tempered and controlled—like a cage that contains the panther pacing at the zoo. It transpires that either someone left the cage door open, or we are now inside the cage itself.

The title of the conference from which the essays in this collection originate was "Sounds: Avant-Garde, Modernism, and Fascism." Even at that time (spring 2019), there was no pretense that the presence of the word fascism was not uninspired by, or innocent of, the exponentially devolving political scene. Since Anglo-American academic discourse in the humanities has traditionally validated itself in recent decades through the claim that it is relevant because it addresses itself to the pressing concerns of the contemporary moment, there was nothing untoward about this. But even though many speakers acknowledged the difficulties of political events in the United States that constituted the larger context in which the papers were being given, the papers themselves employed this fact more as an environmental resonance or atmospheric backdrop rather than as something that was fundamental to the terms of the respective lines of inquiry per se. Little of the foundational architecture of those papers (mine included) would have become unstable if such resonance and atmosphere had been removed, and I am not now going to assume the moral high ground by asserting that they ought to have been then or that all academic work must do so now.

After all, if one feels the great urgency to act, the production of written academic discourse is far from being the most immediately obvious or effective means of doing so. The complex and stringent practices by which such thinking is validated as having been done correctly, mean that academic thinking is a slow thing and, moreover, a quite isolated thing too. By contrast, the battles of the recent political environment mostly seem to require the fast tempo of immediate response and an altruistic openness to participation in communal action. As Hannah Arendt once stated, "One is correct in saying that thinking and acting are not the same, and to the extent that I wish to think I have to withdraw from the world." And a little later in the exchange from which these remarks came from, she puts the point more emphatically: "You know, all the modern philosophers have somewhere in their work a rather apologetic sentence which says, 'thinking is also acting.' Oh no, it is not! And to say that is rather dishonest. I mean let's face the music: it is not the same! On the contrary, I have to keep back to a large extent from participating, from commitment."[3] Since I *am* self-evidently taking the time to prioritize academic thought over political action proper, one would be correct in assuming that such slow temporalities and perhaps vaguely narcissistic acts of withdrawal are still acceptable to me. Indeed, maybe thought's slowness and distance from direct social action is one of the means by which we are able to traverse passages of human history that are marked, like our own, by an instability more emphatic than at other times. In her 1975 acceptance speech on receiving the Sonning Prize, Arendt's remarks about philosophy would seem resonant here. As she states, "Philosophy is a solitary business, and it seems only natural that the need for it arises in times of transition when men no longer rely on the stability of the world and their role in it, and when the question concerning the general conditions of human life, which as such are properly coeval with the appearance of man on earth, gain an uncommon poignancy."[4] Unsurprisingly, for someone whose intellectual development remained so intimately conversant with Heidegger's, Arendt's proposition for philosophy here allows thinking to be conceived as a kind of dwelling, shelter, or habitat. Like Plato, Heidegger saw wonderment as the beginning of thinking, but unlike Plato, for Heidegger one therefore had the responsibility "of taking up and accepting this wondering as one's abode."[5] As Arendt states, "The abode of which Heidegger speaks lies therefore, in a metaphorical sense, outside the habitations of men."[6] Of course, in its ability to offer us protection from exposure, it must therefore take the risk of walking dangerously close to the cliff edge that falls away into dark forms of escapism. For many, therefore, Heidegger was guilty of having fallen off. But without any intention of making excuses for Heidegger, it is nevertheless the case that such are the conditions of thinking in a troubled time. About this, Arendt, more than most, was uniquely qualified to understand.

My thoughts here thus pull in two directions at the same time. For whilst my words self-evidently do not constitute political action proper, I have nevertheless taken the opportunity afforded by recent transformations in our relationship to the word fascism to bring my contemplations upon things from the past from my original conference paper into a perhaps more forceful *engagement*. On the one hand, I therefore withdraw into something that, to develop Arendt's theme, might offer the respite of a form of stability, which, precisely since that is something the world beyond this act of writing can no longer easily offer, therefore has a certain "poignancy" to it. On the other hand, I seem to want to advance in order to trouble the historical past out of its slumber by proposing how aspects of its character and behavior are still wide awake here and now in the present and to wonder what beneficial critical work reflection upon that fact might perform. Quite self-consciously, this essay is thus both at rest and at work, retracting and extending, a relaxing comfort and a provocatory vivification, distracted by the past and irked by the present.

The tension created by the coexistence of these conflicting tendencies is to a large degree constitutive of some of the things I have still to speculate upon—notably, the continuing presence of what I interpret as certain basic norms and strategies of modernist and avant-garde attempts to politicize artistic practice across a number of historical case studies, including the work of Kurt Weill and Bertolt Brecht, and the politicized performance practice of Nina Simone during the civil rights era. But the presence of this tension should also, I assert, be recognized as a sign of ethical and political integrity, and not just the unfortunate residue of a reluctance fully to commit to getting out of bed and getting on with the business of fighting the good fight. In the face of our potential embarrassment at giving value to anything other than the notion that time should be put to good use, I therefore argue just as strongly for the import of the luxury of being able to waste time too.

The reason why I justify attributing value to such an inhabiting of the temporal is roughly as follows. Obviously, the indisputable fact of the shocking conditions of the present, and indeed the centuries-long ongoing and continual duress to which the fight for freedom and democracy has been subjected, easily justifies the *necessity* of a kind of *insomniac* relationship to the labor requisite for successful political activism. The pragmatic truth of this is registered unambiguously in, for example, the title of Angela Y. Davis's much-lauded recent book, *Freedom Is a Constant Struggle*.[7] But what negative things are potentially unleashed, and what long-term damage done, when such an acknowledgment becomes a charter for assuming an unquestioned *desirability*, in and of itself, of participation in the endless labor of political activism? In other words, what happens when we make a virtue out of a necessity? Or to give it a more academic formulation, what happens when we make the "category mistake" of confusing the terms of pragmatism with those of morality?[8]

Undoubtedly, devotion to constant political dissent is a discipline that can be extraordinarily empowering for human subjects, as the memoirs of political activists frequently attest. Further, there seems little doubt that for those whose lifeworlds are not immediately endangered by their political situation, participation in political action, particularly in the United States, can easily become a kind of pleasure: it is the right thing to do, and thereby imbues life with a sense of purpose and moral good. However, if it is the case that one has felt that one has *had* to act, one has therefore also been the victim of temporal theft. I am reminded here of some oft-quoted words of Toni Morrison on the function of racism from a talk entitled "A Humanist View" that she gave in 1975 at Portland State University as part of the Public Dialogue on the American Dream Theme. It is important, she states, "to know the function of racism, which is distraction. *It keeps you from doing your work.* It keeps you explaining over and over again, your reason for being." Racism thus places its victims in a kind of endless waiting room to the experience of their own being: "Somebody says you have no language and so you spend 20 years proving that you do. Somebody says your head isn't shaped properly so you have scientists working on the fact that it is. Somebody says that you have no art so you dredge that up. Somebody says you have no kingdoms and so you dredge that up." For Morrison this is "a deadly prison," where "one spends one's life fighting phantoms, concentrating on myths, and explaining over and over to the conqueror your language, your lifestyle, your history, your habits." And she urges emphatically that one resists inhabiting such a place—however hard that may be. She calls, in effect, for the victims of racism to seek Being instead, which, somewhat surprisingly means, to live the truth of "exactly what every 3-year-old child knows: that the whole business of reproducing and dying by the billions is unsatisfactory and clumsy."[9] And one of the most privileged means of living in such a way is for her through artistic practice. So, to what degree might one argue that the perceived necessity of political action, irrespective of being a source of dignity, must to a degree be a sign of one's poverty too? What damage is done by the efforts that necessitate endangered political subjects from having to deny this poverty in order to act?

This is a particularly intractable problem in the United States of America where, for a myriad of reasons—such as the ways in which the relationship of its ideological value system to European models cross fertilized with the stringencies of the lives lived by initial generations of immigrants in the New World—the Protestant Work Ethic and an unquestioned celebration of work and labor as values, in and of themselves, is something to which a not insignificant percentage of the population continues to hold a particularly rabid ideological identification. Since the United States is also, in terms of the rest of the Western world, the country with the unquestionably worst labor conditions, belief in work, in and of itself, is perhaps one way of surviving the miseries attendant upon work. So, to what degree does this belief in work make us concentrate more on the dignity of political action, as opposed to the unacceptability of having had to have given up one's time to political action in the first place? To gain some purchase on this, I turn now to consideration of instances where aesthetic practice and political practice have been intentionally brought into alignment. I do this because the aesthetic, as a traditional location for the values of noninstrumental play and sensory pleasure, has often been perceived—in Western discourse, at least since Friedrich Schiller's 1794 *On the Aesthetic Education of Man*—as having the potential radically to challenge the value of work.[10] For some, such as Herbert Marcuse famously in 1955 in *Eros and Civilization*, it is precisely this possibility in the aesthetic that defines its potential as a positive political force.[11] For my purposes, by contrast, the advantage of bringing the political into such close proximity with the aesthetic is that it helps to *exacerbate* the very problem of work and its value as they function within the political.

2

For avant-garde modernists, mired in the exponentially growing economic and political turmoil of Europe after the Great War, and increasingly in response, like us now, to the looming presence of potentially fascist governments, the question of the possibly shaming poverty attendant upon political action was rarely acknowledged. For them, the increasing state of emergency meant that everything had to be put to work as a form of resistance effort. To expedite that cause rhetorically, the aesthetic, particularly in the form of its embodiment as high culture, got scripted as a bad habit to which audiences needed to be trained to no longer react in a positive fashion. This was done mostly in the name of an allegiance to Marxist thinking—irrespective of the fact that Marx's writings, even after his mid-career turn to the seeming more sober study of strict political economy, remained consistent in their admiration of the luxury of non-instrumental aesthetic endeavors that, in and of themselves, were self-validating. Nevertheless, in the case of the collaboration between Brecht and Weill, one might quip that what they enacted was an adaptation of the formal strategy of Marx's famous 1845 reconceptualization of philosophy in the eleventh *Theses on Feuerbach* to the conceptualization of art. So, where Marx wrote "Philosophers have hitherto only interpreted the world; the point is to change it,"[12] Brecht and Weill could be seen to have put into action a notion that "High Art has hitherto only sought to please its audiences; the point is to transform them," and thus to change the world.

As with Marx's conceptual realignment from interpretation to transformation, Brecht and Weill's theoretical reorientation of art from pleasure to an essentially practice-based form of public pedagogy had more far-reaching ambitions than just to be an act of academic redefinition and clarification. Just as important as the change in meaning was the shock-inducing intensification of affect incurred from being exposed to that change in meaning. It is the effect of a *coup de théâtre*, and so there is a strong odor in the stating of these redefinitions of the stage and an audience's ability to be gripped by what happens upon it; of spectacle and melodrama; sudden turns of fate and their tragic repercussions. Since Brecht and Weill were both theater men, this is perhaps to be expected. But since such theatricality is also common to the experience of reading Marx, it is interesting in passing to speculate on the degree to which Brecht and Weill's radical implementation of theoretical transformations of music theater resulted as much from the attempt to co-opt the pedagogical effectivity of Marx's own affectively dramatic mode of theorization in prose as from the more literal-minded attempt to simply adapt Marx's ideas to the theater.

Whatever the case, in both instances, reconceptualization is tantamount to a change in our own location as perceivers just as much as it is a change in the location of the object. This is what accounts for the shock—we realize that we are not where we had assumed. Rather than looking at the thing from what we thought was the point of view of a kind of easy nature (for example, where philosophy appears "just the way it is," as an interpretation of the world) we are made to confront the artifice of that naturalizing assumption—to see that such assumptions rest rather on an accumulated set of historical circumstances that are so sedimented into unquestioned convention that we no longer even register them as products of human artifice. Since the distinction between what is nature and what is a product of human history would seem to be (until recent considerations of the Anthropocene) pretty obvious, the situation of being caught out in having confused them can easily shame one into feeling foolish. It is worth noting that the act of shaming with regard to those who unreflexively assume that the way in which things have consciously been made to go wrong is just the way things are, or those who like to pretend that history is actually just nature, remains to this day a recognizable and widely practiced technique of left-wing political action. And so, statues of Andrew Jackson, or Robert Lee, or Christopher Columbus, or Confederate flags are confronted by the force of a politically righteous gravitational pull, and are brought down to the level of the very repellent historical realities that their erection was enacted in order to deny.

The experience of being subject to such potentially shaming disorientation is a threat to which one is consistently made vulnerable in reading Marx's works. Seen through the optic of his prose, even the most seemingly obvious of things become immediately strange to us, robbing us of our sense of security, as in the *tour-de-force* opening of volume 1 of *Das Kapital*, where the seemingly innocent commodity form becomes something so uncanny one can start to feel that one is reading a short story by E. T. A. Hoffmann rather than, as the book's subtitle states, "a critique of political economy." So not only here does the commodity no longer correlate with our expectations, and not only are we confused as to the location from which we have been perceiving it, but even the media (the prose of Marx's book) by which these forms of disorientation come to affect us has become ambiguous. Is it a work of academic analysis, or a Gothic work of literary fantasy in the style of early nineteenth century German Romanticism? To quip on a Marxian theme, reading Marx therefore robs us of a sense of security in our own private property; no *habitus* remains habitable any longer. Forced to find our balance on a conceptual ground that is neither any longer singular nor static, we thus must now expend effort leaping from one unfamiliar moving platform to another. This is a kind of exile in which there is nowhere left to rest, or relax, or to rejuvenate through respite, or reconvene forces, and so, as a result, we must be noticeably alive, vigilant, critically alert, even sober—for there are, regarding the latter, overtones of health regimens and prescriptions for increasing vitality loitering here.

The machinations of Marx's prose aim at an almost physiological transformation in its readership, and to this degree we might see Marx as standing at the beginning of an increasing body of polemic and cultural critique exponentially swelling throughout the later nineteenth century until it overflowed into the next century and saturated so many of the discourses of artistic modernism, including, I would argue, those of Brecht and Weill. A basic message of this body of thought and practice was the need to make people wake up. We can see it, for example, throughout Nietzsche's ongoing diagnoses of cultural lethargy, decadence, and the inability to act; in the vitalism of Bergson; in the pervasive sense, at the beginning of World War I, that war would have a cleansing, revivifying effect on European culture; in the development of eugenics; in the Russian formalist belief in poetry's power to defamiliarize normal language and so, as a result, enhance perception of the familiar; and, not unrelated to this, in Brecht's famous notion of *Verfremdung*, of making strange through techniques that can puncture theatrical illusion, thus compelling the audience into an active critical role in relationship to their artistic experience.

Anything here with the potential for making us somnolent is to be distrusted. From a musical perspective, this is nicely articulated in an oft-quoted newspaper article by Kurt Weill that appeared on Christmas Day, 1928, in *Berliner Tageblatt*. Weill here crafts an imaginary conversation between himself and some schoolchildren that supposedly has transpired on them having just listened to some music by Wagner and his followers. The sense that we are being trained in a more healthy way of being is clearly expressed in the somewhat sinister fashion in which our right of reply is curtailed in favor of the efficiency of being unequivocally *told* what we have just felt: "You saw that it had so many notes in it that I couldn't play them all. You tried to sing along with the melody but that didn't work." Also included in this list of our experiences is the following: that you "felt that the music was making you sleepy, or even a bit drunk, affecting you like alcohol or some other drug."[13] Of passing interest is the fact that the correlation of Wagner with an unhealthy kind of intoxication has a well-known lineage, particularly to European musical discourse in the early twentieth century, stretching back to one of Nietzsche's last books, *The Case of Wagner* of 1888, where of Wagner it is stated unequivocally: "He has made music sick."[14] But for my purposes in this essay, it is the sentence that follows that is most telling: "But you didn't want to go to sleep."[15]

What however if the children *did* want to go to sleep? And what if there were circumstances in which that desire was not necessarily indicative of a moral and ethical fall from grace? When is it a sign of *health* to desire to rest, rather than just a symptom of vitamin deficiency? Since Weill has set the precedent for imagining responses, one could of course imagine an affronted answer to such questions as coming from Brecht and Weill themselves: "Well certainly *not* when the aim is to stay awake!" But such an answer would be belied by the fact of well-known instances when Brecht and Weill's collaborations produced precisely such undisciplined responses. *Die Dreigroschenoper (The Threepenny Opera)* of 1928 is perhaps the most obvious. As Stephen Hinton has shown, the reception of this work has been dogged since its earliest days by the following nagging question: "How could a work of subversive tendency and high artistic merit attract such widespread public acclaim?"[16] In a letter written to Theodor Adorno soon after the premiere, Ernst Bloch, for example, noted that it is curious "how the 'gaiety' masks what is *épatant*. No-one boos, the house is sold out every night." He then adds: "Even the *Friederike* audience is happy."[17] *Friederike* refers to a piece by Franz Lehár, and Bloch's invocation of it suggest that for certain critical intellectuals in 1928, operetta audiences were assumed to be incapable of digesting shocking political critique in the theater. The question of operetta is also raised by Elias Canetti in his recollections of Berlin at the time of the first performances. As he states, "An opera it was not, nor a send-up of opera, as it had originally been"—in other words, in John Gay's eighteenth-century *The Beggar's Opera*, on which *The Threepenny Opera* was modeled. Canetti continues: "it was, and this was the one unadulterated thing about it, an operetta."[18] Like Bloch, Canetti also works with the assumption that operetta audiences tend to seek consolation rather than confrontation. He talks of "the saccharine form of Viennese operetta, in which people found their wishes undisturbed." But for Canetti, the success of the work lay in the fact that Viennese light entertainment had been put into play with a "Berlin form, with its hardness, meanness and banal justifications," which, he importantly concludes, "people wanted no less, probably even more, that all that sweetness." Canetti's assessment of the success of *The Threepenny Opera* is thus ultimately quite damning: "If it is the job of satire to castigate people for the injustice they represent and commit, for the misdeeds which turn into predators and multiply, then here, on the contrary, everything was glorified that one would otherwise shamefully conceal."[19] Or to cast things back into my terms, if the political intention of the work was to wake its audiences up to the horrors of capitalism and their complicity with its practices, the actual result was to make people feel comfortable and at rest even when confronted with such facts. So, if

Marxist-inspired politicized art aimed at forcing people out of bed, why were they still asleep?

An obvious diagnosis of the problem would be to say that politicized art had not been forceful enough. And if one were looking for examples that intensify the kinds of politicized artistic strategies found in Brecht and Weill for precisely this purpose, the work of Nina Simone, and particularly her performance practice during the civil rights era, would be a useful place to start. The connection between the politicized practices of Brecht and Weill and Simone is unambiguous. The 1964 "Mississippi Goddam," which Simone referred to at one time as her "first civil rights song," was written in response to the Mississippi murder of Megdar Evers and the death of four African American children in the Sixteenth Street Baptist Church bombing in Birmingham, Alabama. Simone performed the song in 1964 in one of her famous appearances at Carnegie Hall, at a time when the song was unknown and had only been performed in public once before at the Village Gate. Also on the program was "Pirate Jenny," Simone's extraordinary rendition of "Pirate-Jenny or the Dreams of a Kitchen Maid," from Brecht and Weill's *The Threepenny Opera*. Simone reenvisions the protagonist of the song as a Black maid working in a hotel in a "crummy Southern town" during the Jim-Crow era, and the "black freighter" offshore in the song's refrain as ominously intimating the possibilities of the coming of a Black revolution. Commentators have noted before that there is a strong resonance between Brecht and Weill's *Verfremdungseffekt*, the politicized techniques they employed in order to displace their audience's relationship to aesthetic pleasure and thus wake them up politically, and the strategies Simone employs in "Mississippi Goddam." But rather than the relationship between the two being one of the European avant-garde of the 1920s influencing African-American performance practice in the 1960s, it is more illuminating to conceptualize it as part of a single constellation of autonomous yet analogous practices that communicate with each other by means of what we could refer to as a certain transhistorical act of virtual solidarity. The advantage of this is that it would help us to see artists such as Simone as part of a much broader, racially and politically complex, global picture of artistic modernism, and thus, to appropriate a famous title of Dipesh Chakrabarty, help to "provincialize" the Eurocentrism, which, particularly in standard general histories of music, is still mostly the default position.[20]

By the time of Simone's 1964 performances at Carnegie Hall, the discourse and techniques of modernist and avant-garde political art had already had a long and effective resonance with the self-fashioning practices of African-American musicians and the functions those practices performed in relationship to their political ambitions. Therefore, by invoking the work of Brecht and Weill, Simone was not necessarily doing anything unprecedented for a Black musical performer in the United States. For example, as early as the 1940s bebop musicians had drawn on central aspects of the value system of artistic modernism as a means of conceptualizing the vastly increased difficulty of their music. Such difficulties included bebop's extraordinary rhythmic complexity, breakneck tempos, and the virtuosic demands such musical features placed on its performers; but it also encompassed the decided challenges the music overall posed to audience's powers of comprehension, particularly those attuned to the more commercially orientated big band sound. African Americans appropriated the disdain for the popular that had so often been productive of a certain problematic *hauteur* in modernist aesthetic discourse as a means of enacting, amongst other things, a certain implicit racial critique of the vast industry of economic relations that enabled for the circulation of popular music in the first place. And the terms of this implicit critique were thoroughly congruent with the Marxist practice of unmasking nature as history that I have already broadly articulated.

Specifically, we could understand bebop musicians as intensely involved with distancing themselves from the "feel-good" sound of so much big band music and, in doing so, articulating how it was in large part purchased at the cost of the erasure from representation of the extreme social violence constituting the quotidian reality of Black performers. Such performers appeared on the stage of the big band spectacle as smiling, happy, energized, up-for-it, well dressed, groomed, generous, and socially engaged with their audiences. Such were the terms of contract and labor conditions by which one got to gain economically from big band's participation in the culture industry. But in appearing as such, Black musicians found themselves caught between a certain Scylla and Charybdis that has remained defining of the impossible antagonisms that constitute the vexed experiences of Black entertainers to this day.[21] For such appearances were self-evidently not the product of a simple theatrical realism, and were not therefore just an image of the way things were offstage—even if, for the duration of performance itself, such a way of being was possible and, thus, a certain dignity temporarily made available. If African Americans decided to attempt to capitalize on the rare possibility for economic betterment that in the 1930s and '40s becoming an entertainer afforded, any gains made nevertheless came at the price of a certain censorship. Since such censorship continued to enable audiences to avoid confrontation with the material realities of ingrained political and economic racism, Black entertainers thus found themselves in the negatively dialectical predicament of enjoying the benefits of making economic gains that nevertheless contributed to keeping in place the very conditions that had necessitated them having to become performers in the first place.

One of the many radical features of bebop was therefore its crafting of difficult musical surfaces that, in opposition to the ability of more commercially successful music to mute the registering of the more indigestible aspects of the performer's material conditions, was more easily available as an expression of the often-claustrophobic complexities and antagonisms in which racialized political and economic existence in late capitalist urban modernity took place. If we take a classic instance of bebop, such as Charlie Parker and Dizzy Gillespie's *Anthropology*, we can even argue that the relationship of aesthetic appearance and underlying material conditions is inverted. *Anthropology* is an example of what is called a contrafact, which is a form of jazz composition distinct from jazz standard practice, where, traditionally, a recognizable tune, often from the Great American Songbook, is played up-front and then, keeping its basic underlying harmonic and phrase structures intact, improvised upon. With contrafact, by contrast, a new tune is created then presented up-front and then improvised upon, and in the case of *Anthropology* that is done over the basic chord progression of a famous hit of George Gershwin's, "I Got Rhythm," from the 1930 musical *Girl Crazy*. In a traditional jazz standard practice, Gershwin's tune would be the familiar thing that we would get up-front; the thing that we recognize and that makes us feel at home and in place. Like all highly successful popular tunes, "I Got Rhythm" was available as a reliable sonic bearing in the complicated soundscape of twentieth-century urban life, and its recognizability as a landmark is attested by how incredibly popular the so-called "rhythm changes" of its thirty-two-bar underlying chord structure was, and has continued to be, as a basis for other jazz compositions. Notable instances include Duke Ellington's 1940 "Cotton Tail," and numerous Charlie Parker investigations, such as the 1946 "Moose the Mouche." The Gershwin tune has also, through copyright and the selling of sheet music, existed as a highly successful commodity in and of itself, and was thus available as expressive not only of a certain happiness attendant upon leisure and entertainment but also, particularly to African-American bebop musicians, of the very ambivalences and complicities attendant upon participation in the economic opportunities of commercial music in a racist world.

Gillespie and Parker's *Anthropology*, however, robs us of all the palliatives that the Gershwin in its immediacy might offer and the new contrafact composed over the preexistent chord changes is so densely intricate and almost distractingly virtuosic, in and of itself, that many of the music students I teach, even those conversant with the Great American Songbook, such as music theater majors, are shocked when its well-known foundations are unearthed. If we continue to work with my conceit, and thus to think of popular show tunes as landmarks that help us to gain our bearings within the complex soundscape of urban life in late modernity, then bebop's representation of the cityscape thwarts such attempts at cognitive mapping. Less like a guidebook, and more like the well-known cramped and claustrophobic modernist cityscapes of expressionists such as Ernst Ludwig Kirchner, the tune is now buried and inaudible, lost in a swarm of the more immediately proximate. It is a sonic embodiment of not being able to see the wood for the trees; or, more precisely, not being able to see the wood *unless* one is skilled enough to do so—for example, unless one is an African-American bebop musician. Thus, bebop is to a large degree a highly learned music, a music of cognoscenti, of those in the know. Rather than big band, where the gestures of a relatively large ensemble are put to work for the purposes of expansively opening out towards the audience in order to make them feel good, bebop, with its propensity for a small combo of saxophone, trumpet, piano, guitar, double bass and drums, often turns inwards like chamber music. The musicians talk more with each other than with their audience, as if, and with a kind of classic modernist disdain, they were turning their backs in the gesture of a snub.

The stylistic features of bebop music can easily be drawn into the kind of global constellation of modernist and avant-garde politicized aesthetic practices that I have suggested as a model for "provincializing" the Eurocentrism of our music historiographies. To take but one example, as with the kinds of Marxian processes that I have outlined, this music enacts a radical dislocation of the terms of our understanding of what constitutes a show tune. In the face of the way in which we might assume that our understanding of, for example, "I Got Rhythm" is "just the way 'I Got Rhythm' is," bebop contrafactual practice reveals, to the contrary, that that is simply the result of where you are looking at "I Got Rhythm" from. Bebop thus has the potential to illuminate how our understanding arises from whatever complex intersection of historical, economic, political, and racial forces have led, for example, to you being a white person enjoying yourself at a large night club by dancing to the music of a big band largely constituted by African-American musicians. It has the potential to enact a certain disenchantment of the ear and in bebop practice this often leads to the tune being transformed into a formalized abstraction that can act as a conduit for another music to be heard—both literally, in the demanding virtuosity of the musical sounds themselves, and also metaphorically, in the sense of the material conditions of alternate positions of hearing.

But for the purposes of my argument, and to lead us back to consideration of Simone and the shortcomings of the political effectivity of the Brecht-Weill collaborations, bebop is also profoundly resonant with a Marxist critical practice in the way in which it dislocates any easy non-politicized understanding of what it means to conceptualize African-American performers as mere entertainers. Indeed, I would argue that one of the many reasons for the indisputable political force of African-American music since the middle of the twentieth century lies precisely in the challenges they have posed to our conceptualization of audience-performer relations, and Simone is particularly notable in this regard. If bebop performance practice, in its original historical contexts, held the possibility of enacting the gesture of a snub to an implied audience, Simone's performance practice often exacerbated that potential for audience discomfort to an inordinate degree.

"Mississippi Goddam," for example, begins as if we were about to hear a bit of amusing music-hall schtick. Vamping on the spot to a mechanically inane oompah Simone cracks an absurdist joke to loosen everyone up: "This is a show tune, but the show hasn't been written for it yet." In the recording of Simone's famous 1964 performance of this song in Carnegie Hall the audience laughs, as if settling down into their seats.[22] Comedy puts everyone at ease; things are in place, just as they should be. But as the song proceeds, the inexorable vamping undergoes a kind of inverse transmogrification into a terrifying, predatory perpetuum mobile, and the music-hall banter becomes increasingly infected by evermore excoriating forms of furious address unambiguously directed at the audience. Through an accumulating refusal of compromise, this finally culminates in a proclamation that "this whole country is full of lies," and that "you're all gonna die and die like flies." At this point of excess, where the rage reaches a magnitude threatening to the very confines of the song's basic formal articulation, Simone snatches the whole thing away, as if it had merely been the chimera of some mad witch, and we return once more to the safety of the opening's comic vamping, which now, of course, seems repellent. It is as if we find ourselves with a knife in our hand and a seemingly innocent throat that we are being asked to slit. Indeed, the Gothic melodrama of my image is not unwarranted, since the laughter that this music had initially inspired at the opening now literally gets stuck in the audience's throat, as the physical symptom of its guilt. Death by comedy: for Simone during the era of the civil rights movement, this perhaps seemed like a valid form of execution.

In contrast to the disappointing political results attendant upon the commercial success of Brecht and Weill's *The Threepenny Opera*, the political success of "Mississippi Goddam" is attested by how unambiguous the attempts were to thwart the momentum of its immediately rapid commercial circulation. Fearful of the power of its political message, the song was banned in several Southern states and numerous radio stations across America not only refused to play the song, but also sent the records back cracked in half. As stated earlier, the reason for its success was not so much its difference to the fundamental strategies employed by Brecht and Weill so much as in the vastly increased force and tirelessness of their application. Simone opens the song by presenting herself in a traditional mode as a comic Black performer—as if this were just the way things were—and then systematically destroys the ability of the audience to retain, without being profoundly shamed, a stable relationship to the plethora of semiotic cues she had initially unleashed. Nothing is allowed to remain stable, and the effort needed to keep up such a constant stream of negation is unambiguously fueled by Simone's towering rage and its terrifying, unblinking ability to sustain its focus without a single moment of distraction. Incendiary in its force, it feels as if it possesses the power to set alight some inexorable momentum of political action and Simone herself appears as if she will never stop, as if she had become some kind of political machine or infernal immortal. If part of the song's message is to communicate the terrors of how Black people have been pursued by forces that have sought their annihilation, the tables seemed to have been turned and Simone and the song itself feel like they themselves are now the predators, now furies of retribution. This is not only communicated by the already mentioned perpetuum mobile, shifting and changing back and forth constantly between the comic, the horrific, and an excruciatingly acid ironic stance, but in the 1964 live recording, by the fact that the final cadence of the song leads directly into the repetitive motion of the musician's exit music over which Simone happily chirps, "That's it folks!" As a result, the momentum of the song feels like it has crashed through the barriers that protect and police the boundaries between stage and stalls, artifice and reality, performer and audience, representation and the thing itself. As Simone famously stated, "I want to shake people up so bad that when they leave a nightclub where I've performed, I just want them to be to pieces."[23] If "Mississippi Goddam" is a vehicle, then it is only once we have gotten inside for the ride that we realize that it was designed without brakes and that the only thing that will bring it to rest is when it has run over and killed the forces that keep the state of racial injustice alive. It can never be outrun. It will exhaust you.

But how exhausting must it have been to live so much without sleep in such a condition of unending enactment of livid retribution? And what damage did that condition do to Simone—as indeed to any political activist artist who must perform each night such flawless renditions of tirelessness? All performance is, of course, labor. And the realities of most performers' lives is that although a love of what one does is most often the reason for entering into the profession, it can remain difficult to keep that love in sight when the mountain of labor required to do so—the endless exposure of oneself before the public gaze of often unknown others; the grueling grind of life on the road; the draining anxieties regarding how to remain in circulation and not go out of fashion—keeps growing and growing. At certain points the price one pays for the practice of one's art must by definition periodically blanch out into a means of paying the bills so that one might purchase a night of insomnia-free sleep and recuperate. So how much more draining must it be if, like Simone, the path that led to finding one's art having been consumed by such political engagement was, and however much one remained committed to where it ultimately led, nevertheless a deflection from the art that had been one's first love, and, moreover, a deflection that had been enforced upon one by circumstances beyond one's control.

After all, Simone started out her musical life with the desire to be a concert pianist of Western classical music and, in particular, the music of J. S. Bach. Residents of her hometown of Tryon, North Carolina, had provided the funds for her to attend the Juilliard School, in New York, and from there she applied for a scholarship to attend the Curtis Institute in Philadelphia. But even though she performed well in the audition, she was denied the fellowship. Simone put this down to racism. Forced now to make a living, she started to perform in clubs and cocktail lounges and was required by the terms of her contract to both play the piano and sing at the same time. Simone never rejected her early Western classical practice or left the values she saw in it behind, even though, as in the following famous quotation, she was clear to affirm the greater import of her later political commitments: "I had spent many years pursuing excellence because that is what classical music is all about. . . . Now it was dedicated to freedom, and that was far more important."[24] Western classical aesthetics nevertheless remained a strangely haunting presence among the large palette of the techniques over which she could claim total mastery. In part, this is just part and parcel of the characteristic synthesis constituting her own particular style—a synthesis that, whilst immediately recognizable as Simone's, is nevertheless also characteristic of the virtuosic polyphonic, polyglot, stylistic synthesis of so much Black musical practice in general. But it was also redolent of a happiness that could have been, and indeed the kind of happiness that, to return to some of my earlier formulations, comes from wealth of time—from not having had to have devoted oneself to actions in the name of a freedom that should have been yours by rights anyway. And so, she would readily admit, "I think that the artists who don't get involved in preaching messages probably are happier." However, "I have to live with Nina, and that is very difficult."[25]

Notes

1. *Merriam-Webster Dictionary*, s.v. "fascism," accessed August 1, 2020, https://www.merriam-webster.com/dictionary/fascism.

2. See, for example, Andrew Gawthorpe, "Is This Fascism? No. Could It Become Fascism? Yes," *Guardian*, July 31, 2019, accessed August 1, 2020, https://www.theguardian.com/commentisfree/2019/jul/31/is-this-fascism-no-could-it-become-fascism-yes.

3. Hannah Arendt, *Thinking without a Banister: Essays in Understanding, 1953–1975*, ed. Jerome Kohn (New York: Schocken, 2018), 444–445.

4. Hannah Arendt, "Sonning Prize Acceptance Speech, 1975," *Irenebrination*, accessed August 1, 2020, https://www.irenebrination.com/files/hannah-arendt_sonningprizeacceptancespeech-.pdf, 3.

5. Quoted in Arendt, *Thinking without a Banister*, 426.

6. Arendt, *Thinking without a Banister*, 426.

7. Angela Yvonne Davis, *Freedom Is a Constant Struggle: Ferguson, Palestine, and the Foundation of a Movement* (Chicago: Haymarket, 2016).

8. The expression "category mistake" derives from the philosophy of Gilbert Ryle, which had, as part of its goal, "the replacement of category habits by category disciplines." See Gilbert Ryle, *The Concept of Mind* (London: Hutchinson, 1949), 8.

9. Toni Morrison, "A Humanist View," *Mackenzian*, accessed August 1, 2020, https://www.mackenzian.com/wp-content/uploads/2014/07/Transcript_PortlandState_TMorrison.pdf.

10. The transformative possibilities that are afforded by Schiller's text are attested by the fact that even Gayatri Spivak is prepared to entertain it as a resource—if, admittedly, from the position of learning "to use the European Enlightenment from below." See Gayatri Spivak, *An Aesthetic Education in the Era of Globalization* (Cambridge, MA: Harvard University Press, 2012), 3.

11. Herbert Marcuse, *Eros and Civilization: A Philosophical Inquiry into Freud* (Boston: Beacon, 1974).

12. Karl Marx, "Theses on Feuerbach," in Robert Charles Tucker, ed., *The Marx-Engels Reader*, 2nd ed. (New York: Norton, 1978), 145.

13. Kurt Weill, "Der Musiker Weill," *Berliner Tageblatt*, December 25, 1928; translated in Richard Taruskin, *The Oxford History of Western Music* (Oxford: Oxford University Press, 2005–2011), 4:533.

14. See Friedrich Nietzsche, *The Birth of Tragedy and the Case of Wagner*, trans. Walter Kaufmann (New York: Vintage, 1967), 164 (italics original).

15. Weill, "Musiker Weill," 224.

16. Stephen Hinton, "Misunderstanding 'The Threepenny Opera,' " in Stephen Hinton, ed., *Kurt Weill: The Threepenny Opera* (Cambridge: University of Cambridge Press, 1990), 181.

17. Hinton, "Misunderstanding 'The Threepenny Opera,' " 181.

18. Hinton, "Misunderstanding 'The Threepenny Opera,' " 192.

19. Hinton, "Misunderstanding 'The Threepenny Opera,' " 192.

20. Dipesh Chakrabarty, *Provincializing Europe: Postcolonial Thought and Historical Difference* (Princeton: Princeton University Press, 2008).

21. See, for example, Simone C. Drake and Dwan Kendra Hendseron, eds., *Are You Entertained? Black Popular Culture in the Twenty-First Century* (Durham, NC: Duke University Press, 2020).

22. Nina Simone, *Nina Simone in Concert*, Philips PHM 200–135/PHS 600–135 (mono/stereo), 1964, LP.

23. Liz Garbus, dir., *What Happened, Miss Simone?* (Netflix, 2016), chapter 6 (0:49:50).

24. "Nina Simone Quotes," *BrainyQuote*, accessed November 22, 2020, https://www.brainyquote.com/quotes/nina_simone_203090.

25. Garbus, *What Happened, Miss Simone?*, chapter 8 (1:04:45).

References

Arendt, Hannah. *Thinking without a Banister: Essays in Understanding, 1953–1975*. Edited by Jerome Kohn. New York: Schocken, 2018.

Arendt, Hannah. "Sonning Prize Acceptance Speech, 1975." *Irenebrination*. Accessed August 1, 2020. https://www.irenebrination.com/files/hannah-arendt_sonning prizeacceptancespeech-.pdf.

Chakrabarty, Dipesh. *Provincializing Europe: Postcolonial Thought and Historical Difference*. Princeton: Princeton University Press, 2008.

Davis, Angela Yvonne. *Freedom Is a Constant Struggle: Ferguson, Palestine, and the Foundation of a Movement*. Chicago: Haymarket, 2016.

Drake, Simone C., and Dwan Kendra Hendseron, eds. *Are You Entertained? Black Popular Culture in the Twenty-First Century*. Durham, NC: Duke University Press, 2020.

Gawthorpe, Andrew. "Is This Fascism? No. Could It Become Fascism? Yes." *Guardian*, July 31, 2019. Accessed August 1, 2020. https://www.theguardian.com/commentisfree/2019/jul/31/is-this-fascism-no-could-it-become-fascism-yes.

Hinton, Stephen. "Misunderstanding 'The Threepenny Opera.'" In *Kurt Weill: The Threepenny Opera*, edited by Stephen Hinton, 181–92. Cambridge: University of Cambridge Press, 1990.

Marcuse, Herbert. *Eros and Civilization: A Philosophical Inquiry into Freud*. Boston: Beacon, 1974.

Marx, Karl. "Theses on Feuerbach." In *The Marx-Engels Reader*, 2nd ed., edited by Robert Charles Tucker, 145–47. New York: Norton, 1978.

Morrison, Toni. "A Humanist View." *Mackenzian*. Accessed August 1, 2020. https://www.mackenzian.com/wp-content/uploads/2014/07/Transcript_Portland-State_TMorrison.pdf.

Nietzsche, Friedrich. *The Birth of Tragedy and the Case of Wagner*. Translated by Walter Kaufmann. New York: Vintage, 1967.

Ryle, Gilbert. *The Concept of Mind*. London: Hutchinson, 1949.

Spivak, Gayatri. *An Aesthetic Education in the Era of Globalization*. Cambridge, MA: Harvard University Press, 2012.

Taruskin, Richard. *The Oxford History of Western Music*. Oxford: Oxford University Press, 2005–2011.

Chapter 2

"[C]ounting Your Heads / As I'm Making the Beds"
Piratesthetics, Weill-Brecht to Simone

JACQUES LEZRA

And what does it take to make the slave weep?

—Weil, The Iliad: The Poem of Force[1]

Even the blossoming tree lies the moment its bloom is seen without the shadow of terror; even the innocent "How lovely!" becomes an excuse for an existence outrageously unlovely, and there is no longer beauty or consolation except in the gaze falling on horror, withstanding it, and in unalleviated consciousness of negativity holding fast to the possibility of what is better.

—Adorno, Minima Moralia[2]

Scent of magnolias, sweet and fresh . . .

—Meeropol, "Bitter Fruit"

I take my head-counting from Nina Simone's famous 1964-ish cover of the Blitzstein translation of Weill-Brecht's ballad "Seeräuber Jenny," from *The Threepenny Opera*.³ My "piracy" covers the usual registers—the *Seeräuber*, the sea-thief, the unlicensed borrower of protected materials. A figure, in short, like Macheath himself, but also intended to describe the remarkable—I won't say unique—fate of the 1728 *Beggar's Opera*, whose many appropriations and adaptations are striking in this way: in Brecht-Weill's version the work hinges John Gay's interest in the marginal culture of begging with the 1920s and 1930s vernacular Marxist critique of *appropriation, circulation,* and *commodification*. This folding back of the work's subject matter upon the rough history of its pirating, uses, and reuses in the course of the twentieth and twenty-first centuries finds its way rather wonderfully *back* into the matter of the work—for instance when Louis Armstrong name-checks and inserts, meta-lyrically, Lotte Lenya's name into the list of Macheath's lovers, *in* Armstrong's cover of the "Morität" (later incorporated in the 1959 Bobby Darin/Richard Wess hit version); opening or continuing a tradition followed by Darin; Ella Fitzgerald ("Oh Bobby Darin and Louis Armstrong / They made a record, oh but they did / And now Ella, Ella, and her fellas / We're making a wreck, what a wreck of Mack the Knife"); and (among many others) Sinatra, who picks up Fitzgerald's musical baton ("They did this song nice, Lady Ella too/They all sang it, with so much feeling/That Old Blue Eyes, he ain't gonna add nothing new"). Taken together, the counting figure and the strange, self-reflexive, self-commodifying figure of pirating in *The Threepenny Opera* and in "Seeräuber Jenny" above all crop up at different moments, adding something new at each, causing and expressing differently at each moment what we might safely call *aesthetic outrage*—on two levels. First, as regards the *moment*, the signature, the circumstance in which (say) murder or slaughter, or piracy (extensively), is contemplated or takes place: outrage at the wild economic inequality that marked the jazz age in Europe's bourgeois capitals and in the United States (the opera's concern with counting, accounts, and with those in society who *don't count* re-revalues Armstrong's rendition of the name-check in "Mack the Knife" at a third order, incorporating into the account of Macheath's lovers not just the names of the song and the opera's previous performer, Lotte Lenya, but also the bread lines from the Depression setting: "oh the line starts at the corner," the line of performers, beggars, and lovers). Outrage too at the political and social closure of Cold War society in the United States; outrage, in the 1960s and later, as in Nina Simone's extraordinary 1963 and 1964 renditions of "Pirate Jenny," at racial violence and segregation; outrage expressed as "so much feeling" about one or another historical circumstance, well understood, differently understood, when sung by Lenya, by Simone, or about them.

But second, outrage with respect to an aesthetic mode entwining meta-lyrical self-commodification with the performance of the lyrical *critique* of commodity culture: so we can only refuse both, never only one, when, as here, they're on offer.

"Aesthetic outrage," then. Linked, inseparably, *both* to historical outrage *and* to the outrage the spectator cannot refuse at the added value, the added commodity-value, of the history of uses the work makes patent when it counts the events of its previous performances, and the names of its performers, among the heads or the bodies on display *within* it. But *is* "Pirate Jenny," the counting-song, in any of its iterations, and especially just here, at the extraordinary moment when Jenny switches from *allegretto* to what Weill's score calls *meno mosso* (*wie ein langsamer Marsch*), like a slow march, is "Pirate Jenny" an example of aesthetic outrage?[4] Is aesthetic outrage what we feel today, when this bit of shocking news or that snippet of ghastly comment by a politician crawls across our feed? Surely not, or not easily: it's not what we can say, in good conscience, or think that we're feeling.

I'll switch to the first person: here's *my* signature. Outrage, as well as contempt and disgust, anger too, betrayal, even guilt, are what I felt in June 2017 on hearing the results of the Modern Language Association vote on BDS in 2017—the second of two votes, by the Delegate Assembly and then by part of the membership, to "refrain from endorsing the boycott" of Israeli academic institutions. Outrage and the attendant emotions—but would I have called it "aesthetic" outrage? Will I call it that now? "Moral," yes, or I suppose "ethical," and of course "political" outrage, yes. What sort of qualifier is "aesthetic," exactly? We'd resist agreeing that "outrage" can be unproblematically "aesthetic," I think, out of a sense that whatever it is we feel when we're outraged isn't *merely* of the order of the aesthetic, not merely a question (on a very impoverished definition of the aesthetic) of a lapse in style, a vulgarity, a tasteless crack. In fact we'll feel more than a qualm, we'll feel more than resistance when "outrage" sails into the domain of the "aesthetic": we may be outraged at the suggestion that our immediate, spontaneous outrage at the radical mendacity and depredations on display, for instance by the Trump administration, or by supporters of the racist policies of the Israeli government, could be judged to be an aesthetic matter, again a "merely" aesthetic matter. But the seeming alternative to the aestheticization of outrage taken in this weak, gastronomic, and immediate sense gives us pause as well: on the other side, we are rendering the aesthetic outrageous. The work of art, on this other side, is changed into a matter of technique and becomes a tool with which we are charged to change the world, even to make the world. The rhetoricization of aesthetic experience. On either side worlds are lost, outrageously. Is this the condition we inhabit, then—the twenty-first century's version of the Scholastic donkey, Buridan's ass? Balanced between lost worlds, lacking grounds for grieving one more deeply than the other, we are no longer able to express outrage at outrage's complicity in the loss of our worlds; we can no longer even say, with Brecht's characters, "Die Welt ist arm, der Mensch ist schlecht," or in Blitzstein's translation, "The world is mean, and man uncouth," and in Ralph Manheim and John Willet's, "The world is poor, and man's a shit."[5] The naked imperative, "resist," steps in just here, as the strange noun-verb "hope" did in Obama's campaign—objectless and subjectless expressions, generalized, over-rich in "world," over-rich in the idea of world, overflowing in counterfacticity, but poor in program.

We should not agree to this primitive, pre-Brechtian construction of the alternative. Or rather, *a certain* "we" should, can and does agree, a modern, even Modernist "we"—a strange, denudedly objective, even neutral "we" can, the "we" that includes oneself and the vague "the others" or *das Man*, the "they," as Heidegger has it in paragraph 27 of *Being and Time*.[6] An "everyday" "we" "at the disposal of the whims of the others." But perhaps *we*, another *we*, should not. Will a mandarin contempt for *the* "neutral" they, for the anti-modernist others who count themselves into a collective world and into a collective pronoun prematurely, form "our" we, then? Is there a way of approaching the aesthetics of outrage that will yield a different outcome? A way that doesn't secretly or overtly install a priority of the counterfactual over the factual (or the reverse), of the mediate experience of the aesthetic over the brutal, *lumpen* experience of the facts of the world (or the reverse)? A path that doesn't end in impasse, in symmetry, or in a generalized principle of translation? (It may well begin there.) That doesn't lead to the choice between a populist, anti-modernist collective subjectivity on one side, and a reactionary aesthetic subjectivity on the other?

I think so, but finding it requires at least two things. First, it requires doing violence, grave violence, now rather than later, to "the world" understood as an aesthetic object, as an object-for-show, for-use, or for-enjoyment, for instance for show to the Homeric gods, to the human animal, or to the intellectual or the pundit; an object for the use and pleasure of the consumer. And second, to approach the aesthetics of outrage productively requires that poverty-of-world, Heidegger's notorious characterization of being-without-a-world-language, of merely animal being, be wrenchingly reappropriated. I'm calling these two violent gestures by an old name: piracy.

Let's first rephrase the question. To get at what still, even after Brecht, might make us uneasy about the expression "aesthetic outrage" it's useful to give it a different shape. To do so allows us to imagine how to be outraged at a moment when the beginning of political organization and a rather hazy sense of "resistance"—Black Lives Matter—the moment's art and media-forms (TikTok, the meme), even productive violence (the creation of autonomous zones in Western cities), seems on offer to us. (Here "us" remains still indistinct: both collective subjectivities, as above, are interpellated, all heads are counted, though not equally.)

"'*Fiat ars-pereat mundus*,' says fascism, expecting from war . . . the artistic gratification of a sense perception altered by technology."[7] Thus wrote Walter Benjamin in late 1935 or early 1936. "This is evidently the consummation of *l'art pour l'art*," he famously continues. "Humankind, which once, in Homer, was an object of contemplation [*Schauobjekt*] for the Olympian gods, has now become one for itself. Its self-alienation has reached the point where it can experience its own annihilation as a supreme aesthetic pleasure. Such is the aestheticizing of politics, as practiced by fascism. Communism replies [*antwortet ihm*] by politicizing art," he concludes. Communism answers to the nihilism of fascist aestheticization presumably by world-making rather than by destroying worlds. *Pereat ars*: the *merely* aesthetic, the *merely self-contemplative*, all mere gastronomy, all showing-itself, art for the sake of art alone, this all is to perish. Then—*fiat mundus*, a new world. Benjamin's closing sentences lend to *one* historical-political formation, to his day's fascism, the languages of the *imperium* as well as of the dandy and the aesthete—the Latin of *fiat ars-pereat mundus* and the French of *l'art pour l'art*. Marinetti's Italian lurks somewhere in the wings as well; the Greek philosophical lexicon hangs over the scene, moving pieces onstage as the Homeric gods who contemplate the show-thing of human history intrude at times in it. And then, having lent fascism its languages, Benjamin translates them into workaday-communism's German answer: "Der Kommunismus antwortet ihm mit der Politisierung der Kunst," "Communism answers by politicizing art," *der Kunst*. An outrageous confidence in our hard-gained capacity to separate an art that's self-contemplating from one that isn't seems implied. A symmetrical, facing personification of the two tendencies, fascism and communism, the aesthetic destruction of the world and the worldly destruction of aesthetics, *seems* implied. Mutual translation; a proposal, made in the Latin of general humanist speech, correctly interpreted *because* of its humanist universality, because of the legitimacy granted the proposal by its articulation in the language of classical authority, and answered. (Though not, and this is definitive, *in* that language: not answered in Latin but in workaday, communist German, the new international, the new language of the newly human universal class.)

If *that way*, in the direction of spontaneous outrage, lay the Scylla of unthinking, natural, reflexive emotion, then *this way*, the way of self-contemplating art, and the way of the enjoyment *of* self-contemplating art as such, *this way*, disguised as the critique of mere aestheticism, lies the Charybdis of the most hieratic of modernisms, the most elitist. *That way*, a *lumpen*-aesthetics, and *aisthesis* defined as the body's dumb and passive reception of the senses' impressions. The physical world of hands and bodies lies *that* way. *This way*, a new class is announced, composed of those who experience with supreme pleasure their reflection upon their own birth as the class of producers of the world; *aisthesis* defined as pleasure-in-reflection; a blood-aristocracy of the aesthetic, drawing sustenance and making its world from the reflexive surplus-enjoyment of the world of hands and bodies. *This* way, the world of the aesthete; of cultivation in its secondary, class-marked sense rather than its primary, earth-bound sense; of thought rather than outrage.

I can now rephrase my opening provocation, unfolding "aesthetic outrage" in three directions.

First, stress on the first term: aesthetic rather than, for instance, moral outrage, or political, or personal, outrage, or whatever other modifier we'd choose. We imagine a cluster of sorts of outrage, and our focus today would be in the subclass of "outrage," for instance the outrage that a bourgeois or a liberal electorate or audience might feel at what Hannah Arendt describes, in a passage I'll return to in a moment, as "cruelty, disregard of human values, and general amorality," the hallmarks not just of 1920s Germany, but also of neo-liberal, predatory, and racialized capitalism we witness in this country today; or outrage at unfairness, at economic inequality, at insult, that's expressed in any of the domains that configure the field that since Baumgarten we call aesthetics. Here we run the classic danger of trading, in place of what we'd like to believe is a spontaneous and common feeling, perhaps not-yet articulated, perhaps not-yet available formally, the formal arsenal developed for the field of aesthetics—the generic and other devices used to express what came before, that genuine sense of outrage. Aesthetic outrage—outrage aestheticized, recognized as such in the lexicon or lexicons given us. Think Guernica, always the secondary expression of the shock that the newspapers the painting seems to catch and distress and materialize, would offer.

Second, stress on the noun. Aesthetic outrage: whatever object, or work, in that domain, causes outrage. It's an outrage, this work: it causes that sensation, if that's what it is, a sensation. The object, or the work, works some sort of violence upon the form of expression, its conventions, history, genealogy. This may be in the service of a political or moral outrage, or not.

Finally, a matter hovering between the adjective and the noun: just what is outrage? On the moving map of affects and affections, will it fall closer to the reputable neighborhoods of the feelings of the beautiful and the sublime? Is outrage closer to disgust, that famously resistant term? Has it always been in the same location on this map, or does outrage travel with other affective, philosophical, and psychological forms.

Each of these directions to our expression will have a historic determination, or any number of them: aesthetic outrage, aesthetic outrage. A general relativism is in play; at some point, say now, in 2020, or in 1933, or just after news of the extermination camps became current in Europe and in the United States, at some point the experience has one shape, at another the objects that will elicit, for this or that group of people, an experience—changes. "Aesthetic outrage" for our time, in our time, in our world, is at work where the call-and-answer that Benjamin seems to offer is interrupted, wrenched from its reflexive, symmetrical circuits: where it is *pirated*, where fascism's proposition *fiat ars-pereat mundus* doesn't translate into the answering communist alternative *pereat ars-fiat mundus*, or vice-versa.

Let me show you what I mean. You saw me use, improbably and colorfully, two words—the word *pirate*, in its verbalized form, "pirating," to describe the interruption of the aesthetic circuit joining the aestheticization of politics and the politicization of art into a call-and response mirror-shape; and the word *translation* to define, or characterize, that circuit. My claim was that this mirroring form, this generalized translation, is interrupted at the point where aesthetic outrage enters the game. This becoming-popular of the high-modernist critique of merely outrageous, that is to say, merely spontaneous "art" (which reflects ideology and provides no critical, Homeric vantage outside it, no godlike place for self-consciousness to fail at coinciding with itself) becomes, for instance in the view of anti-modernist critics from Arendt to Russell Berman, an index of "the obsolescence of the categories of the historical avant-garde," which is also, for the same line of critics, the obsolescence of the categories of vanguardist Marxism. About Berman's claim that Simone intends "not to hone rational criticism but rather to appeal to emotion, to the terror and pity that characterize the Aristotelian poetics for which Brecht reserved only contempt . . . Wagnerian sentimentalism . . . sentiment . . . sentiment alone . . ." not much needs to be said.[8] More interesting is Arendt's notorious dislike of *The Threepenny Opera*, tellingly expressed in symmetries that evoke Benjamin's, without the edge to his critique. "Particularly significant in this respect," in signaling a misunderstanding of how the aesthetic presentation of outrage would, rather than produce ironic externalization and critique, produce pleasure at or resignation to the outrageous in all audiences, "particularly significant," Arendt writes,

> was the reception given Brecht's *Dreigroschenoper* in pre-Hitler Germany. The play presented gangsters as respectable businessmen and respectable businessmen as gangsters. The irony was somewhat lost when respectable businessmen in the audience considered this a deep insight into the ways of the world and when the mob welcomed it as an artistic sanction of gangsterism. The theme song in the play, "Erst kommt das Fressen, dann kommt die Moral," was greeted with frantic applause by exactly everybody, though for different reasons. The mob applauded because it took the statement literally; the bourgeoisie applauded because it had been fooled by its own hypocrisy for so long that it had grown tired of the tension and found deep wisdom in the expression of the banality by which it lived; the elite applauded because the unveiling of hypocrisy was such superior and wonderful fun. The effect of the work was exactly the opposite of what Brecht had sought by it. The bourgeoisie could no longer be shocked; it welcomed the exposure of its hidden philosophy, whose popularity proved they had been right all along, so that the only political result of Brecht's "revolution" was to encourage everyone to discard

the uncomfortable mask of hypocrisy and to accept openly the standards of the mob.[9]

The pirate—"*die Figur des Piraten*," Carl Schmitt would call it, though he also refers to "Seeräuber," sea-thieves—did not, at the time that Brecht was writing his adaptation of the Gay opera, have quite the standing in international law that it would come to have in the wake of the 1937 so-called Conference of Nyon, on international piracy. Nor did it have as commonly the specific sense we hear today, the taking over of intellectual property. (Simone uses the word constantly in interviews.) When Jenny sang "Seeräuber Jenny" in 1927–1928, the figure of the "Seeräuber" would more likely have called up Schiller's Karl Moor, in Die Räuber, to a Berlin audience than the arcana of international jurisprudence. The song had been written for Polly Peachum, but Weill rearranged it and gave it to Jenny—as he did with a number of songs in the course of production. But this one's of particular importance: the ballad could have been sung, in fact, by any of the characters. It represents strikingly the relation between the domains of the play's setting—the bleak landscapes of SoHo, the circumstances of Berlin—and the aspirational role played by the character as a pirate queen, unrecognized by all, always unrecognized by all, who, in Marc Blitzstein's translation, will "never know to who you're talking," not now when I, Jenny, scrub the floors for you, not tonight, when I pronounce your death-sentence, and never after, when your heads roll and you're nothing but counters. The complication in Brecht is the characteristic one—having to do not with the violent content of the Pirate song, but rather with its undecidable function. Recall the moment I opened with—when Jenny's song, leaping in Weill's score a perfect sixth into seemingly-lyrical heavens, into fantasy and counterfacticity, leaping out of the physical world of the Southern cheap hotel, of "meine lumpen und dies lumpige Hotel," and into the consoling dream of the kitchen maid, leaping into the genre of the revenge-song, Rachelied, leaping into the world of fantasy, may fall into one construction of aesthetics, into mere aesthetics. Is what's being staged in the kitchen maid's dream song, as Brecht would call it in his *Threepenny Novel*, is the dream-vision supposed to function as an idea planted in the audience's mind, the possibility of a revolutionary change, the destruction of the sorts of classes that maintain the Lumpenproletariat in subjection? Then anyone, unbeknownst to the exploiting class, could be the bearer of their last word, the unacknowledged sovereign, the figure of the pirate at home in their bosom. Or is the role of Jenny's fantasy to maintain the relations just as they are—that is, to make it possible for her to have a counterfactual experience, to cultivate a private smile and an interior fantasy life that keeps her at work in the subjunctive mode—you may think I'm just scrubbing the floors, but mark my words, the day will come, the lonely hour of that promised moment, and then my sovereign right to dispose of you will shine through, and the heads I count silently now, under my breath, will roll, and my robbers and I will command. The revolution, in short, will someday arrive, like a ship sailing into the harbor, and then, only then, will my band of robbers, die Räuber, cash in the heads I'm counting now, silently, to myself. (The extraordinary version of "Pirate Jenny" that Bernard Nicolas's 1977 short "Daydream Therapy" offers stages the seeming decision between these alternatives, a generalized insurrectional subjectivity and a counterfactual, deferred, therapeutic, dream-scenario; subjection or dream, rather than revolt; either Simone's counting-song or Archie Shepp's "Things Have Got to Change."[10]) Or more disturbing, more outrageous still—yet another construction of aesthetics: Jenny takes pleasure in the world from which her revenge-song threatens, or seems, to release her; sacrificially or selfishly, she takes pleasure in abjection, in what Chico Buarque's "Geni e o zepelim," the great Brazilian rewriting of "Seeräuber Jenny," calls the abject, deep, even Christ-like "goodness" that Geni manifests in giving herself to anyone, and in secretly preferring the love of "bichos," a wonderful portmanteau word for the vagrant, the beggar, the lost, the animal, the ugly, the angry; for a bug, for a work—in short, for whatever it is that has no value, for what one finds, indeed, in a *Threepenny Opera*, in "dies lumpige Hotel" and in the *Lumpenwelt* generally. (Geni/Genet.)

The entire opera presents itself under the sign of this di- or trilemma—as if the "Pirate song" were the figure of the play and reigned sovereign over it. Any of the characters in *The Threepenny Opera*, and not just Polly Peachum or Jenny, could have sung "Pirate Jenny," because the opera generalizes the condition the ballad describes and makes it the opera's *subject*: abjection its secret pleasure; aesthetic outrage may be enjoyed, drawn out, like a note sung high and long a perfect sixth above the humdrum march or the mechanical dance of our melodic, impoverished lives; or *any* note, like any event and any one of us, carries the seed of that alternative, revolutionary, perfecting, and harmonizing lyrical resolution, which we reach for one night, when the ship, the black freighter, lies at dock at last.

But this construction of our sovereign and common di- or trilemma is wrong in two important ways. What happens if, and when, we can't decide whether this object at hand, the ballad "Pirate Jenny," the ballad I have been offering you as the figure of the aestheticization of outrage in that other object of which it's a part, the aesthetic object we call *The Threepenny Opera*, this ballad-object I've suggested could really have been sung by any of the characters, inasmuch as it provides the shape of the critique of aesthetic sublimation that is the opera's structuring political concern? What happens if and when we can't decide whether "Pirate Jenny" works to reproduce, or to announce the end of, the regimes of exploitation that Brecht and Weill, and Nina Simone and Chico Buarque after them, depict and obviously deplore? What can we expect if we thus can't decide whether the figure of the sovereign pirate, offered ostensibly as the heroic leader of the vanguard is also, not implausibly, the taskmaster who has armored herself sadistically in the leader's cloak, the better to maintain, or even worse, to naturalize, the outrageous conditions the opera deplores? What happens when we find, with Geni/Genet, that we love the abject, *os bichos*, the beggars as such?

Well then: if in short the ballad is undecided as to its understanding of the sovereign function of the aesthetic image, then how will we decide whether it, the ballad, has or has not reigned sovereign, always and already, over the opera's understanding of itself? It can't be decided, on the model (if it is a model) that's offered by "Pirate Jenny," whether "Pirate Jenny" is or is not the hieratic figure into which the balance of *The Threepenny Opera* can be translated. Its sovereignty over the work—that is, the sovereignty of the ballad, *this* ballad, over the formal and ideological claims of the opera—is subject to the same undecidability as its content, Jenny's vision of herself as sovereign over the pirates. And notice then two things, from a conceptual point of view even more intriguing, even more outrageous. The ballad's sovereign capacity to provide a principle that makes the work cohere, what we might call an immanent principle that furnishes the objectality of the work, that sings it, that translates it into the aesthetic register—surely this, too, will now vanish. And then we will conclude that what makes a work like *The Threepenny Opera* useful, what turns it into a means or a tool for conveying the aestheticization of outrage at historical moments other than those marked in its deictic, historicizing gestures—what makes *The Threepenny Opera* translatable—lies just here, where it does not offer itself as an organized, countable historical object, which is to say, just where it performs the undoing of its objectality.

Brecht's, Weill's, the translator Elizabeth Hauptmann's, Blitzstein's, Simone's, and Buarque's undoing of the aesthetic object makes it untranslatable too—and here perhaps lies the moment of greatest violence in the opera. The general condition that's meant to characterize every character, every way-of-being in the *Lumpenmwelt*, is also not translatable from one situation, one character's experience, one language to another, not from Brecht's verse to Weill's score or back, and not from German to English or to Brazilian Portuguese. At the moment when "Pirate Jenny" suddenly shifts tempo, from the *allegretto* to a *langsam* march, the German says: "Und ein Schiff, mit acht Segeln, wird liegen am Kai." Weill/ Brecht's *wird*- construction is particularly striking, and typical of Brecht, of this opera, and of Weill and Brecht's collaborations at this time—this construction of *wird*- as both a future condition, an active, and a descriptive verb. (For instance in "Surabaya Johnny.") When it comes to translating the expression, Mannheim and Willett have [the ship] "has tied up the quay" for *wird liegen am Kai;* Blitzstein translates the verse in full, with a violent colloquialism, as "There's a ship / The black freighter / With a skull on its masthead, / will be coming in." Neither translation quite captures the conceptual oddity of the expression, though Blitzstein's does some of the German original's work by jamming up the present tense "There's a ship" with the unusual future progressive, "Will be coming in." Brecht's German makes a historical event, the arrival of the revolutionary ship, of the revolution; the conversion of oppression into sovereignty; the translation of outrage into aesthetic form; the conversion of the aesthetic form into a revolutionary, physical reality with the application of revolutionary force—Brecht's verse makes this event into something that *will lie* in the world. One day, it will be disclosed always to have been lying there already, this ship, this event. The possibility of revolutionary sovereignty enters the scene suddenly, one night, with shrieks and violence, a cut, a distinct historical event, something we could count as we count heads; but it *also* lay-there-already, always and already. Weill's score seeks to translate this philosophical-grammatical proposition by showing that *any* melodic line and *any* tempo can be interrupted-completed, perfected, through transposition or through modulation. In the very last verse of Nina Simone's version, the danger of this modulation is apparent: the note to which she leaps threatens not to end; her breath, infinitely drawn out, arrests the event; the love and pleasure of the abject note empties the opera of philosophical, historical, political content; like heads just rolling, the note rolls on and on.

The unfinishing of the aesthetic object, of the aesthetic image, is here accomplished temporally—and it cannot, rightly, make its way from German into English. This violent untranslatability is just what makes possible the ballad's uncomfortable drift into other moments and other times. Never just an instrument, never just self-referring, never having a determinate or indeed determinable effect, "Seeräuber Jenny" drifts from voice to voice, from Lotte Lenya to Judy Collins to Nina Simone to Chico Buarque and others; from the signature of the crises of capital in the European metropolis, to the cheap racism of the Southern hotel, to the hypocrisy of bourgeois mores in the emergent capitalist economy of the Brazilian city. *Drifting* here should appear a violently paradoxical term, since it's on the principle of the work's staging and enjoyment of sovereign *untranslatability* that I'm saying that it "drifts," or moves, modulates, transposes, even *translates* across times, locations, and characters.

I'd be happy to end on that note—on the claim that the piratesthetics that Weill and Brecht, together, diagnose for the crisis of capitalist societies is indeed violent, paradoxical, mobile, singular, modal, abject. Like Jenny's, or Polly's, revenge song, one day it lies there, and the world will change.

Ending there leaves open, though, the question, for whom, to whom—the matter of address, of political subjectivity. I'm now asking whether a work, *The Threepenny Opera* or Nina Simone's counting-song "Pirate Jenny," that piratically performs the undoing of its objectality, does so in order to build (or, more weakly, does so *and* builds) something like a collective subjectivity. If so, we will no longer call this built/produced "we" *either* popular and anti-modernist, *or* aesthetic-modernist. *This* subjectivity constituted-addressed, addressed-constituted might not be content to wait for the appearance, one day, of the always-already-present event of the arrival of revolutionary subjectivity; *this* subjectivity might work toward its production, toward its translation, toward radicalizing its drift, toward making Simone's leap to the hanging note, for a moment, permanent; the crisis, for a moment, permanent. Outrage, drawn out all the length of our breath: *Meno mosso (wie ein langsamer Marsch)*.

Notes

1. Simone Weil, *The Iliad: The Poem of Force*, trans. Mary McCarthy (Wallingford, PA: Pendle Hill, 1991), 9.
2. Theodor Wiesengrund Adorno, *Minima Moralia*, trans. E. F. N. Jephcott (New York: Verso, 1978), 25.
3. Simone included "Pirate Jenny" on *Nina Simone in Concert*, which she recorded in March and April of 1964, off three live performances at Carnegie Hall.
4. The Weill score, from UNIVERSAL EDITION 8851, WIEN 1928; see Michael Bednarek, ed., *Die Dreigroschenoper (The Threepenny Opera)*, by Bertolt Brecht and Kurt Weill, *Michael Bednarek—Classical Music Scores Written with MOZART—and Some Other Stuff*, accessed May 7, 2022, http://mbednarek.byethost7.com/scores-sql.php?sort=1&dir=tpo&dont=.
5. For the German, see Bertolt Brecht, *Die Dreigroschenoper* (Frankfurt am Main: Suhrkamp, 1986), 40. For Blitzstein's translation, see Bertolt Brecht and Kurt Weill, *The Threepenny Opera*, trans. Marc Blitzstein (New York: Tams-Witmark Music Library, 1956). For the Willett-Manheim translation, see Bertolt Brecht and Kurt Weill, *The Threepenny Opera*, trans. Ralph Manheim and John Willett (New York: Arcade, 1994).
6. Martin Heidegger, *Being and Time*, trans. Joan Stambaugh and Dennis J. Schmidt (New York: State University of New York Press, 2010), §126 (italics original): "The everyday possibilities of being of Dasein are at the disposal of the whims of the others. These others are not *definite* others. On the contrary, any other can represent them. What is decisive is only the inconspicuous domination by others that Dasein as being-with has already taken over unawares. One belongs to the others oneself, and entrenches their power. 'The others,' whom one designates as such in order to cover over one's own essential belonging to them, are those who *are there* initially and for the most part in everyday being-with-one-another. The who is not this one and not that one, not oneself, not some, and not the sum of them all. The 'who' is the neuter, *the they* [German, *das Man*; literally, *the One*; as in *one does this or that*]."
7. Walter Benjamin, *The Work of Art in the Age of Its Technological Reproducibility and Other Writings on Media*, ed. Michael William Jennings, Brigid Doherty, and Thomas Y. Levin (Cambridge, MA: Harvard University Press, 2008), 42.
8. See Russell Alexander Berman, "Sounds Familiar? Nina Simone's Performances of Brecht/Weill Songs," in Nora Maria Alter and Lutz Koepnick, eds., *Sound Matters: Essays on the Acoustics of German Culture* (New York: Berghahn, 2004), 181. For a careful argument in favor of Simone's Brechtianism (one version of it, at any rate) and specifically *contra* Berman, see Rafael do Nascimento Cesar, "A Fragata Negra: tradução e vingança em Nina Simone," *MANA* 24, no. 1 (2018): 39–70, especially 56–59.

9. Hannah Arendt, *The Origins of Totalitarianism* (San Diego: Harcourt, 1968), 3:33.

10. See the discussion of Bernard Nicolas's 1977 short "Daydream Therapy" in Michael T. Martin, "Struggles for the *Sign* in the Black Atlantic: Los Angeles Collective of Black Filmmakers," in Allyson Nadia Field, Jan-Christopher Horak, and Jacqueline Najuma Stewart, eds., *L.A. Rebellion: Creating a New Black Cinema* (Oakland: University of California Press, 2015), 211–12. Samantha Sheppard expresses in the strongest, clearest terms the affirmative-therapeutic sense Nicolas's film can have, in Samantha Noelle Sheppard, "Bruising Moments: Affect and the L.A. Rebellion," in Allyson Nadia Field, Jan-Christopher Horak, and Jacqueline Najuma Stewart, eds., *L.A. Rebellion: Creating a New Black Cinema* (Oakland: University of California Press, 2015), 241: "In this case, the woman's transformation is marked in color, literally, where she represents a return to a Black Pan-African nationalism symbolized as more natural and authentic for the African diaspora than America's capitalist and patriarchal society. In waking up from her militant dream to this revolutionary reality, she is liberated and transformed into an activist. Nicolas's film explores the notion of personal awakening but also connects the individual experience of one Black woman with Pan-African struggles for equality. *Daydream Therapy*'s protagonist uses her mind not only to dissociate herself from her oppressive social environment but also to free-associate to her global community."

References

Adorno, Theodor Wiesengrund. *Minima Moralia*. Translated by E. F. N. Jephcott. New York: Verso, 1978.

Arendt, Hannah. *The Origins of Totalitarianism*. San Diego and New York: Harcourt, 1968.

Bednarek, Michael, ed. *Die Dreigroschenoper (The Threepenny Opera)*. By Bertolt Brecht and Kurt Weill. *Michael Bednarek—Classical Music Scores Written with MOZART—and Some Other Stuff*. Accessed May 7, 2022. http://mbednarek.byethost7.com/scores-sql.php?sort=1&dir=tpo&dont=.

Benjamin, Walter. *The Work of Art in the Age of Its Technological Reproducibility and Other Writings on Media*. Edited by Michael William Jennings, Brigid Doherty, and Thomas Y. Levin. Cambridge, MA: Harvard University Press, 2008.

Berman, Russell Alexander. "Sounds Familiar? Nina Simone's Performances of Brecht/Weill Songs." In *Sound Matters: Essays on the Acoustics of German Culture*, edited by Nora Maria Alter and Lutz Koepnick, 171–82. New York: Berghahn, 2004.

Brecht, Bertolt, and Kurt Weill. *The Threepenny Opera*. Translated by Marc Blitzstein. New York: Tams-Witmark Music Library, 1956.
Brecht, Bertolt, and Kurt Weill. *The Threepenny Opera*. Translated by Ralph Manheim and John Willett. New York: Arcade, 1994.
Brecht, Bertolt. *Die Dreigroschenoper*. Frankfurt am Main: Suhrkamp, 1986.
Buarque, Chico. "Geni e o Zepelim." *Letras*. Accessed August 14, 2020. https://www.letras.mus.br/chico-buarque/77259.
Cesar, Rafael do Nascimento. "A Fragata Negra: tradução e vingança em Nina Simone." *MANA* 24, no. 1 (2018): 39–70.
Field, Allyson, Jacqueline Najuma Stewart, and Jan-Christopher Horak, eds. *L.A. Rebellion: Creating a New Black Cinema*. Oakland, CA: University of California Press, 2015.
Heidegger, Martin. *Being and Time*. Translated by Joan Stambaugh and Dennis J. Schmidt. New York: State University of New York Press, 2010.
Kowalke, Kim H. "'The Threepenny Opera' in America." In Stephen Hinton, ed., *Kurt Weill: The Threepenny Opera*, 78–120. Cambridge: Cambridge University Press, 1990.
Martin, Michael T. "Struggles for the *Sign* in the Black Atlantic: Los Angeles Collective of Black Filmmakers." In Allyson Nadia Field, Jan-Christopher Horak, and Jacqueline Najuma Stewart, eds., *L.A. Rebellion: Creating a New Black Cinema*, 196–224. Oakland, CA: University of California Press, 2015.
Sheppard, Samantha Noelle. "Bruising Moments: Affect and the L.A. Rebellion." In *L.A. Rebellion: Creating a New Black Cinema*, edited by Allyson Nadia Field, Jan-Christopher Horak, and Jacqueline Najuma Stewart, 225–50. Oakland, CA: University of California Press, 2015.
Steyn, Mark. "Mack the Knife: Sinatra Song of the Century #95." *Steyn Online*, December 8, 2015. Accessed May 7, 2022. https://www.steynonline.com/7344/mack-the-knife.
Weil, Simone. *The Iliad: The Poem of Force*. Translated by Mary McCarthy. Wallingford, PA: Pendle Hill, 1991.

Chapter 3

Sonic Ordeals

Music, Torture, and *The New Orpheus*

PETER SZENDY

In 1925, Kurt Weill wrote a cantata entitled *The New Orpheus*, on a poem by French-German poet Iwan Goll. The mythical Orpheus, represented by the solo violin, has become "everyone" (*jeder*). He has moved to a big metropolis where he is confronted with new conditions for his music-making: instead of his traditional lyre, "gramophones," "pianolas," that is to say mechanical instruments, and a "torture keyboard (*Qualenklavier*) in a suburban cinema."

Why torture? And what does such a keyboard have to do with the mechanized reproduction of music?

Taking Kurt Weill's *New Orpheus* as a metonymy for the conditions of music today, I will try to sketch out a broad genealogy of sound as a means of torture in the age of technological reproducibility.

∽

In the wake of the news that began to spread, in 2003 and 2004, about the torturing practices of the United States Army at Guantánamo and Abu Ghraib, various studies were dedicated to the use of music in what has been euphemistically called "enhanced interrogation techniques."

Following the publication of a few articles in the press, musicologist Suzanne Cusick was to first to offer an in-depth analysis of torture by means of music, thus paving the way for others.[1]

This emerging body of scholarly work generally inscribes musical torture within a narrow historical perspective, limited to the second half of the twentieth century: Suzanne Cusick identifies the origins of what historian Alfred McCoy termed "no-touch torture" (namely, torture that does not leave marks or stigmata on the body) in the 1950s, a time when the CIA was developing programs designed to use data from psychological experiments to improve their interrogation techniques; others consider that it is an even more recent phenomenon.[2]

John Hamilton is the only one, to my knowledge, who has attempted to expand this narrow historical frame, but at the cost of reversing the perspective, with an approach that raises more problems than it resolves: in going back to olden times (to the sixth century BC) and rereading the story of Phalaris's bull—the brazen bull in which the prisoners of the Sicilian tyrant burned while the pipes of this artificial animal turned their screams into smooth harmonies—Hamilton does not discover a more ancient origin for music as an instrument for torture. Rather, he offers a singular example of "torture as an instrument of music": far from paving the way for a genealogy of musical torture as witnessed in the context of the "war on terror," his approach leads to emphasizing the power of aesthetic sublimation that turns pain into sweet and pleasant sounds.[3] In fact, fascinating as it is, the story of the brazen bull exhumed by Hamilton remains isolated, detached. It is like a philological pearl, a beautiful artifact given over to the curiosity of the archeologist.

I would like to propose an alternative approach: I will attempt to inscribe the recent phenomenon of musical torture in a long-term genealogy—though without yielding to aesthetic sublimation—and I will try to question what is proper to music or sound in this dark history. If there is one question that no musicologist, critic, or historian seems to face entirely, it is this: why music, why sound? There is no doubt some resistance to analyzing what might destine music or sound to such a torturing (rather than simply violent or belligerent) practice. This is why those who approached torture by means of music often content themselves with listing the seemingly obvious connotations and impacts of a given musical genre (rap and hard rock are supposed to be aggressive, right?, and children's lullabies are exasperating, right?), without acknowledging that if nearly *all genres* can be used for torture, it is precisely because, beyond its stylistic determinations, what is at stake is music or sound *as such*.[4]

To understand this, however, we must place the emphasis not on the suffering inflicted or on the violence exerted, but rather on the objective of all torturers practicing "no-touch torture," i.e., confession. Indeed, the reason, the main justification for torture, is always the same; it results from a desperate monotony ("torture is monotonous and sad," says Godard's voice-over in *The Little Soldier*): truth has to be *extracted*, the prisoner must deliver the information expected of them; in short, they must *spit it out*.

What follows, then, is my attempt at capturing what binds music or sound to today's remnants of an old practice known as *ordeal*. I will be guided both by Theodor Reik, who dedicated remarkable pages to trial by ordeal;[5] and by an ad hoc filmography spanning from film noir to Polanski.

Extracting the truth, producing the confession *by means of sound*: this is what is staged in a remarkable scene in *The Big Combo*, a film noir directed by Joseph H. Lewis in 1954, during the same years when the CIA conducted sound experiments designed to break the will of subjects submitted to interrogation. First, we see a slightly deaf gangster, Joe McClure, as he slaps Police Lt. Leonard Diamond, who is half passed out, attempting to extract information from him. But when the boss, Mr. Brown, enters the room, he reminds Joe that he shouldn't have "touched" the cop ("I told you not to touch him," he says). Joe answers: "I didn't hurt him, we're still legal." No laws seem to have been broken yet, then, but everything remains to be done since the lieutenant hasn't given any information. Thus, in order to pursue the interrogation while leaving no stigmata on the victim's body, Mr. Brown turns toward another technology. "The problem with you, McClure," he says to his employee, "is that you never took the time to learn technique."

The technical device in question, the equipment that makes touchless torture possible, combines both a radio and Joe McClure's hearing aid in order to produce what Mr. Brown calls "a little concert": when McClure refuses to speak, Mr. Brown holds the hearing aid up to the radio. Taking advantage of a drum solo, he inflicts an unbearable sound dynamic upon his victim's ears and then he forces him to swallow some alcohol, turning the poor lieutenant into a sort of crawling animal.

The sonic torture, then, is immediately followed by what we will soon be calling, with Theodor Reik, an "oral ordeal" (*orale Ordal*).[6] The contiguity between these two forms of violence—forced inebriation and decibels—isn't due to pure chance springing from the arbitrary cruelty of the torturers: in both cases, the same logic is at work that we have to analyze. Let's simply say, to anticipate, that in both cases a fluid substance, either liquid or sound, penetrates the victim's body in order to be then spit out or vociferated, regurgitated in the form of an oral truth, a confession.

The fact remains that, in *The Big Combo*, it is the sheer volume of the sound that inflicts pain, more than the music itself. Let us turn to another film, then, to Roman Polanski's *Death and the Maiden*, adapted in 1994 from Ariel Dorfman's eponymous theatrical play. Here, it is not about the volume: this time, it is actually the music that seems to cause and to have caused suffering. Schubert's string quartet in D minor (D. 810), nicknamed *Death and the Maiden* after the lied from which the second movement borrows its motif, seems capable of harming its listener after having become the metonymy of an unbearable memory.

"Let's listen to it, for old times' sake," says Paulina Escobar (Sigourney Weaver) to the man she just tied to a chair and gagged: Dr. Miranda (Ben Kingsley), who, we learn, regularly raped her while she was imprisoned and tortured in the time of dictatorship (we are not told the name of the country where the film is set). Paulina is convinced that she has identified him, but he refuses to recognize her. She holds a piece of evidence supporting her conviction: the cassette tape, the phonogram of the quartet that she has just discovered in the car of the man who abused her to the sound of this music.

The torturer and his victim, then, listen to this Schubert piece that takes them back—*pars pro toto*—to many years ago. It is as if, in the form of this phonographic record that has remained indifferent to the passage of time, the music *replayed* the trauma buried in memory. In front of her husband Gerardo who wakes up to discover the scene in astonishment, Paulina says to the doctor: "You know how long it's been since I listened to this quartet? [. . .] it made me sick, physically sick to hear it. But it's time for me to reclaim my Schubert, my favorite composer."

We are on the threshold of a powerful repetition that is about to reproduce the supposed crime, so that its perpetrator will confess it. And it is music that plays the key role in this reconstitution.

Death and the Maiden is the voice of the young girl that Paulina was but is no more, and this voice died with what she lived through. It is her own resurrected voice that testifies to what happened: Schubert's quartet functions in the same way as the musical clues or pieces of evidence that

Theodor Reik analyzes in many narratives and legends, where they are the metonymy of the deceased's voice as it identifies the murderer:

> In *Grimm's Fairy Tales* we find the [. . .] story of the singing bone. A jealous elder brother pushes his younger brother off a bridge into the water and buries him under the bridge. Many years after, a herdsman drives his sheep over the same bridge. He sees there a white bone, picks it up and carves out of it a mouthpiece for his horn. When he puts it to his mouth, the bone itself starts to sing: "O, my dear little shepherd boy, / Out of my bone you've made a toy. / My brother gave me a treacherous blow / And buried my corpse in the sand below." They dig under the bridge and find the boy's skeleton [. . .].[7]

Reik exhumes similar examples "in numerous countries," as this "Sicilian tale" according to which "a bagpipe is made out of the dead man's skin and bones (*Knochen und Haut des Toten*), and gives the murderer away (*den Mord verrät*)" (Reik, 94), or a "Saxon fairy tale from Transylvania" in which "a murder is betrayed by a flute made from a reed which has grown on the victim's grave" (Reik, 98 [93, German original]).

But the cassette tape of *Death and the Maiden*, the object that begins to sing as soon as it is slipped into a cassette player isn't just the metonymy of Paulina's voice returning to accuse her torturer. According to the same metonymic logic, only reversed, the tape is also the culprit's excretion or exudation: it seems to emanate from his body. In fact, if we follow Reik's theory on the metonymic secretion of clues or evidence, there is, always according to the logic of *pars pro toto*, an equivalence between "the murderer" (or, in Dr. Miranda's case, the persecutor) and "everything he has come into contact with," for example, here, the music (57 [54]). This equivalence, according to Reik, explains the criminal's frequent returns to the crime scene, where "the clue is changed back into the person—*totus pro parte*" (63 [60]).

The part for the whole or the whole for the part, for that part that already took the place of the whole: it is within this dizzyingly metonymic circulation of clues that the ritual of the ordeal takes place, its oral form being the focus of Reik's analysis.

The "oral ordeal" actually establishes innocence or guilt by "the incorporation (*Einverleibung*) of a part of the murdered man by the supposed culprit" and observing his reaction (111 [104]); accordingly, "nausea" appears as "the forerunner of confession" and "a primitive form of repentance" (111 [488]). It is as if this repetition of the crime, this "cannibalistic" way of committing it again "in an indirect way and on a substitutive object" (112 [105]), constituted both the confession and the expiation.

In a later sequence of *Death and the Maiden*, Paulina asks her husband Gerardo to take off Dr. Miranda's gag and to prepare his defense, which will look like a mock trial. Once ungagged, the doctor nearly vomits, just like the poor cop in *The Big Combo*. And what he regurgitates, literally and symbolically, is Paulina's underwear that she'd shoved in his mouth to silence him. Even before he says anything, and while he desperately asks for some water, he is forced to spit out the piece of his guilt as a rapist.

And yet, he protests—"this is unforgivable," he pathetically moans— and his words are immediately captured, they are recorded with the same phonographic device that had first voiced the accusation against him by singing, so to speak, *Death and the Maiden*. "There's a mike built into this," Paulina says triumphantly, and she adds: "I want everything on the record, scrupulously recorded."

"Everything on the record," that is to say: the evidence, the confession, the accusation, and the defense. In their dizzyingly metonymic rotation or whirl, things and signs substitute for one another on the stage of this sonic ordeal in the era of phonography, in this old-new ordeal in the age of the technological reproducibility of music.

∽

In the mock trial that Paulina has orchestrated, her husband Gerardo plays the part of the civil rights discourse. A famous lawyer recently named head of the investigation commission of past crimes, Gerardo is the helpless prosopopoeia of enlightened justice when it is confronted with the return of the age-old institution of ordealic torture embodied by Paulina.[8] When Paulina bites and sniffs Dr. Miranda, reenacting on her torturer's body the metonymic equivalents of what she herself has suffered, Gerardo gives voice to what we would like to believe in, to what we *must* hold onto: "Even if he is guilty you can't torture him like this," he says, "he has the right to defend himself."

Gerardo's argument repeats what many other enlightened voices had to say against torture. Like Pietro Verri who declares, in section 11 of his *Osservazioni sulla tortura*:[9] "it's an unjust matter and contrary to the voice of nature that a person becomes his own accuser and that both persons, the accuser and the accused, become one." The confusion that Verri denounces is the driving force of the ordeal as symbolic repetition of the crime. And in the crazy metonymic circulation of clues between the accuser and the accused, as if both belonged to the same great body of the crime, music plays the role of a sort of matrix, indifferent to what passes through and circulates within it: it lends itself to all substitutions, inversions, or superpositions. As the beautiful ending of Polanski's film shows, it is the very element of interchange through which all criminological figures pass, in every direction, and every way.

The last minutes of *Death and the Maiden* take us to a concert. A string quartet on stage is about to interpret Schubert's work. The camera slowly zooms out from the close-up of a bow to show all four musicians seated in a half circle. Then, with a circular panning movement, it shows the concert hall and the audience listening in silence. The camera zooms in on Gerardo and Paulina, who sit side by side; and it bounces back, so to speak, against Paulina's eyes to head towards Dr. Miranda who is seated on the first balcony, surrounded by his wife and two children. Miranda watches Paulina; and the doctor's son watches his father who looks elsewhere. The camera then returns towards Paulina and Gerardo: now, it is the latter who gazes at the doctor before looking at the stage again. Counter shot: we see the semicircular quartet as it continues to play, with an overwhelming indifference.

Death and the Maiden, substituting as *pars pro toto* for music in general, includes all these gazes, all these projections or identifications, all these trajectories, these replacements and metonymies.

It includes them and comprehends them in advance.

∼

I could have easily summoned other scenes from the vast filmography of sound torture. I think, for instance, of Hitchcock's 1940 *Foreign Correspondent*, which features Van Meer, a Dutch diplomat forced by Nazis to listen to a deafening jazz. I also think of Billy Wilder's 1961 comedy *One, Two, Three*, which features Otto, a young activist, who endures an unbearable repetition of the song "Itsy Bitsy Teenie Weenie Yellow Polka Dot Bikini" as a German police officer repeatedly decenters the disc on the phonograph to create a distorted sound. Finally, I think of Kathryn

Bigelow's recent *Zero Dark Thirty* (2012), in which a prisoner suspected of being involved with the 9/11 attacks is subjected to the sounds of the hardcore punk band Rorschach.[10] But rather than multiply these cinematographic scenes where sound plays an active role in torture, I would like to conclude by questioning the privilege of the filmic medium as a way of accessing the element of ordeal in sound torture.

So why film?

In Villiers de l'Isle-Adam's *Tomorrow's Eve*, published in 1886, Edison laments being "a latecomer [. . .] in the ranks of humanity" and he regrets that there is no phonographic record of the harmonious screams coming from the ancient brazen bull:

> Even among the noises of the past, how many mysterious sounds were known to our predecessors, which for lack of a convenient machine to record them have now fallen forever into the abyss? . . . Who nowadays could form, for example, a proper notion of the sound of the trumpets of Jericho? Of the bellow of Phalaris' bull? [. . .] Dead voices, lost sounds, forgotten noises, vibrations lockstepping into the abyss, and now too distant ever to be recaptured![11]

Edison continues his retro-prospective daydreaming, lamenting that photography, too, "has come along very late" (21). What if, the great inventor ponders to himself with a mix of enthusiasm and melancholy, "the industrious Japheth," Noah's son, had "carried a camera with him into the Ark," what if today we could enjoy the snapshots of "all the episodes of the New-Testament" or have "postcards" of Prometheus. Then, when he imagines how photography could meet phonography in these early stages or prehistory of cinema (we are in 1886 and the first silent projections of the Lumière brothers will take place only a decade later), torture begins to occupy again the mind of the scholar (22): "One would want, too, all the scenes of torture, from the very beginning of social life. . . . And the cruel interrogations that have gone on in the prisons of Germany, Italy, France, the Orient, everywhere, why not those too? The camera, aided by the phonograph (they are near of kin), could reproduce both the sight and the different sounds made by the sufferers, giving a complete, an exact idea of the experience."

Why does torture insist and persist in the daydreaming of the inventor of the phonograph? Why does torture return to haunt his dreams at the precise moment when he associates the phonograph to the photographic lens, thus anticipating the birth of film?

It is not only the imagination of the author of the *Nouveaux contes cruels* that shines through here (under this title, Villiers de l'Isle-Adam published in 1888, two years after *L'Ève future*, a collection that includes "A Torture by Hope," a short story about the Inquisition adapted as an opera by Luigi Dallapiccola). It is much more than that: for cinema, as Godard explicitly states or lets his characters state in *Le petit soldat* (1963), is not simply a technical device for the reproduction or the fictionalizing of a scene of interrogation; cinema has *the very structure of interrogation*, in the inquisitorial sense of this word.

It is worth rereading the famous Godardian formula—"cinema is truth twenty-four times per second" (*le cinéma, c'est vingt-quatre fois la vérité par seconde*)—in its original context, a photoshoot in which Veronica (Anna Karina) agrees to pose for Bruno (Michel Subor):

> BRUNO: Okay, I'm going to ask you questions and you're going to answer them, that will be easier. You seem scared, why?
>
> VERONICA: Yes, I'm scared.
>
> BRUNO: Don't be.
>
> VERONICA: I feel it's like a police interrogation.
>
> BRUNO: Yes, yes, a little. Photography is truth. And cinema is truth twenty-four times per second. . . . What's your last name, Veronica?

It becomes clear, upon hearing this series of lines, that photography is akin to interrogation and that the cinema is the *frequentative*, so to speak, of the photographic questioning.

A little later during their photoshoot, there is a brief exchange between Veronica and Bruno during which the latter attributes to music—or rather: to *each* music—the power to mark or index calendrical time:

> BRUNO: Do you have a record?
>
> VERONICA: Yes, what do you want? Bach?

BRUNO (*opening the camera to load a new film roll*): No, it's too late; Bach is eight o'clock in the morning [*Bach, c'est huit heures du matin*]. A *Brandenburg* at eight o'clock in the morning, marvelous.

VERONICA: Mozart? Beethoven?

BRUNO: Too early. Mozart is eight o'clock in the evening [*Mozart, c'est huit heures du soir*]. Beethoven, it's very profound music. Beethoven is midnight [*Beethoven, c'est minuit*]. No, we should really choose . . . here, some Haydn. Good old Joseph Haydn.

It is as if, for the frequentative of photographic interrogation that film is, music were a privileged temporal marker (metonymically linked to an hour, a moment in the day, a precise instant), an index bound to return, to repeat itself (if Bach "is" eight o'clock in the morning, it is eight o'clock in the morning each and every day). It is by embodying this iterative structure that music inscribes in the filmic frequentative of questioning the horizon of an ordealic return.

But there is more: music also has the faculty to slip from diegetic to extradiegetic space—and back—thereby blurring the positions of enunciation exactly as they are blurred in the trial by ordeal: the latter, as we read in Pietro Verri's *Osservazioni sulla tortura*, is "contrary to the voice of nature" inasmuch as it forces "both persons, the accuser and the accused, [to] become one." Let us remember the scene from *Le petit soldat* during which Bruno is tortured by the National Liberation Front activists who kidnapped him. We first hear the voice-over (Godard's own) saying: "Torture is monotonous and sad. It is difficult to talk about. I will hardly speak of it." Immediately after these words, as if music had to fill the empty space they leave, we hear a piano theme while the camera moves along the front of a building. The theme continues into a new scene, in the apartment where Bruno is held captive. Obviously, this music, since it remains identical and impassible as the camera moves from exterior to interior, does not belong to the diegetic space: no one plays it nor listens to it *within the story being told*. And yet, when Bruno's torturer (László Szabó) soon turns up the volume of a small radio to cover the cries of his victim, it is the same music we hear, this time inside the diegetic space where the characters can act upon or with it.

Music or sound, in sum, is the bypass (*échangeur*) from enunciation to statement (*de l'énonciation à l'énoncé*), from confession to accusation, from narrating to narrated voice, from executioner to victim. It is thus the switching point in the traffic of voices that directs or clears their paths within the ordealic questioning. But it is also the indexing of voices in calendrical time: it is what anchors them metonymically to a *given* moment in time, the givenness of which is simultaneously the promise of its return, which is to say of the symbolical repetition of violence.

In the era of these frequentatives of truth that cinema and phonography are, sound torture, though certainly not a new practice, multiplies and unleashes the immemorial power of the phonordeal.

Notes

1. See Moustafa Bayoumi, "Disco Inferno," *Nation*, December 26, 2005, accessed May 7, 2022, https://www.thenation.com/article/archive/disco-inferno; Suzanne Cusick, "Music as Torture, Music as Weapon," *Trans* 10 (2006), accessed May 7, 2022, https://www.sibetrans.com/trans/articulo/152/music-as-torture-music-as-weapon; and Jonathan Pieslak, *Sound Targets: American Soldiers and Music in the Iraq War* (Bloomington: Indiana University Press, 2009), especially 78–99. See also Peter Szendy, "Music and Torture: The Stigmata of Sound and Senses," in Julie A. Carson and Elisabeth Weber, eds., *Speaking of Torture* (New York: Fordham University Press, 2012), 189–204.

2. Alfred McCoy, *A Question of Torture: CIA Interrogation, from the Cold War to the War on Terror* (New York: Owl, 2006), 7: "From 1950 to 1962, the CIA became involved in torture through a massive mind-control effort, with psychological warfare and secret research into human consciousness that reached a cost of a billion dollars annually—a veritable Manhattan Project of the mind. After experiments with hallucinogenic drugs, electric shock, and sensory deprivation, this work then produced a new approach to torture that was psychological, not physical, perhaps best described as 'no-touch torture.'" According to Jonathan Pieslak, though, "It does not appear that the use of music in interrogation originated in the government-funded experiments of the second half of the twentieth century. Rather, the practice of interrogating detainees with music appears to be new. [. . .] Music scholar Suzanne Cusick claims that present detainee interrogation practices can be traced back to interrogation research funded by the Office of Strategic Services and its successor, the Central Intelligence Agency, as well as by British and Canadian intelligence services, since the 1940s. Many such experiments used low-volume noises, like hissing or static, to dull the sense of sound by creating an unchanging

sonic backdrop, but there is no mention of music in these studies. Background noise and soundproofing were used in research to test how the control and elimination of all sensory stimuli affected human behavior and mental processes. The experiments were funded by government agencies in response to fears that Russia had developed powerful behavior modification and hypnosis techniques. Even though certain aspects of the research may have suggested the use of music in interrogation, they did so only peripherally, and there are clear differences in the scope, purpose, and practice of how sound was tested in these experiments and how music is employed in detainee interrogation in Iraq. In the CIA experiments, the purpose of the noises was to dull or entirely block out auditory perception, not to sonically antagonize a person." See Pieslak, *Sound Targets*, 86–87.

3. John Hamilton, "Torture as an Instrument of Music," in Sander van Maas, ed., *Thresholds of Listening: Sound, Technics, Space* (New York: Fordham University Press, 2015), 143–52. Hamilton's initial question—"Would music's torturing function somehow be explained by torture's musical function?"—ultimately receives no satisfying answer: "How, then, can torture's role in the production of music relate to the use of music in acts of torture? In the end, there can only be somewhat wild conjecture, resting on associations that are quite free and without proof, intended more as a provocation than as definitive interpretation. The idea of torture as an instrument of music—exemplified by the brazen bull [. . .]—obliquely opens onto notions of sublimation." See Hamilton, "Torture," 145 and 152. Hamilton's source is Diodorus Siculus's *Bibliotheca historica* 9.19. The Museum of Fine Arts in Boston has in its collection an engraving of the brazen bull (dated before 1562) by the French engraver Pierre Woeiriot.

4. Hamilton "Torture," 152: "the demonic chromaticism of Metallica, the blatant force of hardcore rap—are these not ideal means for obliterating one world and imposing another?" Suzanne Cusick also considers rap as code for violence: "Generally coded masculine in mainstream US culture, metal and rap are musics that those who don't identify with them often hear as embodying the sounds of masculine rage." See Cusick, "Music."

5. Theodor Reik, *Der unbekannte Mörder* (Vienna: Internationaler Psychoanalytischer Verlag, 1932); translated in Theodor Reik, "The Unknown Murderer," trans. Katherine Jones, in *The Compulsion to Confess: On the Psychoanalysis of Crime and Punishment*, ed. John Farrar (New York: John Wiley, 1959), 1–173.

6. Reik, *Unbekannte Mörder*, 106; translated in Reik, "Unknown Murderer," 100.

7. Reik, *Unbekannte Mörder*, 94; translated in Reik, "Unknown Murderer," 89. As Reik himself recalls in a footnote, "this fairy tale was made use of by Gustav in his *Klagendes Lied*"; see Reik, *Unbekannte Mörder*, 486.

8. In his famous "Osservazioni sulla tortura" (written in 1770, revised in 1776, and published posthumously in 1804), the Italian philosopher and economist

Pietro Verri already emphasized how modern torture derives from the immemorial institution of the ordeal: "Forse la metodica introduzione de' tormenti accaduta dopo il secolo XI trae la sua origine dallo stesso principio, che fece instituire i Giudizi di Dio; [. . .] quando col portare un ferro arroventito in mano, ovvero con immergere il braccio nell'acqua bollente, e tal volta coll'attraversare le cataste di legna ardenti, si decideva o l'innocenza o la colpa dell'accusato." See Pietro Verri, "Osservazioni sulla tortura. E singolarmente sugli effetti che produsse all'occasione delle unzioni malefiche, alle quali si attribuì la pestilenza che devastò Milano l'anno 1630," in Pietro Custodi, gen. ed., *Scrittori classici italiani di economia politica* (Milan: Destefanis, 1803–1816), 17:191–312, 17:293.

 9. Verri, "Osservazioni," 17:283: "sarà cosa ingiusta e contraria alla voce della natura che un uomo diventi accusatore di se stesso e le due persone dell'accusatore e dell'accusato si confondano." The argument is repeated almost literally by the great Italian jurist and philosopher Cesare Beccaria in his *Dei delitti e delle pene*, published in 1764 but largely inspired by the first version of Verri's treatise (and maybe even written in collaboration with him).

 10. Consider the song "Pavlov's Dogs," on their 1992 album *Remain Sedate*. The film has been criticized for its endorsement of torture; see Slavoj Žižek, "Zero Dark Thirty: Hollywood's Gift to American Power," *Guardian*, January 25, 2013, accessed May 7, 2022, https://www.theguardian.com/commentisfree/2013/jan/25/zero-dark-thirty-normalises-torture-unjustifiable.

 11. Auguste Villiers de l'Isle-Adam, *Tomorrow's Eve*, trans. Robert Martin Adams (Urbana: University of Illinois Press, 2001), 9–10.

References

Bayoumi, Moustafa. "Disco Inferno." *Nation*, December 26, 2005. Accessed May 7, 2022. https://www.thenation.com/article/archive/disco-inferno.

Cusick, Suzanne. "Music as Torture, Music as Weapon." *Trans* 10 (2006). Accessed May 7, 2022. https://www.sibetrans.com/trans/articulo/152/music-as-torture-music-as-weapon.

Hamilton, John. "Torture as an Instrument of Music." In *Thresholds of Listening: Sound, Technics, Space*, edited by Sander van Maas, 143–52. New York: Fordham University Press, 2015.

McCoy, Alfred. *A Question of Torture: CIA Interrogation, from the Cold War to the War on Terror*. New York: Owl, 2006.

Pieslak, Jonathan. *Sound Targets: American Soldiers and Music in the Iraq War*. Bloomington: Indiana University Press, 2009.

Szendy, Peter. "Music and Torture: The Stigmata of Sound and Senses." In *Speaking of Torture*, edited by Julie A. Carson and Elisabeth Weber, 189–204. New York: Fordham University Press, 2012.

Reik, Theodor. *Der unbekannte Mörder*. Vienna: Internationaler Psychoanalytischer Verlag, 1932.

Reik, Theodor. "The Unknown Murderer." Translated by Katherine Jones. In *The Compulsion to Confess: On the Psychoanalysis of Crime and Punishment*, edited by John Farrar, 1–173. New York: John Wiley, 1959.

Verri, Pietro. "Osservazioni sulla tortura. E singolarmente sugli effetti che produsse all'occasione delle unzioni malefiche, alle quali si attribuì la pestilenza che devastò Milano l'anno 1630." In *Scrittori classici italiani di economia politica*, edited by Pietro Custodi, 17:191–312. Milan: Destefanis, 1803–16.

Villiers de l'Isle-Adam, Auguste. *Tomorrow's Eve*. Translated by Robert Martin Adams. Urbana: University of Illinois Press, 2001.

Žižek, Slavoj. "Zero Dark Thirty: Hollywood's gift to American power." *Guardian*, January 25, 2013. Accessed May 7, 2022, https://www.theguardian.com/commentisfree/2013/jan/25/zero-dark-thirty-normalises-torture-unjustifiable.

Chapter 4

What Makes Weill Weill?

KIM H. KOWALKE

I came up with the title of this essay when I was invited to present a lecture about Kurt Weill for the Glimmerglass Opera Festival in 2012.[1] I intended it to sound a bit enigmatic when spoken aloud. After Kurt Weill arrived in New York in 1935, he altered his pronunciation of his surname from "Vile" to "Wile." It has not been standardized since, becoming something of a "you say either, I say either" situation. If one chooses to pronounce it as an Americanized "Wile," then "What makes Weill Weill?" presents no more confusion than "what makes Puccini Puccini?" But that isn't the case for the German analogue: "What makes Vile Vile?" Depending on inflection, that could be an inquiry about some wretched performance practice of the composer's music or a wholesale condemnation of his entire output. And if one wanted to play into the hands of critics dismissive of his American oeuvre, one could ask "what makes Wile Vile?" On the other hand, if the German and American pronunciations are reversed into "What makes Vile Wile?," my title hints at the central issue in Weill studies since his premature death in 1950. Modernist aesthetic agendas and critical constructs have been hard-pressed to cope with the dichotomies and ambiguities of Weill's career and output: European and American, German and Jewish, serious and popular, *Amerikanismus* and Americanism. Weill does not conform to the unitary stylistic and biographical identity conventionally expected of a "genuine" composer. So "two Weills" had to be created: "While some notable artists have simply stopped creating at a certain stage of their careers and a few have put an end to their lives, Weill is perhaps the only one to have done away with his old creative self in order to make way for a new one. . . . It means that in Weill we have not one, but two composers. The first and important one can and should be evaluated without reference to the second." In fact, David Drew, the pioneering dean of Weill scholarship and author of the Weill entry in the *New Grove Dictionary of Music and Musicians* in 1980, even entitled its concluding section "The Two Weills." In a final flourish, he asserted that the composer's failure to conform to modernist expectations of artistic development resulted in his being "one of music's great 'might-have-beens.'"[2]

Weill's Last Year

To anchor a brief exploration of "What makes Weill Weill?" let's begin by time-traveling back to 1949, the last day of March, a Thursday, 8:30 p.m. If you were living on the East Coast or in certain parts of the Midwest, you could have turned on your black-and-white television set and tuned in to the fledgling and by no means yet nationwide NBC network to catch a half-hour weekly variety program called *The Swift Show*.[3] Each week a segment of the program showcased a musical then running on Broadway, with a small ensemble of singing theatergoers exclaiming that ticket prices started at $1.10 and capped at $8.80. That evening's featured musical was *Love Life*, a vaudeville by Alan Jay Lerner and Kurt Weill, which had opened the previous October. But the primitively produced *Swift Show* was not all that "swift." It lasted for just that one season, as did Weill's most innovative Broadway musical. Seated at a grand piano in his purported "studio," a tongue-twisted Weill was obviously uncomfortable in front of the camera. He accompanied Martha Wright and host Lanny Ross plugging "Here I'll Stay," *Love Life*'s big romantic duet. But the television exposure didn't help ticket sales all that much. Although now recognized as the first nonlinear "concept musical"—the prototype for *Cabaret, Chicago, Company, Assassins*, and even the *Scottsboro Boys*—*Love Life* closed six weeks later, after 252 performances. Two boycotts had prevented the recording of an original cast album as well as radio stations' broadcasting songs from the show. After its run ended in mid-May, Weill would be without a show on Broadway, but for only a few months.

That summer he and Maxwell Anderson were still hard at work adapting Alan Paton's anti-apartheid novel *Cry, the Beloved Country* as a musical tragedy. They had persuaded the original Porgy, Todd Duncan, to take the lead role and recruited Rouben Mamoulian, the director of *Porgy and Bess*, *Oklahoma!*, and *Carousel*, to stage it. In September, Weill wrote to his parents, who had fled Germany to Palestine in 1935, to reassure them that things were going well, that life was good: "Yesterday I finished composing the music and now I must work flat out to complete as much orchestration as possible before rehearsals begin on 19 September." In the next paragraph he reported, with some satisfaction and surprise, that "after twenty-five years of difficult, tireless work, it almost looks like I am to reap some sort of reward—not in a financial, but in a purely idealistic sense. . . . I've suddenly been promoted to the rank of 'classical composer,' and people are even beginning to talk about the historical significance of my work."[4]

On 30 October *Lost in the Stars* debuted at the Music Box Theatre to generally favorable reviews, particularly for Weill's score and the musical's daring treatment of racial injustice in South Africa, and, by extension, in the United States as well. Shortly after the new year, NBC televised its first opera production, Weill's *Down in the Valley* (1948), just three weeks after CBS had beaten it to the punch with its first opera telecast, *Carmen*. By then Anderson and Weill had already started work on a musical adaptation of *Huckleberry Finn*. Workaholic Weill celebrated his fiftieth birthday on 2 March 1950. Two weeks later he suffered a heart attack. At first, he rallied. But on 3 April, he took a sudden turn for the worse and died, almost exactly one year after his appearance on *The Swift Show*.

Obituaries of "The Two Weills"

The morning after Weill's death, the *New York Times* carried a lengthy, unsigned obituary. Its four-part heading read: "KURT WEILL DEAD; COMPOSER, WAS 50/ Wrote Music for 'One Touch of Venus,' 'Lady in the Dark' and Other Broadway Hits/ ALSO TURNED OUT OPERAS/ 'Der Protagonist' and 'Tsar Has Himself Photographed' His Best-Known Works." Note that Weill is identified not as a "songwriter" or "tunesmith," but as a "composer." This was not an unconsidered choice of words. The obituary later quotes the *Times*'s chief drama critic Brooks Atkinson's review of *Lady in the Dark* from 1941: "he is not a song writer but a composer of organic music that can bind the separate elements of a production and turn the underlying motive into song." Note also which of Weill's works qualify for mention. Predictably, the list begins with his two longest-running shows on Broadway, *Lady in the Dark* (1941) and *One Touch of Venus* (1943). But then, an unlikely assertion: "*Der Protagonist* and *Tsar Has Himself Photographed* his best-known works." These were two of Weill's first operas, both one-acts with librettos by the famous German expressionist playwright, Georg Kaiser. Performed separately and as a double bill by a fair number of Germany's opera houses in the late 1920s, they indeed had almost instantly established Weill's standing as the foremost operatic composer of his generation in Germany. But by 1950 both had all but vanished—on both sides of the Atlantic. At the time of his death, they were a far cry from being his "best-known works." *Down in the Valley* would soon lay sole claim to that distinction, with almost six thousand performances in the 1950s.[5]

The Threepenny Opera warranted no marquee billing in the *Times* obituary. Although it had been produced in virtually every major European city before the Second World War, it had flopped when it was mounted on Broadway in 1933, lasting only twelve performances. Not until 1954, when Marc Blitzstein's adaptation would be staged off-Broadway in the Theater de Lys, with Weill's widow, Lotte Lenya, again playing Jenny, did it find success in English-speaking countries. By the end of that decade, *The Threepenny Opera* would displace *Oklahoma!* as the longest-running musical in history, and Bobby Darin, Louis Armstrong, Ella Fitzgerald, and Frank Sinatra would propel "Mack the Knife" to the head of the hit parade. The song sold more than ten million records. Weill's obituary would have read much differently had he lived to be sixty.

Across the Atlantic, delayed news of Weill's death elicited an obituary in the *Frankfurter Rundschau* about two weeks later than the one printed in the *Times*. Its author was no less a figure than Theodor W. Adorno, the apostle of musical modernism and a principal spokesman for the Frankfurt School of Critical Theory. Its headline read: "Kurt Weill—Musiker des epischen Theaters."[6] "Musician of the Epic Theater" has subsequently become a key document in postwar Weill reception, demanding quotation at some length here:

> The image of this composer, who died in America, is scarcely accommodated by the notion of a "composer." His gift, like

his influence, resides far less in musical capacities as such (in creations whose substance and structure would stand on their own) than in an extraordinary and original feeling for the function of music in the theater. . . . Working with limited powers of organization, he made a virtue of the necessity of subordinating the artistic to theatrical effect and to some degree even the political. . . . With flair, mobility and a very individual mode of expression, he defined a new role: that of a "music stage director" [*Musikregisseur*].

After noting that Weill had been a pupil of Busoni, Adorno lamented that Weill's "lack of real craftsmanship, from the simplest harmonization to the construction of large forms, was his inheritance from a school that was more aesthetic than strictly technical." The harshest and least informed judgment was reserved for the American Weill: "with a disarmingly shy and crafty innocence, he became a Broadway composer, with Cole Porter as his model, and talked as if concession to the commercial field were no concession, but only a pure test of his ability, which made everything possible even within standardized boundaries." There is no evidence, however, that Adorno had ever attended a production of any of Weill's American stage works, nor of Weill attending or commenting on any of Porter's stage musicals.[7] Yet with his own supremely crafty confidence, Adorno thereby sowed the seeds of necessity for two Weills: "In this endeavor he had to renounce all those elements in his musical language which had once created a Weillian atmosphere. He could no longer do what he knew how to do." "Wile" could no longer be "Vile," so to speak.

In contrast, on the Sunday following Weill's death, American composer-critic Virgil Thomson had devoted his column in the *New York Herald Tribune* to an appraisal of Weill's historical significance and had come to conclusions very different from Adorno's:

Everything [Weill] wrote became in one way or another historic. He was probably the most original single workman in the whole musical theater, internationally considered, during the last quarter century. . . . Whether Weill's American works will carry as far as his German ones I cannot say. They lack the mordant and touching humanity of Brecht's poetry. But the loss to music and to the theater is real. Both will go on, and so will Weill's influence. But his output of new models—and every work was a new model, a new shape, a new solution of dramatic problems—will not continue.[8]

These three obituaries vividly demonstrate how limited and parochial were mid-century perspectives on both sides of the Atlantic at the time of Weill's death. A few months later Hans Redlich wrote in London's *Music Survey*:

It is a well-known fact that most of the representative composers of this age . . . have been driven into exile by indiscriminate forces of political factions which brutally denied them vital contact with their respective national climates. This sorry fate overtook Kurt Weill while still in his early thirties and nothing can express more poignantly the sinister implications of this enforced exodus than the sinister fact that Weill's mature music, composed by the homeless artist in France, England and ultimately in the United States, has remained a *terra incognita* even to his admirers.[9]

In a review of a memorial concert for Weill at Town Hall a year after his death, even Virgil Thomson now suggested that "after Weill came to live in America, he ceased to work as a modernist."[10]

Little had changed a decade later, when, at the height of the Cold War, Weill's first biographer, Hellmut Kotschenreuther, declared, "Whoever accepts Weill's *Johnny Johnson* forgoes the right to accept *Die Dreigroschenoper*, *Aufstieg und Fall der Stadt Mahagonny*, and *Die sieben Todsünden*."[11] Already the Weill-with-Brecht was being pitted against the Weill-without-Brecht. The construct of the "two Weills," one German, the other American, had been collapsed and simplified into Weill-With and -Without, despite the fact that Weill and Brecht's collaboration had lasted less than four years and was characterized by fruitful but ultimately irreconcilable aesthetic, political, and personal tensions almost from the outset. Such was the starting point for the long and still incomplete process of trying to put Weill back together, to figure out "What makes Vile Wile or Wile Vile."

As the Berlin Wall was being dismantled, the debate around Weill's identity prompted the formidable musicologist Richard Taruskin to declare him to be "perhaps the twentieth century's most problematical major musician."[12] By then the composer was being viewed from both sides of the Atlantic as a key figure reifying the central issues at hand, and not only in musicological discourse: modernism versus counter- or post-modernism; elitism versus popularism; autonomy versus accessibility; originality versus comprehensibility; atonality/serialism versus tonality; stylistic diversity versus authenticity. In asserting already in 1936 that the "recital hall is obsolete" and that absolute music has reached its historically appointed dead end, Weill anticipated what might now be seen as the central "problem" of music in the second half of the twentieth century and beyond.[13] Absent a compelling replacement for a modernist "progress narrative," how can music in a post-Adornian pluralistic, postmodern, and aesthetically entropic world be productively situated?

Weill's Itinerary

"Where does the stable essence of an 'I' reside?" asks Milan Kundera in *Testaments Betrayed*, his remarkable collection of essays on modernism. "Over what period of time can we consider a man identical to himself?" Such Weill-relevant questions arise as Kundera interrogates the modern novel, seeking in particular to understand the differences between Dostoyevsky and Tolstoy. Kundera suggests that the stable identities of Dostoyevsky's characters lie in their personal ideologies, whereas "in Tolstoy, man is the more himself, the more an individual, when he has the strength, the imagination, the intelligence, to transform himself." In *War and Peace* Bezukhov and Bolkonsky surprise—"They make themselves different"—and thereby offer another conception of human identity: "He is an itinerary; a winding road; a journey whose successive phases not only vary but often represent a total negation of the preceding phases."[14] Kundera immediately refines this metaphor, however: "I've said *road*, a word that could mislead, because the image of a road evokes a destination. Now, what is the destination of these roads that end only randomly, broken off by the happenstance of death?"

In the musical realm Kundera focused not on Weill, but Stravinsky, "whose conscious purposeful eclecticism" he finds "gigantic and unmatched." Stravinsky's life, Kundera notes, "divides into three parts of roughly equal length: Russia, 27 years; France and French-speaking Switzerland, 29 years; America 32 years." Despite corresponding radical shifts in Stravinsky's musical language and style, Kundera argues not for three "distinct personalities" but for a single artistic persona who changes as he attempts to master the past, an agenda central to the modernist project. Elsewhere in his book, in a nuanced unpacking of irony entitled "Paths in the Fog," Kundera might well have chosen Weill (instead of Janácek) to stand as the musical counterpart to Kafka: "In the kingdom of irony, equality rules; this means that no phase of the itinerary is morally superior to another."

Juxtaposition of two crucial milestones along Weill's transatlantic itinerary may prove illuminating: *Die Dreigroschenoper* (Berlin, 1928) and *Lady in the Dark* (New York, 1941). They might seem incompatible, if not antithetical. Yet they have much in common. They were respectively Weill's first successful forays into commercial theater in Germany and America. *Die Dreigroschenoper* opted out of the state-subsidized system of theatrical and operatic production to engage a new audience in the Weimar Republic. Its instantaneous and unexpected near-global success came as an embarrassment to *enfant terrible* Brecht, who spent the next several years attempting to rework it, first as a literary version of the play, then as a novel and a screenplay, each reflecting his newly acquired Marxist bent ever more radically. With *Lady in the Dark*, Weill left behind his affiliations with such left-wing collectives as the Group Theatre to embrace mainstream Broadway, with the most illustrious of collaborators, namely Ira Gershwin (in his first return to Broadway since the death of George) and Moss Hart.

Both were generic hybrids, defying conventions of musico-dramatic structure and exploring alternative relationships between text and music, between what was spoken and sung. *Die Dreigroschenoper* ended up as a "play with music," but a play inhabited with singing actors and acting singers from highly disparate backgrounds. *Lady in the Dark* broke the mold of Broadway musical comedy even more boldly, utilizing music to structure the "musical play," with its through-composed dream sequences corresponding to the use of color to differentiate Oz from Kansas in the previous year's *Wizard of Oz*. This was no ordinary book musical in the era between *Show Boat* and *Oklahoma!* It was a radical experiment, one which could not be repeated, but one that inaugurated the possibility of what would be called thirty years later the "concept musical." Each work established Weill as the foremost innovator in the musical theater in its two respective, diverse cultural contexts. And their success allowed him not only to buy a house in Berlin and Rockland County respectively, but also to give him the stature and resources necessary to advance his ambitious agenda to create new models of musical theater. As such, they lay equal claim as signposts, if not beacons, along Weill's winding road.

In that light, we might now re-direct Kundera's question away from Stravinsky toward Weill: "where does the stable essence of Weill's identity reside?" Perhaps we might consider critic Harold Clurman's oft-quoted characterization of Weill as a musical Gulliver, able to "write music in any country so that it would seem as if he were a native," and "fully capable of adapting into a Hottentot composer and in record time." For Clurman, Weill was "all theater, and all mask," a sort of musical shape-shifter who constantly changed identities by assuming characteristics of his collaborators and adapting to his audiences' expectations.[15] Clurman's corollary, that Weill "sold out" to American commercialism, was largely congruent with the aesthetic views of Eric Bentley, as articulated in *The Playwright as Thinker* (1946), the American dramatic analogue to Adorno's *Philosphie der neuen Musik* (1949). Such appraisals by modernist critics on both sides of the Atlantic beg the foundational question: is there anything essential, or even essentialist, that makes Weill Weill?

Making Weill Weill

At the risk of gross oversimplification in an attempt to formulate a necessarily brief and provisional answer, one might first compile a short list of constants, aspects of Weill's aesthetics, musical language, and dramatic strategies that characterize his music for the stage on both continents. If this were not an interdisciplinary forum, one might be tempted to begin with a detailed technical examination of musical vocabulary and syntax that remained recognizable as "Weill" throughout his oeuvre. Such an inventory might include the treatment of strophic and verse-refrain structures: for example, the parallel form and function in the sixteen-measure, strophic units of the "Moritat vom Mackie Messer" and "The Saga of Jenny." One could compile a catalogue of characteristically Weillian harmonic progressions, starting with the resemblance linking the refrain of "Das schöne Kind" (1917) to the climax of Frank Maurrant's "Let Things Be Like They Always Was" from *Street Scene* (1947). Or chart the unfolding of large-scale "double-tonic" structural units with explicit non-triadic cadential resolutions, from the Cello Sonata (1920) to "My Ship" twenty years later. Or the similarity of fifth-generated harmonies and pentatonic melodies in the fourth song of *Frauentanz* (1923) and "What Good Would the Moon Be?" from *Street Scene*. Or the ubiquitous semitone vacillations between major and minor within melodic and harmonic structures, from the String Quartet in B Minor (1918) through *Lost in the Stars*, Weill's last completed work. Such a recital would rapidly grow tedious for most readers, particularly for those whose ears inform them intuitively that the same composer wrote "Die stille Stadt" (1919) and "Lonely House" (1946). Therefore, it may be more persuasive to examine broader and ultimately more decisive imperatives that persisted throughout Weill's career.

First and foremost, already at the age of nineteen when he was working as a *Kapellmeister* (conductor) in a tiny provincial theater in Lüdenscheid, Weill decided that his special field of activity as a composer would be the theater. He confided to his sister Ruth that the musical theater, "where music can best express the unspeakable, will probably turn out to be my life's work."[16] Although he wrote with some success in other genres and media, for three decades he would indeed focus on the musical theater in its widest range, writing about twenty-five dramatic works in three languages for audiences in the opera house, the commercial theater, the school auditorium, the movie theater, the radio, and even the transportation pavilion at the 1939 World's Fair in New York. He wrote "absolute" instrumental music less and less as his stage career progressed, putting into practice his belief that "in our time theater-music is far more important than absolute music."[17] And, as Stephen Hinton has observed, the array of Weill's theatrical works comprised a succession of experimental generic hybrids, each breaking new ground, each laying claim to the status sui generis.[18] In that sense Clurman certainly was right: Weill was increasingly "all theater."

As a teenager Weill also confessed with some embarrassment to his brother Hans: "I need poetry to set my musical imagination in motion, for my imagination is not a bird, but an airplane."[19] He recognized that he would need words to ignite his inspiration, to propel his musical intellect. His earliest surviving compositions were therefore, predictably, lieder. His first two large-scale orchestral works (1919, 1921) were symphonic poems inspired respectively by Rilke's *Die Weise von Liebe und Tod des Cornets Christoph Rilke* and Johannes Becher's *Arbeiter, Bauern, Soldaten*. When composing the orchestral *Fantasia, Passacaglia, und Hymnus* in 1922, he deemed it necessary to derive much of its musical material from pre-compositional stylistic studies he sketched by setting poetry of Rilke.

During the quarter century extending from his first published and produced opera *Der Protagonist* (1924–1925) through his sketches for the unfinished Huck Finn project, Weill recruited and cultivated as collaborators some of the finest literary and dramatic talents in each language and location in which he labored. He boasted in 1947 that "one of the first decisions I made was to get the leading dramatists of my time interested in the problems of the musical theater."[20] Indeed, in Germany his two principal collaborators were arguably the leading playwrights of their respective generations, Georg Kaiser and Bertolt Brecht. In America he successfully recruited Paul Green, Maxwell Anderson, Elmer Rice, Ogden Nash, S. J. Perelman, Moss Hart, Langston Hughes, and Alan Jay Lerner. Despite considerable effort, his attempts to collaborate with the likes of Jean Cocteau, John Steinbeck, Herman Wouk, and Eugene O'Neill did not come to fruition. Like Stephen Sondheim a quarter century later, Weill preferred to work not just as a composer or songwriter, but also as a "collaborative dramatist," side by side with the author(s) drafting librettos, which were usually then completed before Weill started composing: "I need a subject before I can compose. I've never just taken a libretto and made music to it. It must be a libretto I believe in."[21] In 1944 Weill confessed to Lenya some frustration in this regard while working on *The Firebrand of Florence*: "I don't get credit for anything but the music. But I am sure that Verdi or Offenbach or Mozart contributed as much to their libretti as I do without getting credit for it. This is a part of a theater composer's job, to create for himself the vehicle he needs for his music."[22] This was as true with Kaiser and Brecht as with Anderson or Lerner.

And Weill's relationships to those texts was never uncomplicated. In 1933, for example, in an attempt to persuade the designer Caspar Neher that Brecht's lyrics for the "ballet with singing" *Die sieben Todsünden* wasn't just "literary trash," Weill argued: "Everyone who knows anything about me knows that every text I've set looks entirely different once it's been swept through my music."[23] He frequently cited the example of the "Zuhälterballade" from *Die Dreigroschenoper*, where "a rather obscene text is sung to a tango that is as elegant and seductive as that found in many an operetta."[24] Such ironic counterpoint, even dissonance, between text and music became a Weillian signature, producing complex layers of reciprocal commentary. In furnishing Langston Hughes with a blueprint for the Nurses' Lullaby in act 2 of *Street Scene*, Weill provides a glimpse into the workshop where its "Brechtian irony" was still being crafted:

> Whatever we will do with the last scene, I am sure the nursemaids will be in, and they need badly an amusing song. As you remember, it should be a sort of waltz song about the newspaper reports and pictures, using the whole Daily News terminology which is typical of fifty million women in America who are more interested in murder stories than anything else. . . . This part could be a regular little waltz chorus, then it would be interrupted by a little ditty in a different rhythm (short lines) where they are scolding the babies in the carriages to be quiet. . . . I know that this kind of lyric which should be gay and funny and bitter at the same time is not easy to write.[25]

The subtle, shifting, and sometimes subversive relationships among words, notes, rhythms, and instrumentation remained a crucial Weillian characteristic throughout his career.

Unlike most creators of American musical theater, Weill seldom worked with any librettist or lyricist more than once, Maxwell Anderson and Ira Gershwin the two exceptions. Such inconstancy was both a curse, in that the composer was always breaking in newcomers to the musical stage, and a blessing, in that by working with different writers he avoided repeating himself, by falling back into formulas in the way perennial collaborators such as Gilbert and Sullivan, Rodgers and Hammerstein, or Lerner and Loewe frequently did. Rather, as Weill put it, "each show has to create its own style, its own texture, its own relationship between text and music."[26] And because he required that each work have its own *Klangbild* or sonic world, he insisted on doing his own orchestrations throughout his entire career, virtually unique among Broadway composers of his time. He remained fiercely protective of them whenever his music was performed in the theater, whether a *Schauspielhaus* in Germany or an orchestra pit on Broadway.

Almost all of Weill's stage works dealt with serious contemporary issues of relevance to the audience at hand. But such engagement with issues and audiences in the present came with a price. The topicality of what was called *Zeittheater* in Germany is, of course, double-edged: today's urgent issue (whether disarmament, psychoanalysis, or apartheid) frequently becomes tomorrow's ever more dated memory. The standard repertory of American musical theater in particular has been resistant to politically or socially engaged works. Weill thus walked a precarious tightrope, hovering precipitously between popularizing the "serious" and transforming the "popular" within substantive discourse.

Weill maintained in private and public that all his works were stepping stones along the path toward an accessible modern musical theater, an accessibility demanding that he take into account his changing audiences. "A creative artist," he wrote in an essay from 1937 entitled "The Future of Opera in America," "must know for whom he is creating."[27] Citing Mozart as a model, Weill seldom wavered from a credo he most clearly articulated in 1949: "I have learned to make my music speak directly to the audience, to find the most immediate, direct way to say what I want so say, and to say it as simply as possible."[28] In attempting to reform opera, to rescue it from what he called its "splendid isolation" and to reach out to the broader audience for theater, even to society at large, adapting popular idioms and song forms for serious dramatic purposes became an emblematic strategy. In fact, an astonishing polystylism, an eclectic counterpoint of musical idioms, conventions, and styles in the service of dramatic function, characterizes virtually every one of Weill's two dozen stage works. This may be the most distinctive and stable component of his compositional procedure. As he put it, "the musical score itself becomes its own form of storytelling."[29]

And this musical storytelling went far beyond such "intratextual" techniques as reminiscences and leitmotifs, which Weill had inherited from operatic predecessors extending back to *Die Zauberflöte*. Instead, he often employed "intertextuality" as a type of metadramatic musical commentary on a character or situation. This might involve use of such musical idioms as a tango, foxtrot, or chorale to capture what he once called the "*Gestus*" of a scene.[30] Or, he would invoke allusions to or quotations from works familiar to many in the audience: the "Chorale of the Armed Men" from *Die Zauberflöte* and the "ewige Kunst" of "Gebet einer Jungfrau" in *Aufstieg und Fall der Mahagonny*; in *Street Scene*, the fate motive from *Carmen* and the "Strawberries" sales pitch from *Porgy and Bess*; most poignantly the final vocal utterance in act 2 of *Madama Butterfly* for Sam and Rose's "lilac duet."[31]

Although such examples of the constants throughout Weill's *Lebenswerk* put the lie to Adorno's assertion that in America Weill "could no longer do what he knew how to do," generalizations of any sort are inadequate with respect to either Weill. Unmasking one work reveals little about the stylistic identity of another. Thus, even chronologically contiguous pieces such as *Street Scene, Down in the Valley, Love Life,* and *Lost in the Stars* differ from each other as much as they do from any European predecessors in Weill's oeuvre. The same could have been said about *Happy End, Der Jasager, Die Bürgschaft,* and *Der Silbersee.* Yet Weill was still unmistakably Weill in all of them. Contrary to Adorno's assertion, to the end of his tragically foreshortened career, Weill was doing what he knew how to do, from the Kurfürstendamm to the Great White Way, for a post–World War I audience in Berlin and a very different post–World War II one in New York.

Weill's Own Answer

Four months before he died, Weill himself was asked to consider the question "What makes Weill Weill?" His last appearance on radio took place in December 1949. The occasion was "Opera News on the Air," the intermission feature for a broadcast of the Metropolitan Opera's production of Puccini's *Manon Lescaut.* Host Boris Goldovsky first inquired of Weill (and another guest), "what makes Puccini Puccini?" Weill responded, "I'm convinced we have been looking for it in the wrong place."[32]

> Of course, we could pursue this matter further into a somewhat technical analysis, but even then I doubt if we would have the answer. The answer lies deep within the composer himself and only a sort of musical psychoanalysis, I would say, could get to the root of it. . . . You will notice that in his various operas Puccini consciously colors his music to fit the time and place of his action. For instance, oriental color in *Butterfly* and *Turandot.* But when he hits one of those dramatic situations which he finds most stimulating to himself, the unconscious takes over. He writes pure unadulterated Italian Puccini.

Goldovsky inquired, "Tell me, Mr. Weill, as a composer yourself, are you conscious of any particular emotional appeal that brings forth the most characteristic in you; that brings out the Weill in Weill, so to say? [laughter from audience]" Weill answered without hesitation:

> Well, I'm not conscious of it when I actually write music, but looking back on many of my compositions, I find that I seem

to have a very strong reaction in the awareness of the suffering of underprivileged people—of the oppressed, the persecuted. I know, for instance, that in the music I wrote for *Lost in the Stars*, I consciously introduced a certain amount of South African musical atmosphere, and yet, in retrospect, I can see that when the music involved human suffering, it is, for better or worse, pure Weill.

Lenya liked to tell the story about Weill's staking out an identity as a composer already as a student in Berlin: "One day during the masterclass in composition at the Akademie der Künste in Berlin, his teacher Ferruccio Busoni had poked fun at Kurt's youthful aspirations to create a popular, but serious and socially-engaged musical theater: 'What, you want to become a Verdi of the poor?' 'Would that be so bad?' Weill responded." Perhaps pursuing that goal went a good way toward making Weill Weill.

Notes

1. Earlier versions of this essay were presented as lectures at the Glimmerglass Opera Festival, Cincinnati College Conservatory, Oberlin College, the University of Minnesota, and the University of Buffalo. I am grateful for colleagues' comments, suggestions, and critiques offered on each of those occasions. Dave Stein, archivist of the Weill-Lenya Research Center, was particularly helpful in preparing this print version at a time when COVID-19 limited access to some of my sources.

2. David Drew, "Weill, Kurt (Julian) (*b* Dessau, 2 March 1900; *d* New York, 3 April 1950)," in Stanley Sadie, ed., *The New Grove Dictionary of Music and Musicians* (London: MacMillan, 1980), 20: 309. Drew apparently borrowed the "unhappy might-have-been" epithet from Gerald Abraham, whose target for the phrase had been Max Reger; see Gerald Abraham, *A Hundred Years of Music* (London: Duckworth, 1938), 230.

3. For the *Love Life* sequence from the telecast of *The Swift Show* on March 31, 1949, see Kurt Weill Foundation, "Weill on Swift Show NBC 490331," *Vimeo*, August 3, 2020, accessed May 7, 2022, https://vimeo.com/444251513.

4. For the letter in German from Weill to Albert Weill and Emma Weill, dated 6 September 1949, see Lys Symonette and Elmar Juchem, gen. eds., *Kurt Weill: Briefe an die Familie (1914-1950)* (Stuttgart: Metzler, 2001), 419-20. All translations from the German are my own.

5. See Kim H. Kowalke, "Kurt Weill and the Quest for American Opera," in *Amerikanismus, Americanism, Weill: die Suche nach kultureller Identität in der*

Moderne, ed. Hermann Danuser and Hermann Gottschewski (Schliengen: Argus, 2003), 283–301.

6. Theodor Wiesengrund Adorno, "Kurt Weill—Musiker des epischen Theaters," *Frankfurter Rundschau*, April 15, 1950; reprinted in Theodor Wiesengrund Adorno, *Gesammelte Schriften*, gen. ed. Rolf Tiedemann (Frankfurt am Main: Suhrkamp, 1973–1986), 18: 544–47.

7. No records establish contact between Porter and Weill, though Porter did introduce himself to Lenya in April 1938 when she was singing at the Ruban Bleu nightclub in New York. It is likely that Adorno heard on the radio songs such as "Speak Low," the closest Weill approached the Porter of "Begin the Beguine." Another possibility is that Adorno, like so many others, mistook the almost unrecognizable Hollywood adaptations of *Lady in the Dark* and *One Touch of Venus* for a reasonable facsimile of Weill's original stage scores.

8. Virgil Thomson, "Music in Review: Kurt Weill," *New York Herald Tribune*, April 9, 1950, C7.

9. Hans Redlich, "Obituary," *Music Survey* 3 (1950): 4. A variant of Redlich's observation about Weill's fate has been preserved, without identification of source, as a photocopy filed as Ser.80.200 in the Weill-Lenya Research Center: "The tragedy of our contemporary world is nowhere more vividly expressed than in the fact that the compositions of the mature Kurt Weill, written between his 34th and 50th year, have so far remained a closed book even to his most faithful admirers in the Old World. It must have been a keen disappointment to him that the country of his origin cold-shouldered him even after the defeat of Nazidom in 1945."

10. Virgil Thomson, "Memorial to Weill," *New York Herald Tribune*, February 5, 1951, 11.

11. Hellmut Kotschenreuther, *Kurt Weill* (Berlin: Max Hesse, 1962), 92.

12. Richard Taruskin, "To the Editor," *Kurt Weill Newsletter* 6, no. 1 (1988): 3.

13. Ralph Winett, "Composer of the Hour: An Interview with Kurt Weill," *Brooklyn Daily Eagle*, December 20, 1936, C11–C12, C11.

14. Milan Kundera, *Testaments Betrayed: An Essay in Nine Parts*, trans. Linda Asher (New York: Harper-Collins Perennial, 2001), 211–13.

15. Harold Clurman, *All People Are Famous* (New York: Harcourt Brace Jovanovich, 1974), 128–29. The original formulation of this Hottentot metaphor appeared in *The Saturday Review of Literature* on December 31, 1949.

16. For the letter from Weill to Ruth Weill, dated January 28, 1920, see Symonette and Juchem, *Kurt Weill*, 257.

17. Winett, "Composer," C11.

18. See Stephen Hinton, "Fragwürdiges in der deutschen Rezeption," in *A Stranger Here Myself: Kurt Weill Studien*, ed. Kim H. Kowalke and Horst Edler (Hildesheim: Georg Olms, 1993), 23–32.

19. The letter to Hans Weill, dated June 27, 1919, is reprinted in Symonette and Juchem, *Kurt Weill*, 234.

20. "Two Dreams Come True," published in 1947 as a liner note for the original cast recording of *Street Scene*, CBS OL 4139.

21. Winett, "Composer," C12.

22. The letter from Weill to Lenya, dated August 12, 1944, is reprinted in Lys Symonette and Kim H. Kowalke, trans. and eds., *Speak Low (When You Speak Love): The Letters of Kurt Weill and Lotte Lenya* (Berkeley: University of California Press, 1996), 417.

23. This letter from Weill to Erika Neher, undated but from May of 1933, is held in photocopy in Weill-Lenya Research Center.

24. The letter from Weill to Universal Edition, dated September 10, 1928, is published in Nils Grosch, ed., *Kurt Weill: Briefwechsel mit der Universal Edition* (Stuttgart: Metzler, 2002), 135.

25. The letter from Weill to Langston Hughes, dated September 20, 1946, is held in photocopy in the Weill-Lenya Research Center. Hughes thought that Weill continually tried to make *Street Scene* into something more like *Die Dreigroschenoper* than what Elmer Rice would allow.

26. Kurt Weill, "Score for a Play: 'Street Scene' Becomes a 'Dramatic Musical,'" *New York Times*, January 5, 1947, D3.

27. Kurt Weill, "The Future of Opera in America," *Modern Music* 14, no. 4 (1937): 184.

28. The original letter from Weill to G. F. Stegmann, dated February 14, 1949, is held in the Weill-Lenya Papers, Irving Gilmore Music Library, Yale University, Ser.IV.A, box 47, folder 14.

29. Kurt Weill, "Broadway Opera: Our Composers' Hope for the Future," ed. Edward J. Smith, *Musical Digest* 29, no. 4 (1946): 16.

30. For Weill's most comprehensive explanation of the metadramatic function of music in fixing the "Gestus" of a dramatic moment, see Kurt Weill, "Über den gestischen Charakter der Musik," *Musik* 21, no. 6 (1929): 419–23; translated in Kim H. Kowalke, *Kurt Weill in Europe* (Ann Arbor: UMI Research Press, 1979), 491–93.

31. For a detailed analysis of Weill's utilization of the metadramatic techniques of intertextuality and intratextuality in *Street Scene*, see Kim H. Kowalke, "Kurt Weill, Modernism, and Popular Culture: *Öffentlichkeit als Stil*," *Modernism/Modernity* 2, no. 1 (1995): 27–69. Sondheim's use of "pastiche" in many of his stage works is a variation on this type of intertextual borrowing.

32. Consider Boris Goldovsky's "Opera News on the Air," an intermission feature during the broadcast of Metropolitan Opera performance of *Manon Lescaut* on December 10, 1949. For a transcription of the audio recording of the feature, see Boris Goldovsky, mod., "Opera News on the Air (1949)," *Kurt Weill Foundation for Music*, accessed May 7, 2002, https://www.kwf.org/pages/wt-opera-news-on-the-air-1949.html.

References

Abraham, Gerald. *A Hundred Years of Music*. London: Duckworth, 1938.
Adorno, Theodor Wiesengrund. *Gesammelte Schriften*. Edited by Rolf Tiedemann. Frankfurt am Main: Suhrkamp, 1973–1986.
Adorno, Theodor Wiesengrund. "Kurt Weill—Musiker des epischen Theaters." *Frankfurter Rundschau*, April 15, 1950.
Clurman, Harold. *All People Are Famous*. New York: Harcourt Brace Jovanovich, 1974.
Drew, David. "Weill, Kurt (Julian) (*b* Dessau, 2 March 1900; *d* New York, 3 April 1950)." In *The New Grove Dictionary of Music and Musicians*, edited by Stanley Sadie, 20: 300–10. London: MacMillan, 1980.
Goldovsky, Boris, mod. "Opera News on the Air (1949)." *Kurt Weill Foundation for Music*. Accessed May 7, 2002. https://www.kwf.org/pages/wt-opera-news-on-the-air-1949.html.
Grosch, Nils, ed. *Kurt Weill: Briefwechsel mit der Universal Edition*. Stuttgart: Metzler, 2002.
Hinton, Stephen. "Fragwürdiges in der deutschen Rezeption." In *A Stranger Here Myself: Kurt Weill Studien*, edited by Kim H. Kowalke and Horst Edler, 23–32. Hildesheim: Georg Olms, 1993.
Kotschenreuther, Helmut. *Kurt Weill*. Berlin: Max Hesse, 1962.
Kowalke, Kim H. "Kurt Weill and the Quest for American Opera." In *Amerikanismus, Americanism, Weill: die Suche nach kultureller Identität in der Moderne*, edited by Hermann Danuser and Hermann Gottschewski, 283–301. Schliengen: Argus, 2003.
Kowalke, Kim H. *Kurt Weill in Europe*. Ann Arbor: UMI Research Press, 1979.
Kowalke, Kim H. "Kurt Weill, Modernism, and Popular Culture: *Öffentlichkeit als Stil*." *Modernism/Modernity* 2, no. 1 (1995): 27–69.
Kundera, Milan. *Testaments Betrayed: An Essay in Nine Parts*. Translated by Linda Asher. New York: Harper-Collins Perennial, 2001.
Kurt Weill Foundation. "Weill on Swift Show NBC 490331." *Vimeo*, August 3, 2020. Accessed May 7, 2022. https://vimeo.com/444251513.
Redlich, Hans. "Obituary." *Music Survey* 3 (1950): 4.
Symonette, Lys, and Elmar Juchem, gen. eds. *Kurt Weill: Briefe an die Familie (1914–1950)*. Stuttgart: Metzler, 2001.
Symonette, Lys, and Kim H. Kowalke, trans. and eds. *Speak Low (When You Speak Love): The Letters of Kurt Weill and Lotte Lenya*. Berkeley: University of California Press, 1996.
Taruskin, Richard. "To the Editor." *Kurt Weill Newsletter* 6, no. 1 (1988): 3–4.
Thomson, Virgil. "Memorial to Weill." *New York Herald Tribune*, February 5, 1951, 11.

Thomson, Virgil. "Music in Review: Kurt Weill." *New York Herald Tribune*, April 9, 1950, C7.
Weill, Kurt. "Broadway Opera: Our Composers' Hope for the Future." Edited by Edward J. Smith. *Musical Digest* 29, no. 4 (1946): 41–42.
Weill, Kurt. "The Future of Opera in America." *Modern Music* 14, no. 4 (1937): 183–88.
Weill, Kurt. "Score for a Play: 'Street Scene' Becomes a 'Dramatic Musical.'" *New York Times*, January 5, 1947, D3.
Weill, Kurt. "Über den gestischen Charakter der Musik." *Musik* 21, no. 6 (1929): 419–23.
Winett, Ralph. "Composer of the Hour: An Interview with Kurt Weill." *Brooklyn Daily Eagle*, December 20, 1936, C11–C12.

Chapter 5

A Walk on the Weill Side

Musical Theater and Rock Music in the 1960s

William Solomon

I want to be the rock & roll Kurt Weill.

—Lou Reed

At the end of his magisterial study *Weill's Musical Theatre: Stages of Reform*, Stephen Hinton notes "the inspiration [Kurt] Weill has provided to rock musicians" and proposes this as a topic worth considering in greater detail. As evidence of the fact that the songs of the German-Jewish composer, who died of a heart attack in New York City in 1950, have had "an enduring impact outside the musical theatre for which they were originally but not exclusively conceived," Hinton points to *Lost in the Stars*, a 1985 tribute CD produced by Hal Willner and Paul D. Young.[1] Although only one of the "new renditions of Weill's music" contained on the "eclectic collection" is specifically in the rock idiom—Lou Reed's version of "September Song"—several other participants in the project—Tom Waits, Marianne Faithfull (backed by Chris Spedding), Sting, Van Dyke Parks, and Todd Rundgren—have been associated at one time or another over the course of their respective careers with rock music. Robert Christgau's semi-ecstatic response to the album makes an even stronger case for the significance of Weill in the history of the musical phenomenon. Upon hearing *Lost in the Stars* for the first time, the longtime *Village Voice* music critic counterintuitively quips, "I started muttering, 'Kurt Weill invented rock and roll,' which I report only to indicate how turned on I was, because it's ridiculous—Weill really only invented rock. Milking abrasive pop for outreach and meaning, he had more in common with Dylan and Newman than with Porter and Berlin, and the rock artists who take their turns on this . . . [hour-long disc] sound completely at home." Quibbling with some of the choices—he would have preferred David Johansen do "Mack the Knife" rather than Sting, and would have selected the Clash over Stanard Ridgway for "Cannon Song"—Christgau nevertheless gives the collection an A grade in his Consumer Guide and instructs his readers to purchase it, either to "introduce yourself to one of the century's greatest songwriters and composers" or as a welcome addition "to your collection" of his work.[2]

Christgau was less impressed with the similarly oriented project released more than a decade later, *September Songs* (1997), the audio recording of what was initially a video documentary, produced and directed by Larry Weinstein in 1994. In his review of this collection, another testament to the influence of Weill on popular music in the latter half of the twentieth century, Christgau lists three performances: William Burroughs's spoken-word version of "What Keeps Mankind Alive?"; P. J. Harvey's cover of "Ballad of the Soldier's Wife"; and David Johansen doing "Mack the Knife." The image of a pair of scissors follows, an indication that these were the choice cuts on an album that was otherwise a dud. Of Elvis Costello's "Lost in the Stars," also included alongside a reprise of Lou Reed's previous take on "September Song," Christgau says nothing. But taken together, the members of the cast suggest that the range of Weill's impact extended to new wave, postpunk, and (if only distantly by way of David Johansen's original band, the amusingly outrageous, cross-dressing New York Dolls, whose first album was produced by the aforementioned Todd Rundgren) glam rock.

David Bowie's intermittent acknowledgment of his debt to Brecht-Weill collaborations supports the latter portion of this claim. In 1982, his final release for RCA records before signing with EMI was an EP titled *Baal*, comprised of materials associated with the play (a BBC production of which he starred in that same year) including Weill's "The Drowned Girl." Two years earlier, Bowie had put out "Alabama Song" as a single (with an acoustic "Space Oddity" as the B-side), which despite its unusual key changes sold well enough to reach No. 23 on the UK charts. More pertinently, the title of his groundbreaking fifth album, *The Rise and Fall of Ziggy Stardust and the Spiders from Mars* (1971) seems to be a nod to Brecht and Weill's 1930 opera, *The Rise and the Fall of the City of Mahagonny*. But it is the *New York Times* music critic John Rockwell's assessment of *Images 1966–1967*, a compilation of very early Bowie material, some of which had never been heard before, that solidifies the notion that the popular singer had a longstanding debt to the Weimar Republic duo:

> What is most intriguing about this documentation of his evolution" Rockwell remarked, "is that it reveals how Bowie came to rock from a tradition of cabaret and musical theater, rather than following the most conventional pattern of a rocker picking up sophistication as he goes along. "Images" . . . is full of deft patter, strings and light, mocking arrangements that recall Kurt Weill more than Little Richard. Come to think of it, though, Brecht and Weill are hardly bad models for a contemporary art form based on generational and class antagonisms.[3]

Here I propose to take this theatrical model as a way to interrogate prevailing views on rock performance in the 1960s. If "rock ideology . . . is first and foremost an ideology of authenticity," the historical significance of David Bowie is that he offered in the 1970s a viable alternative to this dominant or major paradigm of soulful "realness."[4] Whereas the counterculture privileged affectively charged performances rooted in the embodied subjectivity of the performer, Bowie's irony and accompanying penchant for role-playing, for developing multiple personae, emphasized the degree to which rock stardom involved (non-method) acting and artificiality ("I feel like an actor when I'm on stage, not a rock artist").[5] In the wake of folk rock's affirmation of expressive sincerity and psychedelic rock's swirling pursuit of moody intensities or (chemically enhanced) mystical states of mind, Bowie helped facilitate the rise of a dramaturgical perspective, one in which identity had the status of a mere costume, or mask one might don for a period of time until it wore out, whereupon one was free to fabricate a new or different character.[6] Rather than insist on being true to himself, Bowie demanded the right to become other, to transform into whomever or whatever he wished to appear as at a given moment in time (man, woman, alien visitor from outer space, etc.).[7] Brazenly calculating, he anointed himself "the avatar of the new age," casting himself in an ostensibly post-counterculture manner as an internally vacuous, unfeeling creature, "as a chameleon without a past or an identity," thus making it "easy either to embrace him as the wave of the future, or to reject him as a soulless poseur."[8] Correlatively, the members of the audience are henceforth maintained in their prescribed position as passive spectators at a show, rather than encouraged as they were throughout the preceding decade to feel like they were active participants in a communal performance, were immersed in a collective experience à la "the love crowd" (as Otis Redding put it) at the Monterey Pop Festival or belonged to the tribal nation (as Abbie Hoffman put it) gathered together at Woodstock.

From this perspective, the emergence and subsequent embrace of Bowie as a popular icon marks the end of the countercultural commitment to revitalizing (romantic) paradigms of lyric self-expression and the beginning of a post-countercultural (re)investment in the kind of dramatic methods of self-objectification or "extinction of personality" previously endorsed by (modernist) poets like Ezra Pound and T. S. Eliot. And indeed it makes sense to say that the '60s witnessed a widespread devotion to performance as a confessional "turning loose of emotion," and that the next contrasting trend in music was toward a detached or depersonalizing "escape from emotion."[9] Yet there is a different way of looking at or historicizing this, one that seizes upon Bowie's histrionics as a means of retroactively illuminating the theatrical impulses more subtly operative before his rise to cultural prominence. For rock stars in the earlier decade were just as dependent as were their glam rock successors on acts of self-fashioning, though such procedures were for the most part kept private rather than boldly exhibited in public. My concern below, then, is with a minor (or modernist) strain of rock performance in the '60s, one predicated on an avowed staginess and that frequently (though not always) coincided with an interest in the work of Weill.[10] Often this interest manifested itself in the form of compositional borrowing, though it is most immediately apparent in the various rock covers of his tunes. I will therefore start where all discussions of Weill's impact on the musical genre do, with Jim Morrison and the Doors' version(s) of "Alabama Song (Whisky Bar)."

The song had recently appeared on record in this country as an instrumental track on a 1960 collaboration between modern jazz greats, John Lewis and Eric Dolphy; though it seems Ray Manzarek got the idea that the Doors should cover it on their self-titled debut album (released in January of 1967) after hearing Lotte Lenya reprise her role as Jenny Hill on a cast recording of *Mahagonny*. It was an apt choice given that before signing with Elektra, the Doors had honed their sound the preceding year while working regularly as the house band at the Whisky A Go Go. The six-month stint came to an abrupt end when Morrison spontaneously concluded an LSD-fueled performance of "The End" at the Sunset Strip Club with a cathartic declaration of incestuous desire ("Mother I want to fuck you.") Muffled on record, the notorious oedipal obscenity shocked the venue's owner, who promptly fired them, forcing the group to search, metaphorically speaking, for a new whiskey bar in order to continue plying their trade.

In any event, the most significant alteration the band made to the original version was to shift the gender of the singer from female to male—a shift implicit in the substitution of girl for boy as the prepositional object in the second verse ("Show me the way to the next little *girl*"). The pronominal switch adds a predatory dimension to the tune. Whereas the prostitute was articulating the need to find a customer as a condition of survival, the character Morrison creates appears to be on a more sinister, lust-driven search for a victim, either to satisfy a sexual urge, or worse to gratify an impulse to kill. The desire to cause death rather than stave it off through the acquisition of money justifies the excision from the Doors' version of the line "Show me the way to the next little dollar." It is less cash for services rendered than murder that the protagonist has on his mind. It is therefore fitting that on occasion the band would combine in concert "Alabama Song" with "Mack the Knife," thus producing a kind of thematic medley of violent villainy.

A telling case in point is a bootlegged 1968 show in Stockholm, where after playing portions of the two Weill numbers the band segues—by way of a wild intro featuring Morrison's strangled vocals and Robby Krieger's heavily distorted guitar vamping—into Howlin' Wolf's "Back Door Man." The first album also contained a slower-burning cover of the famous blues song (written by bass player Willie Dixon); yet there it led off the B side of the LP, and was further separated from "Alabama Song" by the group's biggest hit, "Light My Fire," a suspect plea for sex as shared self-immolation ("our love become a funeral pyre") that brought side A to an end. The turn to one of the legendary Chicago blues man's signature statements may be considered a textbook example of post-Beat White Negro primitivism (or romantic racialism) in the sense that

Morrison here grounds his defiant persona—as Elvis so influentially had done a decade before—in an idealized figure of uninhibited, boldly assertive black virility. If, as Eric Lott convincingly argues, Wolf mobilizes in "Back Door Man" an embodiment of "strident masculinism to redress Jim Crow humiliation through sexual transgression and bravado," then the Doors lead singer both emulates and exploits this stereotyped image of braggadocio for his own (commercial) purposes.[11] It is through an imaginary act of cross-racial identification that he acquires for himself highly marketable traits—erotic prowess and daring—while eliminating in the course of the appropriative process the latently political dimension in the original of African-American resistance to legally enforced discriminatory practices. However, locating materials drawn from two Weill-Brecht plays alongside the Howlin' Wolf tune has a distancing effect (*Verfremdungseffekt*), raising questions as to the degree of seriousness involved in Morrison's reliance on the latter as a role model. Indeed, upon critical reflection, Morrison's growlingly empathic identification of himself ("*I am* . . . a back door man") as a marginalized minority strikes one as an instance of parodic excess, as if Morrison were casting himself in over-the-top style as a character as distinctive as was Mack the Knife in *The Threepenny Opera*.[12]

In sum, the sequencing hints at Morrison's reflexive awareness of the pretense involved in his sonic imitations of African Americans. What might otherwise be taken as naively mystified instances of manly mimicry appear in this light as the comically amplified acts of a skilled ventriloquist, one willing to make a mockery of the extent to which his charismatic personality was derived from a caricature of blackness. In other words, the Lizard King knew quite well how much of his fame depended on his capacity to shed his skin and drape himself in that of a racial other, though it took his fan base a while to catch on ("However theatrical his poses appear in retrospect, Morrison's vision seemed genuinely tormented—aggressively fascinated with death, reptiles, and forbidden varieties of sex.")[13]

Eric Lott has spent a considerable portion of his academic career unpacking the mixed motivations structuring the kind of interracial interplay in question, beginning with his celebrated 1993 study *Love and Theft: The Racial Unconscious of Blackface Minstrelsy*. I won't rehearse in detail here his influential, and multifaceted handling of the topic, but will instead look to the cover of Eric Clapton's 2005 album *Me and Mr. Johnson*—a work by the pop artist Peter Blake, who designed the famous sleeve for the Beatles' *Sgt. Pepper's Lonely Hearts Club Band*—as a condensed illustration of the psychoanalytic (or Lacanian) dimensions of Lott's critical approach. The depiction on the album cover of a photograph and painting of the semi-mythic Delta bluesman, with the Caucasian guitarist seated in the right foreground posed with an acoustic guitar in a manner resembling Johnson's stance in the image on the back wall, implies an understanding of the specular nature of Clapton's long-term investment in his African-American precursor. Mirroring himself on this impressive Depression-era figure was one of the mimetic conditions of possibility of the British musician's attainment in the 1960s of a widely acclaimed degree of instrumental mastery, his virtuosity a product of an imaginary act of (mis)recognition, of an identification across racial (and national) lines with an idealized other. Crucially, for Lott such a procedure, one of the linchpins (by way of Elvis at Sun Studios) in the rise of rock 'n' roll in the US in the mid-1950s, is part of the genealogical legacy of a nineteenth-century form of popular (and racist) entertainment in this country (blackface minstrelsy). The emotional attitude may have changed dramatically, from condescension to idolization, yet it remains the case that ostensibly well-intentioned devotees like Clapton were implicated in a cultural tradition of "cooning" and caricature, or racial masquerade that, its psychosocial complexities notwithstanding, originally functioned as a means of mocking oppressed minorities.[14]

This structure of feeling would seem well suited to account for key components of Bob Dylan's career—from his extraordinary rendition on his first album of Blind Lemon Jefferson's "See that My Grave Is Kept Clean" to his thirty-first studio album, *Love and Theft* (2002)—the title presumably an admission of the applicability of Lott's interpretive framework to his (Dylan's) body of work in its entirety.[15] And indeed near the end of *Chronicle*, his 2004 autobiography, the singer-turned-raconteur recalls that upon signing his first contract with Columbia Records, four decades earlier, the prominent talent scout John Hammond (father of John Hammond Jr.) had given him a copy of Robert Johnson's *King of the Delta Blues Singers*: "I'd never heard of Robert Johnson, never heard the name, never seen it on any of the compilation blues records. Hammond said I should listen to it, that this guy could 'whip anybody.'"[16] (Dylan 2004, 281). Dylan goes on to describe listening to the album for the first time with Dave Van Ronk. Dylan was blown away, his friend and folk-music mentor, less impressed:

> From the first note the vibrations from the loudspeaker made my hair stand up. The stabbing sounds from the guitar could almost break a window. . . . The record that didn't grab Dave very much had left me numb, like I'd been hit by a tranquilizer bullet. . . . Over the next few weeks I listened to it repeatedly, cut after cut, one song after another, sitting staring at the record player. Whenever I did, it felt like a ghost had come into the room, a fearsome apparition. . . . There's nothing clownish about him or his lyrics. I wanted to be like that, too.[17]

Next, after a recapitulation of the impact of Johnson on his songwriting technique (especially at the level of lyric imagery), Dylan quotes Rimbaud's "Je est un autre" and translates it as "I is someone else," the implication being that he is well aware just how important to his artistic development was his complicity in a racialized variant of the process of imagining oneself as an other: "When I read those words the bells went off. It made perfect sense. I wished someone would have mentioned that to me earlier. It went right along with Johnson's dark night of the soul."[18]

However, the story is a bit more complicated, for Dylan had recounted a few pages earlier an equally transformative first encounter with Brecht and Weill. Here too his musical "perspective" changed radically. "My little shack in the universe was about to expand into some glorious cathedral, at least in songwriting terms." Upon hearing the songs featured in a revival of *The Threepenny Opera* at the Theater de Lys (where his girlfriend Suze Rotolo had a job backstage) in Greenwich Village, he realized how he might extend his repertoire beyond the traditional folk materials he had inherited from among others Woody Guthrie.[19] ("You couldn't call this a play, it was more like a stream of songs by actors who sang").[20] "Aroused straight away by the raw intensity of the songs," by their "erratic, unrhythmical and herky-jerky" elements," Dylan was immediately drawn to the "weird visions" and distinctive sounds generated by the opera's shady cast of characters: "the singers were thieves, scavengers or scallywags, and they all roared and snarled."[21] Shortly thereafter, Dylan found himself compelled to analyze the show-stopping ballad "A Ship the Black Freighter" (recorded in 1977 by the British folk rock group Steeleye Span), which he only later learned was actually titled "Pirate Jenny." Stunned by the forcefulness of the piece, which "demanded to be taken seriously" despite the fact that it "wasn't a protest or topical song" since "there was no love for the people in it," he found himself "taking the song apart, trying to find out what made it tick, why it was so effective . . . it was the form . . . the structure and disregard for the known certainty of melodic patterns [that] . . . gave it its cutting edge . . . I wanted to manipulate and control this particular structure and form which I knew was the key that gave 'Pirate Jenny' its resilience and outrageous power."[22]

Perhaps this is why in the records piled on the chaise lounge in the photograph used for the cover of his 1965 release, *Bringing It All Back Home*, a copy of Johnson's *King of the Delta Blues Singers*, is partially obscured by *Lotte Lenya Sings Berlin Theatre Songs by Kurt Weill* (with a copy of *Keep On Pushing*, by the Impressions, the vocal group led by Curtis Mayfield, barely discernible beneath both, and the *Folk Blues of Eric Von Schmidt* placed on top). The stacked albums would thus supply a visual image of the layering in Dylan's mind of the myriad sources of his densely fabricated musical identity, of the little bit of faux in his folk persona. In other words, the performer was dramatically oriented from the beginning, his ethical earnestness galvanized by a distinctly theatrical sensibility, his vocals those of a skilled actor[23]: "In a few years' time, I'd write and sing songs like 'It's Alright Ma (I'm Only Bleeding),' 'Mr. Tambourine Man,' 'Lonesome Death of Hattie Carroll,' 'Who Killed Davey Moore,' 'Only a Pawn in Their Game,' 'A Hard Rain's A-Gonna Fall' and some others like that. If I hadn't gone to the Theater de Lys and heard the ballad 'Pirate Jenny,' it might not have dawned on me to write them, that songs like these could be written."[24] Thus the only thing missing from Grace Elizabeth Hale's excellent summary of Dylan's sociocultural intervention in the 1960s is the pivotal role Weimar cabaret played in it: "Dylan helped create a new kind of popular musician who fused the seeming contradictions of the folk revival's obsession with authenticity with the playacting of minstrelsy, a performer whose authenticity lay in expressing the emotions he shared with the folk. This paradoxical melding of [self] invention and authenticity, of freedom and grounding helped generate the seductive power of mid-sixties rock and roll."[25]

The cover art mentioned above inspired Patti Smith at a formative stage of her career to begin exploring the words and music of Brecht and Weill. "I started reading Brecht because of Bob Dylan," she recalls. "I bought my copy of *Bringing It All Back Home* in 1965, and one of a batch of records on the cover is by Lotte Lenya. I wanted to listen to whatever Bob was listening to, which then opened a whole world to me, of Bertolt Brecht and Kurt Weill."[26] And as her fascination with Weill's wife grew, she managed to get Jann Wenner, the editor of *Rolling Stone*, to let her review for the magazine a recently released collection of Lenya's performances. Notably, in her poem "Autobiography" Smith indicates that what she found in the chanteuse (and in Dylan) was an example of how one might become a musical performer by appearing on stage as who you are not. After a verse in which Smith recalls learning early in life how to mask herself, to construct false identities, for protective purposes—"I paraded in thirty disguises / and when people laughed at my carnival family / We didn't care . . . We had armor"—she implies that in the years to come her role models would teach her this same mimetic lesson: "I joined the fire eaters and sang in the streets . . . using all I learned / from Bob Dylan . . . Lotte Lenya . . . and motorcycle rock 'n' roll."[27] The education of the poet as entertainer involved discovering the virtues of becoming a collective entity, of developing multiple personalities.

Her first public reading, at St. Mark's Church on February 10, 1971, indicated both that a fondness for charismatic criminality would be a component of many of her myriad alter egos, and that it was Brecht-Weill who supplied Smith with a template for this stance. Given that the date of the show was Brecht's birthday, it makes sense that she decided to open with a delightfully amateurish rendition of "Mack the Knife" accompanied by Lenny Kaye on electric guitar.[28] But at roughly the halfway mark of the twenty-minute performance it becomes evident that outlaw defiance will be one of the set's structuring motifs. It is at this point that she reads a piece in defense of Jesse James ("a saint / I ain't saying he is / I ain't saying he ain't"). The narrator turns out to be a woman who was sleeping with both the famous bank robber and Billy the Kid and who witnessed the former's shooting of the latter one "fateful night" as a consequence of the love triangle. Next, she dedicates a "little prayer" she has written to François Villon, who was "really neat because he was a poet" and, she adds with a sheepish laugh, because "he was a murderer too." The final number, "for Sam [Shepherd, who was the one who advised her to inject some rock 'n' roll into her poetry]," was "The Ballad of a Bad Boy," the story, narrated in the first person and thus from beyond the grave, of a juvenile delinquent whose mother cut off all his fingers and then killed him as punishment for his evil behavior. In looking back on the evening at the Poetry Project decades later, Kaye compares Patti to the first of the figures they memorialized on stage together, proposing that his mischievous musical collaborator could be as suavely menacing as Macheath. He concludes his comments by asserting that this "is a character Patti has stepped in and out of over the years" and that in retrospect he feels privileged to have been "a part of her Threepenny Opera."[29]

It is fitting that Lou Reed was in the audience that night, for a consideration of this mercurial figure is the next logical step in a genealogy of Weill's impact on rock music in the US. Let me start with *Take No Prisoners*, a live album recorded and released in 1978. A decidedly strange show, it captures a performer who appears more interested in doing stand-up comedy ("What am I Henny Youngman?") than in playing any of his musical material. Adopting the stance of bitterly jaded rock star, he seems determined to offend anyone and everyone, including former disciples (at one point he disses Patti Smith as if she were a pretender to his crown: "Fuck Radio Ethiopia [the title of her second album], man I'm Radio Brooklyn"). An equal-opportunity insulter, he doesn't spare himself, or at least mocks the frequently copied persona he has constructed: "Watch me turn into Lou Reed before your very eyes," he barks at the crowd. "I do Lou Reed better than anybody so I thought I'd get in on it." Early in the set he does "I Wanna Be Black," his caustic denunciation of white college students' fascination with images of black militancy (and masculinity); and shortly thereafter an unrecognizable "I'm Waiting for the Man" (the second track on the Velvet Underground's debut album) that devolves into an improvised junkie monologue that resembles an outtake from a scene in Shirley Clarke's *The Connection* (1961). Just before this he has led his back-up band through the title cut of *Berlin*, an artistically ambitious yet commercially calamitous album (also critically raked over the coals upon its release in 1973) that Ben Sisario has described as "rock filtered through a Brecht-Weill sensibility."[30] This controversial achievement would seem to be pertinent to the present discussion but I want to turn instead to some of the off-the-cuff remarks he makes later on during the nearly seventeen-minute version of "Walk on the Wild Side."

Really never actually gets around to playing the signature song of his solo career, repeatedly interrupting his quasi-singing of the lyrics to rant about something or other. His lengthiest diatribe is against the intellectualism, or pseudo-academicism of rock journalists like the *Times*'s John Rockwell and the *Voice*'s Robert Christgau, Reed particularly incensed by the latter's grading system (Christgau responded in kind by awarding the double LP that namechecks him a C+ in his column). What is of interest here is Reed's explanation of how he came to write "Walk on the Wild Side." After *Loaded* (1970), the Velvet Underground's last album, Reed quit the group (despite the fact that a couple of singles—"Rock and Roll" and "Sweet Jane" were getting significant amount of airplay) found himself, he tells the audience, working as a typist for his father when "the guys who did *The Threepenny Opera*" (almost certainly the aforementioned Theater de Lys production) contacted him, saying "We think you're a very literate rock and roll person, after Ray Davies, we think you're the person who could take Nelson Algren's book *Walk on the Wild Side* and do like a musical thing for off-Broadway."[31] The project fell through when Carmine Capalbo and his associates took up a different enterprise, an ultimately unsuccessful production of *Mahagonny*, which Reed confuses with the 1975 motion picture, *Mahogany*, a Diana Ross vehicle directed by Berry Gordy himself in which the Motown star plays a hardworking fashion designer who eventually rises to the top of her profession. The lyrics of the film's theme song (burned into my eleven-year-old brain by too much AM radio) would seem perfectly applicable to Reed's quandary at this stage of his career: "Do you know where you're going to? Do you like the things that life is showing you? . . ."

However he might have responded to these queries, given his embittered state of mind at the end of the 1970s, it had been quite clear to Reed earlier in life what he hoped to accomplish: his aim was "to be the rock & roll Kurt Weill." But what exactly did such an aspiration mean to Reed at this time? Here is how he put it: "My interest—all the way back with the Velvets—has been in one simple and guiding-light idea: take rock & roll, the pop format, and make it for adults."[32] This is helpful but conceptually insufficient. A brief explication of Kim Kowalke's critical account of the challenge Weill's work posed in his era to prevailing musical canons and hierarchies is therefore necessary if we are to refine our understanding of this ambition.

Rejecting the "two-Weill" model in scholarship since it tends to privilege his German phase and disparage his subsequent assimilation in the US of the Broadway idiom, Kowalke argues that the composer remains a key figure for those concerned to dismantle the mythology of high modernism. The commonplace notion that Weill in exile ceased to be a serious composer and became instead a sellout, an aesthetic hack devoid of integrity primarily interested in box-office receipts, misses this point entirely. For even before leaving Europe he had begun to renounce the New Music's insistence on isolating itself from the musical marketplace, Weill's project to find a way to appeal to non-specialist audiences, the benefits of an art-for-art's sake autonomy outweighed by the potential social virtues of cultural accessibility. As he explained it while still residing in Berlin:

> The fact that my *Dreigroschenoper* music has been commercialized doesn't speak against it, but for it, and we would be falling back into our old mistakes if we were to deny some music its importance and artistic value simply because it found its way to the masses. . . . I am the only creative musician who for years has worked consistently and uncompromisingly in the face of opposition from the snobs and aesthetes towards the creation of a new, simple, popular musical theatre. Even my least significant music theatre works during this time have been written with this sense of responsibility and have grown out of a constant effort to further a development which seems to me the only one possible.[33]

Whereas proponents of the twelve-tone technique affirmed formal recalcitrance over and above the demands of the music industry, Weill sought to negotiate his way through tensions endemic to twentieth-century cultural production. Rather than stay ensconced in a moribund passion for operatic originality, he felt upon arrival in this country that making "some concessions to Broadway showmanship" was a legitimate method of maintaining the health of the American theater (quoted in Kowalke, 33).[34] In sum, his search was for that most elusive of phenomena, a populist modernism, which would function as the "third term" between Schoenberg and Hollywood film, and in so doing overcome the great divide between art and mass culture.[35]

Reed's claiming of Weill as his hero, then, makes sense at the level of intention: following the composer's lead, what he wished to accomplish with the Velvet Underground was the reconciliation of the urge toward formal experimentation with the desire for economic viability. Having acquired the skills necessary to generate pop hits (Reed had put in some time at the Brill Building and was in 1964 "writing kitsch songs for a company called Pickwick Records"), he found in the classically trained John Cale (just off a stint as violist for La Monte Young's Theatre of Eternal Music) a partner able to help integrate dissonance and drone (feedback and "the everlasting fifth") into the group's music.[36] Saddled per Andy Warhol's instructions (for their debut album) with the German model turned chanteuse Nico (previously Jim Morrison's girlfriend), the Velvet's were in good shape to mediate between rock repetition and aesthetic innovation, to bridge the gap between the auditory pleasures of familiarity and the sonic painfulness of originality. The wish to bring minimalism to the masses may have failed to come to fruition in the economic sphere (the enterprise was not financially remunerative), but the attempt amounts to an extension of Weill's career-long project. What the German-Jewish composer struggled to do on the Weimar and Broadway stages was what Reed endeavored to do in the musical venues history made available to him.

A related claim can be made for Frank Zappa's undertaking with the Mothers of Invention. Paddison, for instance, proposes an analogy between Weill's and Zappa's early records on the grounds that the latter performed "a remarkable balancing act between the spheres of popular and of radical music—largely through the creative use of parody and Brecht-like alienation techniques as well as elements from twentieth-century serious music."[37] Correlatively, Currier has argued that the score for the film *200 Hotels* can be compared to the music of Brecht and Weill; and Fisher Lowe has asserted that "Weill is especially important in understanding Zappa's musical project" whether this be in regard to his penchant for stylistic pluralism, recourse to popular idioms, or general commitment to transgressing the boundaries separating artistic and commercial undertakings.[38] Indeed, "Holiday in Berlin" and its "Overture," both on *Burnt Weeny Sandwich* [1970], allude stylistically to Weill; however, Borders argues of these two tracks that, although their "off-key treatment" and "boozy saxophone solos" evoke Weill's *Mahagonny*, they are "self-parodies" of previous Zappa compositions and that the rock performer "by his own admission (. . .) was not a fan of Weill's music."[39]

Reed's contemporary, Randy Newman, once stated in an interview that when he is searching for a substitute for the blues, and when his songs consequently become "a bit more complex" and he has to "think about the chords, and write them down, and move the voices around," he often finds himself reflecting on Weill's "harmonic vocabulary." "It is something I think about. In fact I'm thinking about it too much."[40] Indeed, from the "mocking German Expressionist twists" of his self-titled first studio album (1968) to "Putin," a satirical track on his most recent (*Dark Matter* [2017]), which prompted Greil Marcus to declare that "it is so German, so 1920s, so after-hours Berlin with everyone doped to the gills and shouting along" that "Kurt Weill and Bertolt Brecht must be jumping up and down in their graves in happiness," Newman has displayed an affinity for Weimar-era arrangements.[41] A pertinent case in point would be "In Germany before the War," a tune from his 1977 album *Little Criminals* that in the chorus adopts the point of view of Hans Beckert, the serial child killer portrayed by Peter Lorre in the Fritz Lang classic *M*. Employing one of Weill's trademark tactics, the articulation of distasteful attitudes in an audibly pleasing way, the song thus exhibits one of the traits that drew Tom Waits to the German composer's work: "I like to hear a beautiful melody telling me something terrible."[42]

It also makes rhetorical use, as so much of Newman's work does, of the dramatic monologue, which in turn requires of listeners that they maintain their distance from the thoughts and feelings of the troubled characters he mimics. Rather than solicit identification, Newman's theatrical ventriloquism is designed to produce an effect of dis-identification or distantiation. We are not encouraged to empathize with the emotions his racists ("Underneath the Harlem Moon" [a rare cover] and "The Yellow Man") and rapists ("Suzanne") express; rather the task is to separate ourselves from (and perhaps analyze) the disturbing ideas and fraught passions the authorial subject reproduces: Newman "always writes, and what is harder, sings, in the voices of his characters . . . ; no matter what grotesquerie is involved, he does not sing about, he sings *as*."[43] For Marcus, the exasperating lack of public appreciation for Newman's talents was a sign of a widespread failure on the part of the masses to measure up to the critical challenge his manipulations of point of view posed: "Audiences are no longer used to the idea that someone might make something up, create a persona and effectively act it out, the way Chuck Berry and Bob Dylan used to do. Audiences take everything literally, partly because sensitive personal confession, 'honesty,' and one-to-one communication between singer and whoever is listening is so attractive and reassuring."[44] In contrast to the comforts offered by autobiographically inclined singer-songwriters like James Taylor, whose output may be consumed as if one were reading the pages of a diary, Newman's dangerously disconcerting role playing draws upon the legacy of the stage.

His riskiest maneuver is of course his vocal indulgence in racial caricature. Newman switched, Marcus argues, around the time he was putting together his second album (*12 Songs*), "from a style that could be called Jewish to one that can only be called black"—though the qualities he derived from this imitative procedure are not what the bulk of white rock 'n' roll singers customarily seek to appropriate from their racial other: "assertiveness, aggression, melancholy, sexual power."[45] Rather it is the stereotyped lassitude, the laidback drawl, of the (deviously) somnambulant, ostensibly dim-witted dunce, that Newman impersonates: "it is as if Randy's real blues hero wasn't Howlin' Wolf, but Stepin Fetchit."[46] If hyperbolic amplification of the more commonly adopted role model enabled Morrison to detach himself, however slightly, from the blackface mask he metaphorically donned, in Newman's case it is irony that cracks the façade, thus salvaging his work from the accusation that it perpetuates aspects of the minstrel tradition ("Old Kentucky Home," for instance, also on *12 Songs*, structures its chorus around elements of the verse of the similarly titled Stephen Foster ballad).

Coda

If that's all there is my friends, then let's keep dancing.

—Peggy Lee, "Is That All There Is?"

In the late 1960s, the illustrious songwriting team and production duo Jerry Leiber and Mike Stoller, who had helped invent rock 'n' roll in the preceding decade by composing a string of mini-dramas or comic playlets for the Coasters, "had been talking about stretching out as writers." Jerry had been reading a Thomas Mann story titled "Disillusionment" and felt prompted "to look deep into the existential hole that sits in the center of our souls." Out of this turn to the nothingness within came "a series of loosely connected verses" spoken by a disenchanted woman. Mike seized upon these vignettes, which "ached with the bittersweet irony of the German cabaret," as a perfect opportunity to expand their compositional horizons, writing music "he hoped caught the spirit of Kurt Weill and Bertolt Brecht."[47] When Peggy Lee, whom they considered "the funkiest white woman alive," agreed to work with them again on a new tune (they had had an "across-the-board hit" with her on "I'm a Woman" in 1963), they naturally chose Randy Newman to do the arrangements. "We heard in Randy's work an irony and theatricality that we thought appropriate" for "Is That All There Is?"[48] A wonderfully weird work of art, the song was also a commercial sensation in 1969, climbing the charts and staying there alongside "the Beatles' 'Get Back' and 'Come Together,' the Stones' 'Honky Tonk Women,' Elvis's 'Suspicious Minds,' and Sly and the Family Stone's 'Everyday People.' "[49]

In the same year James Brown, backed by the Louie Ellison Orchestra as conducted by Oliver Nelson, released a terrific version of Weill's "September Song" (originally featured in the Depression-era Broadway musical *Knickerbocker Holiday*) on the album *Soul on Top*. That a tune that would serve many years later as the point of departure for a deadpan rock performance (Lou Reed) had previously functioned as a touchstone for a five-minute burst of lively funk is another multi-generic testament to the faint yet sustained resonance of Weill's oeuvre in the history of postwar American popular music. Brown's surprising decision to take on "September Song" also supplies me with an opportunity to restate my thesis: that attending to the Weill motif is one way to excavate the theatricality hidden at the center of the field of cultural practice under investigation. Accepting the premise that the ideology of rock music was predicated on a notion of authenticity, there is little need to rehearse the powerful influence of the Godfather of Soul on the postwar rise of the phenomenon. Mentioning the fact that on the other side of the Atlantic the Who covered two of his emotionally intense, rhythm and blues tunes ("I Don't Mind" and "Please, Please, Please") on their first record (*My Generation* [1965]) and that David Bowie and the Spiders from Mars in the early 1970s used to do a medley of Brown's material on stage should be sufficient. But he was also the self-proclaimed "hardest working man in *show business*," which is to say he was well aware of the importance of spectacle and artifice in the realm of professional entertainment. A notorious taskmaster and stickler for details, his performances were meticulously planned out, his moves carefully choreographed, his backup band a disciplined unit. Nor was the lead singer of the Famous Flames above faking it, his closing "cape routine" less a manifestation of a real passion to perform than a campy portrayal of physical fatigue. In other words, it only requires a slight shift in critical perspective to become aware that what still sounds on record like raw nature shrieking expressively was a construct designed to thrill an audience. Though exciting, his conventionalized gestures were by no means spontaneous, and there is no guarantee that their source was the genuine feelings of an embodied self on stage. Soulful affect was perhaps simply a fictive effect generated by an empty subject. And if in the end (as in the beginning) that is all there is, then there is only one thing left to do: in Bowie's words, "Put on your red shoes and dance the blues."

Notes

1. Stephen Hinton, *Weill's Musical Theatre: Stages of Reform* (Berkeley: University of California Press, 2012), 472.

2. Robert Christgau, "Lost in the Stars: The Music of Kurt Weill (A&M, 1985)," *Robert Christgau*, accessed May 7, 2022, https://www.robertchristgau.com/get_album.php?id=1488.

3. John Rockwell, "The Bowie Boom," *New York Times*, May 25, 1973, 30. Two years later, Rockwell would say something similar about Roxy Music, commenting as many would after him on their front man's stylized, German cabaret affectations. See John Rockwell, "Bryan Ferry: Enfant Terrible of Rock," *New York Times*, February 19, 1975, 20: "The lyrics of the group's songs (all written by Mr. Ferry, who also provides most of the music) often strike a similar posture, mixed with just a hint of delicately sadistic detachment. The music, deliberately eclectic in its sources, leans heavily on a steady, almost funereal beat, persistently grinding distortions, crooning saxophones and a clipped ballad form reminiscent of Kurt Weill's songs for Brecht. And again dominating things is Mr. Ferry's peculiar crooner's baritone, alternately mellow and bleating." Ferry would go on to record "September Song" for a 1999 album, *As Time Goes By*. More recently, his nostalgic "Bitter-Sweet," commissioned for the soundtrack of the TV series *Babylon Berlin*, has been widely regarded as a return to his Weill roots. On his fondness for Lotte Lenya, see Jon Savage, "Bryan Ferry on How Roxy Music Invented Artpop," *Guardian*, February 1, 2018, accessed May 7, 2022, https://www.theguardian.com/music/2018/feb/01/bryan-ferry-roxy-music-invented-new-pop-game-for-anything.

4. Jack Hamilton, *Just around Midnight: Rock and Roll and the Racial Imagination* (Cambridge, MA: Harvard University Press, 2016), 14–15.

5. See Timothy Ferris, "The Iceman, Having Calculated, Cometh," *Rolling Stone*, November 9, 1972, accessed May 7, 2022, https://www.rollingstone.com/music/music-news/david-bowie-in-america-56227; quoted in Philip Auslander, *Performing Glam Rock: Gender and Theatricality in Popular Music* (Ann Arbor: University of Michigan Press, 2006), 109.

6. David E. James, *Rock 'n' Film: Cinema's Dance with Popular Music* (New York: Oxford University Press, 2016), 384. See also the indispensable chapter "Who Can I Be Now? David Bowie and the Theatricalization of Rock," in Auslander, *Performing Glam Rock*, 106–49.

7. *Transformer* is the name of the 1972 Lou Reed album that David Bowie produced in the hopes of revitalizing Reed's career by turning him into a glam rocker. The LP contains "Walk on the Wild Side."

8. Tom Carlson, "David Bowie," in Jim Miller, ed., *The Rolling Stone Illustrated History of Rock & Roll* (New York: Rolling Stone, 1980), 386–87.

9. T. S. Eliot, *Prose Keys to Modern Poetry*, ed. Karl Shapiro (New York: Harper & Row, 1962), 71. The correlation of Bowie and Eliot is not entirely fanciful. It may even be the case that the rock star copped a trope from the poet's "The Love Song of J. Alfred Prufrock." The first line of "Rock 'n' Roll Suicide," the final cut on *Ziggy Stardust*, is "Time takes a cigarette, puts it in your mouth." Compare this to Eliot's gloomy, temporally obsessed protagonist's query as to how he might "spit out all the butt-ends of [his] days and ways"; see T. S. Eliot, *Selected Poems* (New York: Harcourt Brace, 1964), 13. See also the similar figuration in "Preludes I." Bowie, however, would no doubt have dismissed such speculations. See Claire Armitstead, "Did David Bowie Pinch a Cactus from T. S. Eliot?," *Guardian*, March 21, 2013, accessed May 7, 2022, https://www.theguardian.com/books/booksblog/2013/mar/21/did-david-bowie-steal-from-ts-eliot.

10. The carnival sideshow aesthetic of the Detroit-based band Alice Cooper owed nothing musical as far as I can tell to Weimar Cabaret, though the band's main producer, Bob Ezrin, must have been well versed in the latter tradition, for it was he who, while working with Lou Reed on *Berlin* (1973), "substituted violas and cellos to evoke 'a Kurt Weill / Bertolt Brecht atmosphere which would suit the lyrics' "; see Peter Hogan, *The Dead Straight Guide to the Velvet Underground and Lou Reed* (Falmouth, UK: Red Planet, 2020), 162. Moreover, Ezrin was given partial writing credit for his contribution to Pink Floyd's "The Trial," "an homage to the early 20th century operettas of Kurt Weill and Bertolt Brecht." Ezrin reportedly altered the track, the penultimate one on *The Wall* (1979), so that it could function as "a big, over-the-top theatrical finale" for the double album. See M., "The Trial," *The Wall Complete*, April 1, 2017, accessed May 7, 2022, https://thewallcomplete.com/2017/04/01/pink-floyd-the-wall-the-trial.

11. Eric Lott, "Back Door Man: Howlin' Wolf and the Sound of Jim Crow," *American Quarterly* 63, no. 3 (2011): 701. I am also drawing on Eric Lott, "White Like Me: Racial Cross-Dressing and the Construction of American Whiteness," in Amy Kaplan and Donald Pease, eds., *Cultures of United States Imperialism* (Durham, NC: Duke University Press, 1993), 474–98. It is feasible that the decision to cover this song was determined by its title, which in its altered context could function as a reference to the band's name and thus as a declaration on Morrison's part of belonging: "I'm a back *Doors* man."

12. It was during a drunken performance of "Back Door Man" in 1969 that Morrison infamously (albeit allegedly) unzipped his black leather pants and exposed himself to the crowd. "Back Door Man" also offers a template for the protagonist of The Rolling Stones' "Midnight Rambler," which Keith Richard once referred to as a "blues opera"; see "Midnight Rambler," *TrackTalk*, accessed May 7, 2022, http://timeisonourside.com/SOMidnight.html. Though it alludes to the real-life actions of the Boston Strangler, the 1969 song (on *Let It Bleed*) also evokes to my mind

Mackie Messer (that is, *Mick* the Knife as cutthroat rapist), especially its phallic final line: "I'll stick my knife right down your throat baby, and it hurts." See also "Stray Cat Blues" for Jagger as seducer of young girls, which makes one wonder if *Beggar's Banquet* might be described as a decadent reworking of John Gay as mediated by Brecht and Weill. Not for nothing did Terry Southern characterize the latter as "the original glimmer twins" in the liner notes he wrote for the aforementioned tribute CD, *Lost in the Stars*. (The Glimmer Twins is the pseudonym Jagger-Richards used to receive credit as music producers.) Determining whether or not this analogy holds is beyond the scope of the present discussion, though my sense is one way to pursue this would be to consider "Salt of the Earth" (the final cut on *Beggar's Banquet*) alongside Brecht and Weill's "The Cannon Song" (from *The Threepenny Opera*) as parallel attempts to disrupt the ideological appeal of drinking or barroom singalongs. For an excellent analysis of "Cannon Song" from this point of view, see Nicholas Brown, "Musical Affect, Musical Citation, Musical Immanence: Kurt Weill and the White Stripes," *Postmodern Culture* 25, no. 2 (2015), accessed May 7, 2022, doi:10.1353/pmc.2015.0005.

13. Geoffrey Stokes, with Ed Ward and Ken Tucker, *Rock of Ages: The Rolling Stone History of Rock & Roll* (New York: Rolling Stone, 1986), 366. See along related lines the genesis of the Muddy Waters inspired moniker "Mr. Mojo Risin" (an anagram of Jim Morrison). This linguistic playfulness (which occurs in the bridge of "L.A. Woman") suggests a self-conscious understanding of the silliness of his racially inflected claim to possess folk magic or hoodoo powers. John Hammond, Jr., from whom The Doors got the idea to do "Back Door Man," would seem, in contrast, to have been deeply invested in such imaginary acts of interracial identification and has been frequently excoriated on this count. See for example Marcus's comment on the folk singer's "ludicrous blackface vocals" in Greil Marcus, *Mystery Train: Images of America in Rock 'N' Roll Music*, 3rd ed. (London: Penguin, 1990), 203.

14. For a fuller treatment of Clapton from this perspective, one that probes the politically unsavory repercussions of his artistic adulations, see Ulrich Adelt, *Blues Music in the Sixties: A Story in Black and White* (New Brunswick: Rutgers University Press, 2010), 57–77. Also valuable are the essays gathered together in Eric Lott, *Black Mirror: The Cultural Contradictions of American Racism* (Cambridge, MA: Harvard University Press, 2017); see especially 139–56 for an eye-opening discussion of Joni Mitchell's Black pimp alter ego.

15. See Lott, *Black Mirror*, 195–207. Hamilton stresses the impact of early rock 'n' roll vocal performances on Dylan's rendition of the blues classic; see Hamilton, *Just around Midnight*, 71–73. For a different opinion, see Keith Nanby and John M. Radosta. *Bob Dylan in Performance, Stage, and Screen* (Lanham, MD: Lexington, 2019), 33.

16. Bob Dylan, *Chronicles: Volume 1* (New York: Simon and Schuster, 2004), 281.

17. Dylan, *Chronicles*, 283–85.

18. Dylan, *Chronicles*, 288. It is fitting that the term "white negro" can be traced back to the author of *Illuminations* by way of a Paul Verlaine epitaph; see Charles Nicholl, *Somebody Else: Arthur Rimbaud in Africa, 1880–91* (Chicago: University of Chicago, 1997), 312.

19. Opening in 1955, starring Lotte Lenya, and directed by Carmen Capalbo, for a decade this version of the opera held the record as the longest running off-Broadway show. But Dylan's memory may be somewhat faulty here; he seems to have conflated the *Threepenny* revival with a 1963 production called *Brecht on Brecht (An Improvisation)* at the Sheridan Square Playhouse. Rotolo also worked there and arranged for Dylan to come to one of the rehearsals where he would have listened to an African-American actress named Micki Grant sing "Pirate Jenny"; see William Farina, *The German Cabaret Influence in American Popular Music* (Jefferson, NC: McFarland, 2013), 168–69. For Southern's take on the "Brecht-Weill renaissance" in the early 1960s, see Terry Southern, *Now Dig This: The Unspeakable Writings of Terry Southern, 1950–1995* (New York: Grove Press, 2001), 147–52. Thomas Pynchon remarks apropos the 1960s folk artist and novelist Richard Fariña (and friend of Dylan's) that two "albums of the period I know he was crazy about were Mose Allison's 'Back Country Suite' and [. . .] the English version of Weill and Brecht's *Threepenny Opera*"; see Thomas Pynchon, "Introduction," in Richard Fariña, *Been Down So Long It Looks Like Up to Me* (Harmondsworth: Penguin, 1983), ix.

20. Dylan, *Chronicles*, 272.

21. Dylan, *Chronicles*, 272–73.

22. Dylan, *Chronicles*, 275–76.

23. Hence the recollection in Robbie Robertson, "Bob Dylan," *Rolling Stone*, December 3, 2010, accessed May 7, 2022, https://www.rollingstone.com/music/music-lists/100-greatest-artists-147446/jimi-hendrix-5-30413: "His voice seemed interesting to me. But it wasn't until we started playing together that I really understood it. He is a powerful singer and a great musical actor, with many characters in his voice."

24. Dylan, *Chronicles*, 287.

25. Grace Elizabeth Hale, *A Nation of Outsiders: How the White Middle Class Fell in Love with Rebellion in Postwar America* (New York: Oxford, 2011), 124.

26. Ed Vulliamy, "Some Give a Song. Some Give a Life . . . ," *Guardian*, June 3, 2005, accessed May 7, 2022, https://www.theguardian.com/music/2005/jun/03/meltdownfestival2005.meltdownfestival. She even insisted Robert Mapplethorpe, several years before the iconic portrait of her on her first album *Horses* (1974), help her self-reflexively recreate the *Bringing it All Back Home* shoot by posing alongside that album cover, the cover of *Blonde on Blonde* (a title perhaps derived from the Brecht on Brecht production mentioned above) and the cover of *Lotte Lenya Sings Berlin Theatre Songs by Kurt Weill* (1955).

See "f3d93f6d256f433285001e0b8d783af5," *Pinterest*, accessed May 7, 2022, https://i.pinimg.com/originals/f3/d9/3f/f3d93f6d256f433285001e0b8d783af5.jpg; and KRISTENHOWELL, "Patti with Bob Dylan Albums, I'm Pretty Sure This Is Circa 1969," *Pinterest*, accessed May 7, 2022, https://in.pinterest.com/pin/195695546281943150/?nic_v1=1am50eaK7DLE2%2FjNUK55h8eUqw08kPAO%2Bhno7zmXGQ9LhKw57frj%2B3EuVagw%2F9tJtD. See also Patti Smith, *Just Kids* (New York: Harper Collins, 2010), 154.

27. See the September 1971 poem "Autobiography," in Patti Smith, "Autobiography," *A Patti Smith Babelogue*, accessed May 7, 2022, http://www.oceanstar.com/patti/poetry/autobio.htm. I owe my awareness of this poem and several other details of the Smith/Lenya nexus to Fariña, *German Cabaret Influence*, 179.

28. See Nero54ad1, "Patti Smith's First Performance, St Marks Church 2/10/71," *YouTube*, October 12, 2016, accessed May 7, 2022, https://www.youtube.com/watch?v=klpUlOZyGIs. Fariña points out that a few months later, on November 10, 1971, Smith gave a performance under the heading of "Rock and Rimbaud," which included a version of Weill's "Speak Low" from *One Touch of Venus*.

29. Sarah Conkey, prod., "Mack the Knife," *Soul Music*, BBC, December 8, 2015, https://www.bbc.co.uk/sounds/play/b06r50wk. His remarks begin at 18:30 of the broadcast. Richard Hell described television as "the most peculiarly successful melding of the Velvets, the Beatles, the everly brothers [sic], and Kurt Weill." His bandmate and cofounder of the group, Tom Verlaine, dated Patti Smith for a while; see Bryan Waterman, *Television's Marquee Moon* (New York: Continuum International, 2011), 87.

30. Ben Sisario, "Revisiting a Bleak Album to Plumb its Dark Riches," *New York Times*, December 13, 2006, E1.

31. Auslander mentions that the narrative vignettes of the Kinks' anticipated Bowie's "music hall style"; see Auslander, *Performing Glam Rock*, 110. Ray Davies's flirtation with Weill-inspired music would begin with "Just Friends," part of the soundtrack to the 1971 comic film *Percy* and would pick up steam with the rock opera *Preservation Act I and Act II* (1973, 1974)—not generally considered among his best work. Christgau calls *Act II* "sloppy Weill"; see Robert Christgau, *Record Guide: Rock Albums of the '70s* (New Haven: Ticknor & Fields, 1981), 214. See also Andrew Hickey, "The Kinks' Music: Percy," *Head of State*, May 16, 2012, accessed May 7, 2022, https://andrewhickey.info/2012/05/16/the-kinks-music-percy. Incidentally, *Percy*, based on a novel by Raymond Hitchcock, is a sex farce about the world's first penis transplant; the author's amusingly eccentric son Robyn named his first band—how could he not?—The Soft Boys.

32. Bill Flanagan, *Written in My Soul: Conversations with Great Rock Songwriters* (New York: Rosetta, 2010), 291. Reed adds that he does not have in mind "taking 'Mack the Knife' and making it into a hokey thing like Bobby Darin did. I thought that was grotesque"; see Flanagan, *Written in My Soul*, 291. See also Roy Kotynek and John Cohassey, *American Cultural Rebels: Avant-Garde*

and Bohemian Artists, Writers and Musicians from the 1850s through the 1960s (Jefferson, NC: McFarland, 2008), 201.

33. Quoted in Kim H. Kowalke, "Kurt Weill, Modernism, and Popular Culture: *Offentlichkeit als Stil*," *Modernism/Modernity* 2, no. 1 (1995): 32.

34. Quoted in Kowalke, "Kurt Weill," 33.

35. Kowalke calls the object of Weill's quest an "extroverted modernism" but the idea is basically the same. The dialectical formulation is Theodor Adorno's, one of Weill's harshest critics, and comes from a letter to Walter Benjamin, whose Brechtian enthusiasms worried Adorno greatly; see Theodor Wiesengrund Adorno, "Letters to Walter Benjamin," in Ronald Taylor, ed., *Aesthetics and Politics* (London: Verso, 1986), 123. For more on Weill and modernism, see Daniel Albright, "Kurt Weill as Modernist," *Modernism/Modernity* 7, no. 2 (2000): 273–84.

36. Alex Ross, *The Rest Is Noise: Listening to the Twentieth Century* (New York: Picador, 2007), 554.

37. Max Paddison, "The Critique Criticised: Adorno and Popular Music," *Popular Music* 2 (1982): 217.

38. See, respectively, Kevin Currier, *Dangerous Kitchen: The Subversive World of Frank Zappa* (Toronto: ECW, 2002), 226; and Kelly Fisher Lowe, *The Words and Music of Frank Zappa* (Lincoln: University of Nebraska Press, 2007), 95.

39. James Borders, "Form and the Concept Album: Aspects of Modernism in Frank Zappa's Early Releases," *Perspectives of New Music* 39, no. 1 (2001): 145.

40. Paul Zollo, "Randy Newman: The Bluerailroad Interview," *Bluerailroad*, accessed May 7, 2022, https://bluerailroad.wordpress.com/randy-newman-the-bluerailroad-interview.

41. See Stephen Holden, "The Evolution of the Singer-Songwriter," in Anthony DeCurtis and James Henke, gen. eds., *The Rolling Stone Illustrated History of Rock & Roll: The Definitive History of the Most Important Artists and Their Music* (New York: Random House, 1992), 488; and Greil Marcus, "Masters of Reality: How Bob Dylan, Randy Newman, and John Oliver Make Us Face Ourselves," *Pitchfork*, October 17, 2016, accessed May 8, 2022, https://pitchfork.com/features/greil-marcus-real-life-rock-top-10/9965-masters-of-reality-how-bob-dylan-randy-newman-and-john-oliver-make-us-face-ourselves.

42. Patrick Humphries, *The Many Lives of Tom Waits* (London: Omnibus, 2008), 257.

43. Marcus, *Mystery Train*, 104. All the songs listed above appear on *12 Songs* (1970). Marcus asserts that "Suzanne" is in intertextual dialogue with—or is an "answer song"—to Leonard Cohen's tender-hearted ballad of the same name. I mention this here because Tom Robbins has described the Canadian cult figure as someone who strikes him as "an electrified de-Germanized Kurt Weill"; see Tom Robbins, *Wild Ducks Flying Backward: The Short Writings* (New York: Bantam, 2006), 78.

44. Marcus, *Mystery Train*, 104.

45. Marcus, *Mystery Train*, 99.
46. Marcus, *Mystery Train*, 99.
47. Jerry Leiber and Mike Stoller with David Ritz, *Hound Dog: The Leiber and Stoller Autobiography* (New York: Simon & Schuster, 2009), 237–38. When Walter Becker and Donald Fagen visited the Brill Building to hawk a demo to Jerry Leiber and Mike Stoller the former showed some interest and commented that it "reminded him of some German art songs brought into the contemporary style." Later in this interview Fagen recalls that "we used to listen to the Brecht/Weill songs." See Mojo Magazine, "The Return of Steely Dan," *Steely Dan Reader*, October 1, 1995, accessed May 7, 2022, http://steelydanreader.com/1995/10/01/return-steely-dan. The bridge on "Glamour Profession" (a track on the 1980 LP *Gaucho*) is taken from Weill's "Speak Low." See David Breskin, "Steely Dan Interview," *Steely Dan Reader*, accessed May 7, 2022, http://steelydanreader.com/1981/03/01/steely-dan-interview. Though little known today, David Ackles functioned as a conduit between the Brecht-Weill tradition and a few major figures who emerged in the 1970s in England. Elton John and Elvis Costello, for example, shared a deep admiration for the American singer-songwriter Bernie Taupin (John's lyricist) producing Ackles's third album *American Gothic* (1972). On Weimar tendencies in the US in the 1970s, see John Rockwell, "Yesterday's Folkies Are Today's Cabaret Singers," *New York Times*, November 28, 1976, 115. He has in mind among several others Joni Mitchell, Paul Simon, Laura Nyro, and Judy Collins. After proposing that "folk and cabaret do not, as one might have first thought, represent opposite poles of naturalness and arch artificiality," Rockwell points to the fact that Bruce Springsteen's music (though devoid of cabaret overtones) "has always been marked by a rhetorical, ornate quality very close to Broadway musicals. It's so marked that he offends some rockers with his very theatricality."
48. Leiber and Stoller, *Hound Dog*, 242.
49. Leiber and Stoller, *Hound Dog*, 245–46.

References

Adelt, Ulrich. *Blues Music in the Sixties: A Story in Black and White*. New Brunswick: Rutgers University Press, 2010.
Adorno, Theodor Wiesengrund. "Letters to Walter Benjamin." In *Aesthetics and Politics*, edited by Ronald Taylor, 110–33. London: Verso, 1986.
Albright, Daniel. "Kurt Weill as Modernist." *Modernism/Modernity* 7, no. 2 (2000): 273–84.
Armitstead, Claire. "Did David Bowie Pinch a Cactus from T. S. Eliot?" *Guardian*, March 21, 2013. Accessed May 7, 2022, https://www.theguardian.com/books/booksblog/2013/mar/21/did-david-bowie-steal-from-ts-eliot.

Auslander, Philip. *Performing Glam Rock: Gender and Theatricality in Popular Music*. Ann Arbor: University of Michigan Press, 2006.

Borders, James. "Form and the Concept Album: Aspects of Modernism in Frank Zappa's Early Releases." *Perspectives of New Music* 39, no. 1 (2001): 118–60.

Breskin, David. "Steely Dan Interview." *Steely Dan Reader*. Accessed May 7, 2022. http://steelydanreader.com/1981/03/01/steely-dan-interview.

Brown, Nicholas. "Musical Affect, Musical Citation, Musical Immanence: Kurt Weill and the White Stripes." *Postmodern Culture* 25, no. 2 (2015). Accessed May 7, 2022. doi:10.1353/pmc.2015.0005.

Carlson, Tom. "David Bowie." In *The Rolling Stone Illustrated History of Rock & Roll*, edited by Jim Miller, 386–87. New York: Rolling Stone, 1980.

Christgau, Robert. "Lost in the Stars: The Music of Kurt Weill (A&M, 1985)." *Robert Christgau*. Accessed May 7, 2022. https://www.robertchristgau.com/get_album.php?id=1488.

Christgau, Robert. *Record Guide: Rock Albums of the '70s*. New Haven: Ticknor & Fields, 1981.

Conkey, Sarah, prod. "Mack the Knife." *Soul Music*. BBC, December 8, 2015. https://www.bbc.co.uk/sounds/play/b06r50wk.

Currier, Kevin. *Dangerous Kitchen: The Subversive World of Frank Zappa*. Toronto: ECW, 2002.

Dylan, Bob. *Chronicles: Volume 1*. New York: Simon and Schuster, 2004.

Eliot, T. S. *Prose Keys to Modern Poetry*. Edited by Karl Shapiro. New York: Harper & Row, 1962.

Eliot, T. S. *Selected Poems*. New York: Harcourt Brace, 1964.

Farina, William. *The German Cabaret Influence in American Popular Music*. Jefferson, NC: McFarland, 2013.

"f3d93f6d256f433285001e0b8d783af5." *Pinterest*. Accessed May 7, 2022, https://i.pinimg.com/originals/f3/d9/3f/f3d93f6d256f433285001e0b8d783af5.jpg.

Ferris, Timothy. "The Iceman, Having Calculated, Cometh." *Rolling Stone*, November 9, 1972. Accessed May 7, 2022. https://www.rollingstone.com/music/music-news/david-bowie-in-america-56227.

Fisher Lowe, Kelly. *The Words and Music of Frank Zappa*. Lincoln: University of Nebraska Press, 2007.

Flanagan, Bill. *Written in My Soul: Conversations with Great Rock Songwriters*. New York: Rosetta, 2010.

Hale, Grace Elizabeth. *A Nation of Outsiders: How the White Middle Class Fell in Love with Rebellion in Postwar America*. New York: Oxford, 2011.

Hamilton, Jack. *Just around Midnight: Rock and Roll and the Racial Imagination*. Cambridge, MA: Harvard University Press, 2016.

Hickey, Andrew. "The Kinks' Music: Percy." *Head of State*, May 16, 2012. Accessed May 7, 2022. https://andrewhickey.info/2012/05/16/the-kinks-music-percy.

Hinton, Stephen. *Weill's Musical Theatre: Stages of Reform*. Berkeley: University of California Press, 2012.

Hogan, Peter. *The Dead Straight Guide to the Velvet Underground and Lou Reed*. Falmouth, UK: Red Planet, 2020.

Holden, Stephen. "The Evolution of the Singer-Songwriter." In *The Rolling Stone Illustrated History of Rock & Roll: The Definitive History of the Most Important Artists and Their Music*, edited by Anthony DeCurtis and James Henke, 480–91. New York: Random House, 1992.

Humphries, Patrick. *The Many Lives of Tom Waits*. London: Omnibus, 2008.

James, David E. *Rock 'n' Film: Cinema's Dance with Popular Music*. New York: Oxford University Press, 2016.

Kotynek, Roy, and John Cohassey. *American Cultural Rebels: Avant-Garde and Bohemian Artists, Writers and Musicians from the 1850s through the 1960s*. Jefferson, NC: McFarland, 2008.

Kowalke, Kim H. "Kurt Weill, Modernism, and Popular Culture: *Offentlichkeit als Stil.*" *Modernism/Modernity* 2, no. 1 (1995): 27–69.

KRISTENHOWELL. "Patti with Bob Dylan Albums, I'm Pretty Sure This is Circa 1969." *Pinterest*. Accessed May 7, 2022. https://in.pinterest.com/pin/195695546281943150/?nic_v1=1am50eaK7DLE2%2FjNUK55h8eUqw08kPAO%2Bhno7zmXGQ9LhKw57frj%2B3EuVagw%2F9tJtD.

Leiber, Jerry, and Mike Stoller with David Ritz. *Hound Dog: The Leiber and Stoller Autobiography*. New York: Simon & Schuster, 2009.

Lott, Eric. "Back Door Man: Howlin' Wolf and the Sound of Jim Crow." *American Quarterly* 63, no. 3 (2011): 697–710.

Lott, Eric. *Black Mirror: The Cultural Contradictions of American Racism*. Cambridge, MA: Harvard University Press, 2017.

Lott, Eric. "White Like Me: Racial Cross-Dressing and the Construction of American Whiteness." In *Cultures of United States Imperialism*, edited by Amy Kaplan and Donald Pease, 474–98. Durham, NC: Duke University Press, 1993.

M. "The Trial." *The Wall Complete*, April 1, 2017. Accessed May 7, 2022. https://thewallcomplete.com/2017/04/01/pink-floyd-the-wall-the-trial.

Marcus, Greil. "Masters of Reality: How Bob Dylan, Randy Newman, and John Oliver Make Us Face Ourselves." *Pitchfork*, October 17, 2016. Accessed May 8, 2022. https://pitchfork.com/features/greil-marcus-real-life-rock-top-10/9965-masters-of-reality-how-bob-dylan-randy-newman-and-john-oliver-make-us-face-ourselves.

Marcus, Greil. *Mystery Train: Images of America in Rock 'N' Roll Music*, 3rd ed. New York: Penguin, 1990.

"Midnight Rambler." *TrackTalk*. Accessed May 7, 2022. http://timeisonourside.com/SOMidnight.html.

Mojo Magazine. "The Return of Steely Dan." *Steely Dan Reader*, October 1, 1995. Accessed May 7, 2022. http://steelydanreader.com/1995/10/01/return-steely-dan.

Nanby, Keith, and John M. Radosta. *Bob Dylan in Performance, Stage, and Screen.* Lanham, MD: Lexington, 2019.

Nero54ad1. "Patti Smith's First Performance, St Marks Church 2/10/71." *YouTube*, October 12, 2016. Accessed May 7, 2022. https://www.youtube.com/watch?v=klpUlOZyGIs.

Nicholl, Charles. *Somebody Else: Arthur Rimbaud in Africa, 1880–91.* Chicago: University of Chicago, 1997.

Paddison, Max. "The Critique Criticised: Adorno and Popular Music." *Popular Music* 2 (1982): 201–218.

Pynchon, Thomas. "Introduction." In *Been Down So Long It Looks Like Up to Me*, Richard Fariña, v–xiv. Harmondsworth: Penguin, 1983.

Robbins, Tom. *Wild Ducks Flying Backward: The Short Writings.* New York: Bantam, 2006.

Robertson, Robbie. "Bob Dylan." *Rolling Stone*, December 3, 2010. Accessed May 7, 2022. https://www.rollingstone.com/music/music-lists/100-greatest-artists-147446/jimi-hendrix-5-30413.

Rockwell, John. "The Bowie Boom." *New York Times*, May 25, 1973, 30.

Rockwell, John. "Bryan Ferry: Enfant Terrible of Rock." *New York Times*, February 19, 1975, 20.

Rockwell, John. "Yesterday's Folkies Are Today's Cabaret Singers." *New York Times*, November 28, 1976, 115.

Ross, Alex. *The Rest Is Noise: Listening to the Twentieth Century.* New York: Picador, 2007.

Savage, Jon. "Bryan Ferry on How Roxy Music Invented Artpop." *Guardian*, February 1, 2018. Accessed May 7, 2022. https://www.theguardian.com/music/2018/feb/01/bryan-ferry-roxy-music-invented-new-pop-game-for-anything.

Sisario, Ben. "Revisiting a Bleak Album to Plumb Its Dark Riches." *New York Times*, December 13, 2006, E1.

Smith, Patti. "Autobiography." *A Patti Smith Babelogue.* Accessed May 7, 2022. http://www.oceanstar.com/patti/poetry/autobio.htm.

Smith, Patti. *Just Kids.* New York: Harper Collins, 2010.

Southern, Terry. *Now Dig This: The Unspeakable Writings of Terry Southern, 1950–1995.* New York: Grove Press, 2001.

Stokes, Geoffrey, with Ed Ward and Ken Tucker. *Rock of Ages: The Rolling Stone History of Rock & Roll.* New York: Rolling Stone, 1986.

Vulliamy, Ed. "Some Give a Song. Some Give a Life . . . " *Guardian*, June 3, 2005. Accessed May 7, 2022. https://www.theguardian.com/music/2005/jun/03/meltdownfestival2005.meltdownfestival.

Waterman, Bryan. *Television's Marquee Moon.* New York: Continuum International, 2011.

Zollo, Paul. "Randy Newman: The Bluerailroad Interview." *Bluerailroad.* Accessed May 7, 2022. https://bluerailroad.wordpress.com/randy-newman-the-bluerailroad-interview.

Chapter 6

Marguerite Duras's Musical Return of the Real

Fernanda Negrete

Music courses through Marguerite Duras's writing, holding open its essential word-hole (*mot-trou*). Music is also recurrently associated with the mother figure in Duras's works and personal history, especially in her texts from the Barrage Cycle.[1] Yet both music and the word-hole respond to something beyond any maternal or parental ideals or norms. The purpose of music is to transmit something of the real, the order of remainders excluded from consciousness because they are unacceptable within the field of shared reality, or language. Therefore, the presence of music in Duras's work is not only an element in the world her characters inhabit or an audible adornment of her creations, although works of music certainly populate her films and plays. In addition to these two manifestations of music, there is a musicality proper to her writing and filmmaking.[2] In all of these registers—thematic, sonic, formal-poetic—music seeks to catalyze and welcome the return of the real. The author's treatment of words to create scenes of love, desire, and sex, to name a few major themes, is less concerned with representing these experiences or with using words meaningfully, than with making a fundamental gap in meaning felt in its full intensity. The same occurs in her turn to theater, screenplays, and film direction, through strategies that evacuate meaning and disclose a singularly empty time and space, in fact an altogether different, non-chronological time that I would also call distinctly musical.[3] In this essay I discuss this musical time in Duras's 1977 play *L'Éden Cinéma*, beginning with a brief discussion of forms of repetition in Lacan, and Deleuze, and Guattari, whose musical implications I underscore. At the end of the essay, I specify the real of Duras's aesthetic transmissions.

The register of the real in the Lacanian sense is not representable, so it necessitates repetition or *returning* as its distinctive mode of emergence. Indeed, the real concerns the subject's unmediated encounter with what seems impossible from the perspective of its symbolic universe; it thus also exceeds what can ever be accessed in the ordinary or lived present, to the extent that this verb tense is bound by a work of representation within the limits of language, or the receivable.[4] Duras's writing consistently aims at just this encounter and excess. In a famously evoked passage from *Le ravissement de Lol V. Stein* this excess appears in terms of a *mot-trou*, a word-hole whose force provokes and organizes the whole novel. This word-hole, one reads, "could not have been said but could have been made to resonate. Immense, without end, an empty gong . . . " [*on n'aurait pas pu le dire mais on aurait pu le faire résonner. Immense, sans fin, un gong vide . . .*].[5] The conditional past for the verb *pouvoir*, which indicates possibility, what is, or is not, in someone's power, temporally situates the enouncing subject (and any speaker, as the impersonal pronoun *on* suggests in connection to the verb *dire*, "to say") as removed from the word-hole; the moment is "too late," and yet, the sentence claims, making it resonate is what one could have done. This is the called-for action, like an ethical imperative, even if or precisely because it is failed, and also excessive, as the novel's sentence declares: immense, endless, hollow resonance. From this standpoint, the relevance of the real ultimately lies not in the distant past or missed moment, and not in a relative future (relative to the present), but rather in a musical time, a time of the event. To transmit the real, according to these formulations, is not to crop its immensity and infinity down with a ready-made signifier, nor to cork it up with the illusion of meaning. Rather, it is to render something beyond meaning audible with a resonance of its own.

In *Le ravissement*, the narrator, Jacques Hold, who describes the word-hole at the core of the ravishing feeling that Lola Valérie Stein undergoes, cannot know what exactly gave rise to her experience.[6] What he witnesses in his body, instead, are the effects of her ravishing, which she seems to spread around her irresistibly, from a certain point onward, a point at which something that had lain dormant in her for a decade at least manages to reawaken. The novel shows, first, that something of the "madness" ascribed to her by the people around her is contagious. Second, it indicates that while this madness is so-called because it is inexplicable within the social link Lol inhabits, within the field of what can be said or represented, it follows a precise logic, a pattern, even, that Lol's body seems to write repetitively and incomprehensibly through her long walks around the city. The walks' odd disconnection from her social life and familial roles, and the irresistible push to spend hours drifting, indicate that, to Lol, this writing and its effects in the world around her are much more important than social acceptance or inclusion. Likewise, to Duras the novel is not a mirror for shared reality, or even a means to tell stories per se (on this level Duras offers mostly variations on very few stories, and one might even ask whether these stories themselves aren't also variations on a stubborn theme). In the novel and in other forms Duras thus constructs spaces where the singularity of a rhythm and a music take precedence over signification, where something of the real gets transmitted. The constraints of this transmission decenter writing from the site of signification and deliver it to an intensive field of sound and silence, of resonance and, thus, repetition, which contributes significantly to turning sequences of sound and silence into music.

Repetition is important in psychoanalysis as well, where it also takes hold with the help of a certain sound pattern. Jacques Lacan set forth repetition as one of the four fundamental psychoanalytic concepts because it discloses the site for the real to erupt as missed encounter, accident, or act intruding upon the pleasure and reality principles, which are instead homeostatic. Lacan's commentary on Sigmund Freud's discussion of these principles distinguishes repetition from them, in order to sketch out the site of the real as the experience of a gap for a subject, provoking a creative response. The example in question is the child who invents the *fort-da* game in confronting the void that his mother's absence causes him to experience "at the edge of his crib, that is to say a pit,"[7] by throwing and retrieving from it a reel. Lacan contends that this reel is not a substitute for the absent mother, but instead "a little something of the subject that detaches itself all while still being very much his, still retained."[8] It is with this detached yet retained "little something of the subject," in other words with this part of himself that has split—a reel qua bit of the real—that the child "leaps over the borders of his territory (*domaine*) transformed into a pit and that he begins the incantation."[9] The incantation, made up of the sounds "o-a," marks or punctuates the oscillation of this partial detachment and retrieval, and it also remarks the ungraspable pit or hole that causes the entire game, whose distinctive mode is at once repetitive and original.

In the extraordinary essay "1837: de la ritournelle" (Of the Refrain), Gilles Deleuze and Félix Guattari begin, precisely, with a scene of a child reshaping the frightening darkness through song. While they initially emphasize this elementary procedure as one of constituting a territory, what matters most here is the fact of being confronted with chaos, with a real, and also the fact of a musical response to this, which requires playing, in this instance vocally, and perhaps also by "skipping," as the essay states: "Perhaps the child skips as he sings, hastens or slows his pace. But the song is already a skip: it jumps from chaos to the beginnings of order in chaos and is in danger of breaking apart at any moment."[10] Playing, as Lacan's comment on inventing the *fort-da* game indicates, has to do for the child with a little real/reel that splits off yet remains his own, in a dynamic whose precariousness and risk Deleuze and Guattari underscore. The real may not be graspable with words or in the ordinary present, yet it might resonate within a different, extraordinary time, configured by a *fort-da* incantation, or by a key, tempo, time signature, and timbre. While the timbre in the cited passage from *Le ravissement de Lol V. Stein* is of a mysterious gong where an endless void resonates, in Duras's work the privileged instrument is the piano,[11] and the signature, often, waltz time, as I will show. Instead of the back-and-forth *fort-da* proposes, waltz time introduces repetition in three pulses, and, as the waltz is a dance, a return to "one's territory," to adopt Lacan's expression on the child's body in the crib. Yet that territory is significantly displaced or transformed at each revolution. The German word *Walzen* indicates that both the dance and the musical form play, indeed, a turning, spinning, revolving motion. It is thus perhaps the waltz's continually displaced return that offers to Duras a recurrent, rhythmic transformation of territory into a hole, or into an opening that sensorially relays something of the real, in an unbounded movement beyond pulsed time.

In both Lacan's reading of the *fort-da* incantation and Deleuze and Guattari's articulation of the child's song and skipping, the child finds herself alone. The child's mother has disappeared, even if the creative act is not a substitute for the mother, as Lacan suggests. In Duras the mother and music are closely linked. How does the mother, or her absence, open up a space for the creative act? It has been noted that Duras's childhood in French Indochina is the scene where her love of cinema (for its fascinating images of romantic love) was born, and that this love is tied up with a love of the mother.¹² Duras herself writes about both loves in autofictional and nonfictional texts, pointing out that going to the movie theater in Saigon as a child was possible for her because her mother played piano to animate silent film screenings in the 1910s and '20s. In what follows I explore the close connection between the pianist mother and the return of the piano in Duras's writing[13] (a connection perhaps even closer than that between cinema and the mother as early love objects decisive in her writing) by focusing on passages from the play *L'Éden Cinéma*. I also argue that the mother is ultimately not an object of nostalgia, but instead performs or inscribes something like a musical silence on the side of creation, like a rest marked with a fermata, to be sustained indefinitely longer.

In *L'Éden Cinéma* (1977) the stage directions indicate that the siblings Suzanne and Joseph (two characters based on Duras's adolescence in Indochina with her mother and two brothers)[14] discuss childhood memories while their mother stands by, though she appears "absent" from the temporality in which her children speak of the past. The brother and sister discuss the mother and her effects on them, while the directions mark the moments when they turn toward or away from her as they speak, whereas she "*will remain immobile in her chair, without expression, as though transfixed, distant,* separated—*like the stage—from her own story*" (emphasis in original).[15] This description of the mother as basically petrified, "transfixed," "distant," and, with typographical emphasis, "separated," offers an important indication that the children address their words, memories, and love to a fundamentally Absent Other. Consequently, the relevance of this Other is not, ultimately, as someone absent now but formerly present, more or less approachable, more or less connected, even if on the level of the story the mother was in the past alive and, according to Suzanne and Joseph in the play, closely attached to them.

Renate Günther has pointed out the ambivalence in Duras's biographical descriptions of her mother's attitude toward her, highlighting the feeling of rejection by the mother. With this in mind, Günther has interestingly suggested that Duras's films "reinscribe the maternal through a displacement of unrequited love for the mother on to the figure of Anne-Marie Stretter, the mythical heroine of Duras's most acclaimed film *India Song* (1975)."[16] According to that logic, the return to the Barrage story two years later in the play *L'Éden Cinéma* would entail a return to more directly inscribing the distant biographical mother on stage. My reading instead considers the crucial issue in this play's stage directions and writing choices (and in Duras's writing as a whole) to go beyond an attempt at inscribing the experience of maternal love, rejection, or distance. In this sense the spatial determinations to stage the conversation between Suzanne and Joseph are telling. Duras begins with a description of the stage as "a great empty space that surrounds another rectangular space."[17] The inner rectangle, she adds, is a bungalow furnished with very old, poor, colonial chairs and tables, whereas the great empty space around it designates the Plains of Kam between Siam and the sea. In these simple descriptions Duras establishes a fictional space for the story the play will tell, without its space-time ever fully actualizing itself in the space-time in which the play unfolds. A gap between the two moments is sustained through a work of staging that remains out of sync with the dialogues and with itself to some extent. Thus, Duras's writing seems less interested in recreating childhood memories than in opening up another dimension by outlining a precise form. Staging here consists in producing an empty space at whose center something crucial yet not representable about the story, and not limited to the child's attachment to the mother, comes through somewhere *between* the story's fragmentary remainders, which take the forms of colonial furniture and a few key dialogues, in a few salient bodily gestures (of dancing, laughing, singing, embracing, as well as freezing still), and certainly also in the music and the mother's position and almost unconscious presence on stage.

Beyond the love and loss of the mother there is space for radical creativity[18]; like the *mot-trou*, the *fort-da* incantation, and the *ritournelle*, the mother and the music in *L'Éden* insist upon this. The Absent Other, and my purpose in writing it in uppercase is to suggest this, marks a speaker's encounter with the structural void that even the closest others around that speaker—even the mother whose body housed the speaker before birth—cannot fill, and since language does not cover over this structural void either, this encounter reveals that the object that causes the address is not someone or even something out in the world somewhere; it resides within the subject.

With her stasis and silence, the mother in *L'Éden Cinéma* thus serves above all to introduce the Absent Other into the space of speech and performance. This becomes very clear as Duras's stage directions for the mother go on:

> *The others touch her, caress her arms, kiss her hands. She lets them: what she represents in the play exceeds what she is and she is not responsible for that.*

> *What could be said here is said directly by Suzanne and Joseph. The mother—object of the narrative—will never have a say about herself.*
> Music. (emphasis in original)[19]

The intimate closeness to the mother is therefore at the same time exposure to an infinite, irreducible distance that she represents and that exceeds her. She is "the object" of the story, which is to say, the silent, enigmatic object that allows these speakers to at once evoke and address themselves to that excessive realm *beyond* "what could be said directly." As in the word-hole passage from *Le ravissement*, Duras's text here insists on what could be said and what exceeds such a realm, not in order to remind us that we must thereof be silent, but rather to make it resonate. As Joseph finishes proffering his sentence that the mother will never have a say about herself, music enters the script and stage, reminding us of its having first played before the characters on the great empty space that is the stage began to move or speak. The absence the mother makes present serves to open up in the space of the stage the field of what always remains out of language, the censored whose drives uniquely shape speaker's bodies, and that here also uniquely shapes the space and time of the stage.

Just after Joseph's first lines in the play, where he briefly describes the mother's Northern French background, the stage directions return to insist on the presence of music, and to indicate the relationship between the music, what is spoken, and the mother:

> Music.
> *They wait for the time of the music to go by [que s'écoule le temps de la musique].*
> *This music is also the story of the mother.*[20]

These directions call attention to an intimate dynamic between the characters on stage and the music, while also associating the music with the silent mother. Interestingly, in the sentence where the characters wait, we read that the music has its own time. In this *temps* it is relevant to read at once tempo and time signature, if not also the temperature and climate constituting that flow of time before which the characters stand by, and which is also the unspeakable story of the mother.

Early on, Joseph describes a physical proximity between the children and their mother, and also between the children and the piano she played in the movie theater:

Joseph:
She took us with her to the Eden.
We slept around the piano on pillows.
Music.
She never could separate herself from her children, the mother.
Wherever she went
She would drag us clinging to her body [*nous traînait agrippés à son corps*].[21]

In the first sentence above, the name of the movie theater in Saigon makes evident some of its weight and effects as a signifier. "Eden" is of course also Adam and Eve's blissful garden, before the fall into sin and the knowledge of good and evil. Through the mother, Joseph and Suzanne have access to this bliss, which leads them to lie down and sleep as though cradled by the piano music. As one interrogates the stakes of this blissful image of the children asleep at the movie theater, it is striking to notice the placement of the directions for music throughout the play's script. For instance, "music" in this passage comes immediately after the description of lying down to sleep by the piano, drawing attention to the children's soundscape in the movie theater. For the staged play, music would plausibly bring the audience into the moment being recollected, giving more direct access to the past being evoked. Yet what I have previously emphasized as the mother's strange separation on stage logically discourages an interpretation where an undoubted, full coexistence in the present would be the standpoint from which to recall and consider a once-present past. So, music is not just a way into the recollected past. To what, then, does music give access, if not time past?

On the level of the text alone, the indication for music between Joseph's spoken thoughts accentuates them, as well as the characters' bodily gestures. Simultaneously, music introduces for readers caesuras that they must imagine as resonant, and more specifically as the music composed by Carlos d'Alessio for this play, which includes a "Valse de l'Éden Cinéma" for piano. Indeed, Duras's final remarks at the end of the written play, addressing potential directors, make clear that d'Alessio's music "must be kept" (*devra être gardée*), although its order can vary, as can the order of the dialogues, as long as the story is preserved.²² If the music, and not only the story, is essential to the play, it is because both carry something singular. It is especially striking to note that to Duras the music is not merely an accompaniment that could be replaced or omitted without distorting the play. And it is important too that the music to be kept is not what her mother actually played in the movie theater when Duras was a child, but instead an original composition for this 1977 play, a musical work that responded to Duras's desire.²³ Marc Phéline has highlighted a distinctive trait of d'Alessio's compositions that was key to Duras's immediately enthusiastic response and invitation to collaborate. Phéline writes that Duras attended a performance of a play by the group TSE called *Luxe*, "a semi-parodic homage to music hall"²⁴ for which d'Alessio, who was part of the audience that night, was the composer. "In the narrow margin between pastiche and citation, the score finds the exact tone to say not 'it's music hall,' but rather 'it would be music hall.'"²⁵ Coming back to *L'Éden Cinéma*, an evocative distance is certainly sustained, although I believe there is more at stake there than the link between d'Alessio's piano and what the mother would have played at the movie theater. At stake is what d'Alessio, speaking of the effect of his *India Song* theme in the film, called its "oneiric puissance,"²⁶ which results from having composed after Duras's *Le ravissement* and *Le viceconsul*. I will address this oneiric puissance at the end of this essay.

In any case, both Joseph's words and d'Alessio's "Valse de l'Éden Cinéma"²⁷ indicate that this music is also very specifically piano music. Let me briefly describe d'Alessio's waltz in C minor, which unfolds in a sequence of changing moods.²⁸ The theme starts on the pickup, without any grand announcement or call for attention, as if the melody's first phrase instead went straight to the point, which presents a situation of unavoidable suffering and needs to be sung in a tone of complaint, possibly accusation. From the beginning, the accompaniment appears dragged by the motif. It clings, like the children to the mother's body in Joseph's initial memory. Unfolding over two bars, the pattern of the accompaniment continues this "dragging" effect as the waltz continues. The antecedent phrase begins expressing the situation in question and strives to develop its logical consequences, although they are left unresolved by the open cadence. The repetitive and syncopated descent gives a sense of reeling, in the attempt to hold on to something along the way from i to v. The melodic line on the consequent phrase is also syncopated, leading to an authentic cadence. The "question" of the motif is then restated, the tonic center briefly shifting to F minor, before returning over a longer phrase—an insistent tresillo sequence that causes a galloping percussiveness (calling to mind Ernesto Lecuona) and multiplies the already circular feeling of the passage. After a brief presentation of the theme in the relative major, again with tresillos in the consequent phrase, there is a move back towards C minor, ending on the dominant. The latter's mood is nostalgic, evoking old-fashioned romance and popular song from another period, for instance a tango waltz, especially given the recurrent dramatic halts for oscillating thirds, before reintroducing the waltz time. The melody in this section also evokes "Ramona," a dreamy song both the girl and her older brother loved and danced together as adolescents (on which more to follow). The section closes echoing 1920s cabaret melodies. Next, an interlude[29] insists on the motif with galloping eighth notes that form a kind of spiral; here the melody seems to give up on its complaint and to accept the consequences of the event. It then repeats the nostalgic, romantic melody before concluding in a return to the initial theme, starting at the third phrase, and repeating in a syncopated rhythm, the vertiginous tresillo motif to reach the end.

Two elements from the waltz stand out with regard to the question of what kind of time or dimension music gives access to, or more broadly of how the return of the real occurs, aside from its evocation in the insistent circular, turning, reeling patterns. First, the nostalgic section of the waltz is interesting in that gives an initial impression of going back to old times, which I have said is *not* the main function of music in the play (this main function even requires overcoming the illusion of accessing a lost past). Its old-fashioned, popular feel precisely calls to mind *modern* waltzes such as tangoes or "Ramona," and this gesture is especially striking in connection with Duras's final stage notes, where in addition to stating that the original music must be preserved, she writes, "For me, the waltzes, are the mother's music, that of the Éden Cinéma. And the one-steps, that of the children, of Ream [in Cambodia], already modern."[30] This apparently simple comment that fits into a chronological sequence of music and dance forms corresponding to two generations is actually not so clear-cut. For one, the mother herself might have already played one-steps to accompany 1910s and '20s films while the young children slept. Moreover, the insistence on "Ramona," a waltz, as a song the children loved and that made audible the move away from childhood and into adolescence, also away from the mother and toward other love objects, undoes this generational distinction almost at once, "steps back" as it were, by virtue of keeping the waltz form.[31]

"Ramona" comes from the eponymous 1928 film by Edwin Carewe, which had a synchronized score and sound effects but no sound dialogue. It therefore marks a shift from the "ancient" to the "modern" in cinema, which is highly relevant in the universe of the Barrage Cycle because the end of silent film put the mother out of a job.[32] With her savings, the mother then buys a plot of land from the colonial administration to cultivate rice, yet the crop always gets flooded by the Pacific waves in July. Despite the mother's effort at building a dam against the ocean, both the money and the crops go to waste, so they end up living from her small pensions. The play stresses the children's awareness of having to leave their insane mother and their decaying rural home near the sea in Prey-Nop behind, and their waiting for an opportunity to do so.[33] Both the mother and the life she has provided are unsustainable, and to continue their lives the children wait for others who can sweep them away from their stagnant situation. In *Le barrage contre le Pacifique*,[34] the siblings play "Ramona" on an old gramophone to feed this hope: "With *Ramona*, it was inevitable, the hope that the automobiles that would take them far would not be long to stop became more vivacious."[35] Joseph's entry into adolescence is through an encounter with an older woman, a kind of femme fatale. As for Suzanne, Duras in *L'Éden* strikingly introduces her encounter with the Chinese billionaire who falls for the girl as "her first prostitution,"[36] stressing throughout the play that her mother is in fact the pimp in this arrangement.

"Ramona" exemplifies the transition toward sound film and its illusions of synchrony, indeed of full presence. If, on the one hand, Duras includes scenes of the siblings dancing and listening to a gramophone recording of "Ramona," as a film director, she artfully takes these very illusions apart, in her own experimental cinema of the 1970s, with d'Alessio's compositions in many cases. These illusions Duras dismantles are of course also those of romantic love, which cast the encounter of the ideal partner and forming a unity with him/her as the culmination of desire, as if its object were someone somewhere already in the world. Such an encounter would purportedly stop up the word-hole that Duras instead shows as a resonant force that unleashes the inexhaustible movement of desire and maintains the inadequacy of language and culture to contain or satisfy it.[37]

In relation to this, the second element from the waltz I want to interrogate concerns its melody, which I qualified as initially complaining and gradually accepting its situation. What would the song say, anyway, if it had words? Duras wrote lyrics for the *India Song* theme that launched her collaboration with d'Alessio, although these lyrics were never used in the film or play. Instead, they were used to record Jeanne Moreau's interpretation for a 45 rpm released by Polydor.[38] These lyrics offer a kind of answer to the question of what the *L'Éden Cinéma* melody would have to say. To the hypnotic refrain in d'Alessio's bluesy melody, Moreau's sultry low voice adds: "Chanson, toi qui ne veux rien dire, toi qui me parles d'elle, et toi qui me dis tout" (Song, you who mean nothing, you who speak to me of her, and you who tell me everything). The singer addresses the song, and this apostrophe has the effect of an internal split; the song's own speech is beyond the words sung by Moreau, which is appropriate if the song means nothing, all while paradoxically "speaking" about "her," even "telling me everything." Moreau's melisma on the word "tout" at the end of the strophe breaks open the totality *tout* is supposed to enclose, allowing us to hear a supplementary *où*, "where," and, given the paradox of meaninglessness and full speech, the location is outside-meaning, and also beyond the conscious will at stake in the French expression *vouloir dire* (in which "meaning" is literally "wanting to say").

Thus, I would say music in *L'Éden Cinéma* carries something of Eden's bliss, an ineffable moment of ravishment. Beyond time past, this is the difference music gives access to. From this perspective, instead of re-presenting the recollected past, "music"—both the indication on the script and d'Alessio's piano compositions—marks the way in which speech reaches the limits of what can be said, represented, as well as the way in which what exceeds those limits takes a distinct quality and form. In the text the emergence of music appears after Joseph's speech, each intervention occupying its own line or space-time; music and speech are two contiguous elements, like sand and sea. Certainly, the line between them is not immobile and their meeting point marks an intimate encounter as well as their separation, although not without some degree of contagion.

But what is the bliss evoked by music about if not the past or romantic love? The music is also the mother's story, the stage directions indicate. And the children are tethered to the mother like the mother is tethered both to them and to the piano. Must maternal love be the horizon of this intensity once the romantic illusion is dismantled? As a dance form, the waltz reinforces the couple, and its pose is of loving, physical closeness and contact. Approaching the link between the real and the piano as key instrument of the real's transmission in Duras's writing does seem to necessarily involve the mother. But is it only possible to do so in terms of a first love object that precedes full entry into language, or that is longed for after entering language, that is, in preoedipal and oedipal terms? Such a reading carries the sense of a fall (indeed, from Eden); it emphasizes the writing's often melancholic mood[39] and what one could call, borrowing a musical term, the minor tonality that undoubtedly marks Duras's sentences. In such a reading that tonality would give voice to a fundamental loss that haunts all human relations in her writing. Yet my sense of Duras's articulation of space and time—with the absent mother and with the relationship between speech and music—is that what is ultimately at stake in the transmission of the real exceeds even the certainly important link to the mother, and its loss. Not only is transmission decidedly not recognition, substitution, or reparation of loss; it is above all a creative act that implies—and furthermore affirms, embraces—an essential, irreducible lack, or as Deleuze and Guattari prefer to call it "an opening" in the circle traced to keep "the forces of chaos" out: "One opens the circle not on the side where the old forces of chaos press against it but in another region, one created by the circle itself. As though the circle tended on its own to open onto a future, as a function of the working forces it shelters. This time, it is in order to join with the forces of the future, cosmic forces. One launches forth, hazards an improvisation."[40] This *other opening* that leads to a different dimension and escapes the opposition between home and chaos is, I believe, what the aesthetic transmission of the real is concerned with above all, including in Duras's use of the piano with d'Alessio. As I explained, the second section of the waltz may be nostalgic, yet it is precisely that section that evokes what Duras situates as the children's "already modern" music breaking away from the mother's ancient waltzes. D'Alessio's waltz then includes other rhythms that distort or rupture the waltz form, calling forth the future that confronted Suzanne and Joseph as adolescents. The purpose of the creative opening Deleuze and Guattari highlight is to release what the authors call "the forces of the future" or "cosmic forces" in improvisation or "lines of drift."[41] Such forces are not, therefore, turned toward the past or the lost maternal home, or womb; they instead involve a creative, undetermined engagement with space and time that transforms them. At stake is a future no longer subordinated to the present as a stable territory, but instead engaged with the cosmos and its drifting motion. This improvisatory attitude, which Deleuze and

Guattari present as a function of the refrain (*ritournelle*),[42] allows them to say that "the refrain fabricates time" and (decentering Kant) that "Time is not an a priori form; rather, the refrain is the a priori form of time, which in each case fabricates different times, meters, tempos."[43] Duras once stated that "in music there is a fulfillment, a time we cannot actually receive. There is a sort of annunciation in music of a time to come, one you can hear."[44] If music to Duras accomplishes the feat of bringing "a time we cannot actually receive," then it is committed to creatively transmitting the unreceivable force of the unbound drive. How might Duras's piano play such times, meters, and tempos? And if the piano is tightly, inseparably woven to the mother figure, then how does the work of fabricating time enable a different kind of return of the real, neither leaving the mother out of these lines of drift, nor letting her trap everything within the familial space? What, indeed, might the mother become if she is brought along in hazarding an improvisation aiming to embrace an outside?

This risk and embrace—of an outside or an Eden, a bliss that does not reside in the remote past before some fall but that is instead accessed by stepping out of chronological time to introduce something unprecedented, unheard-of—are, I believe, what Duras's writing seeks, always in unique combinations of sonorities, timbres, lines, modes, tempos, time signatures. This effort's logic is that the bit of the real incommensurable with anything preexistent in language or the world seeks an outlet and might come through in an original work of composing non-chronological time.[45] When Deleuze and Guattari begin with the simple scene of a child singing and skipping, finding a way to "venture from home on the thread of a tune,"[46] they also show how for the child and whoever undertakes the endeavor of the refrain, everything is at stake. The vital operation of creating a space-time, or a "ritournelle," particularly where stepping out, through an outlet, and releasing "cosmic forces" is concerned, can be understood as an act that involves a great risk, whose logic is intrinsic to the act and what drives it, and not the result of some judgment coming from the culture where this act makes its intervention. After all, if it measured itself against the criteria of a culture, how could the act possibly make an intervention in it?

Cultures tend to evoke the real that caused them through myths that relate archaic or primal figures and scenes, with emphasis on a disruption to the temporal continuum, wherein a censored element breaches the culture's sense of stable coherence in the world, or inaugurates a new one.[47] At both the cultural and the intimately personal levels, the crucial problem is that the censored element in question cannot be managed by the signifier; it irrupts in an "out of sync" and bodily manner.[48] Furthermore, the real returns *après coup*, one says in French, literally, after the blow. Yet the real's mark is indeed confirmed by the *coup*, the blow it forcefully delivers in spite of, or even through, its very temporal lag. It is this forceful effect, often in the form of a myth, that evokes, then, an inaccessible cause mobilizing a culture, or a human being.

But while myths and rituals for the most part serve to contain or manage the real they evoke, and to manage it in the service of preserving a culture, in practices such as Duras's writing the outcome is different. For the point here is no longer to manage and limit the real (as a field of chaotic forces), but rather to "open a space between words for the return of the real"[49] and so to release its forces sensorially. While the return of the real is frequently associated with acts of violence, indicative of unprocessed trauma, both private and collective, it is also, albeit differently, at stake in what one can call aesthetic acts of transmission. If trauma can call up events that actually took place, the unprocessed status of experiences related to those events makes room for scenes that do not simply reproduce the events. Instead, in departing from shared reality, these scenes that Freud found rehearsed in formations such as dreams, screen memories, and symptoms point to the inaccessible core of trauma, or to the unconscious proper, which is no longer a matter of a once-actual scene and resides even beyond the interpretable elements of those other scenes. The only way to reach this real unconscious dimension and release it from the imaginary grip of the Other in order to sustain it is therefore creative, by constructing a unique object to transmit that which has no equivalence in the reality defined by language. When writing holds open a space between words to sensorially release forces beyond language, they can have aesthetic effects that also alter the field of shared reality. And how are these effects verified?

In the psychoanalytic clinic the transference (another one of Lacan's four fundamental concepts) is a crucial first operation on the way to that creative act, and it implies in itself an unconscious transmission from the analyst to the analysand, through which the latter is able to take the risk of speaking beyond cultural norms and ideals. At the other end of the analytic trajectory there is another transmission, this time of the constructed, unique object or signifier, in the procedure Lacan set up in his school and named "the conclusive pass," which verifies the end of analysis and the shift from analysand to analyst.[50] These transmissions belong within a very specific and sustained process that only unfolds over an extended period of the analysand's life. Yet a work of art—in its creative, singular quality, and in its ability to reach us in some way that is not simply cognitive or useful—can, I believe, effect an aesthetic transmission of the real as well, and this is art's single most important function.[51]

To shed light on this operation of transmission in Duras via piano, I must now shift my own position, from that of a literary critic extracting relevant details and comparatively showing their relevance to concepts in psychoanalytic theory, to that of a more intimate, truly close reader, where closeness involves taking the risk of being moved, mobilized beyond what one can consciously recognize in the present, in way that can only return *après coup*. To attempt this shift of gears, I will offer an account of how I became aware of the piano in Duras after many years of working on other aspects of her writing. In other words, while I focused on love, sexuality, and loss in Duras, and on her stylistic strategies for approaching the edge of language, an unconscious transmission had occurred, with different, specific components; key among them was the piano. I started to realize this after a dream I had in spring 2016:

> *My grandmother's living room. As usual, her piano stands against the wall next to the house's main entrance. My grandmother and I stand next to each other a few feet back, by the house's supporting column, facing the wall space between the front door and the piano. The piano's surface, suddenly, is soaking wet, and I worry about the most precious object in her house being ruined, knowing the woman's apprehensiveness and need for control over almost anything (and anyone) under her roof.* (During my childhood, this grandmother was also my piano teacher, and she had me wash my hands and cut my nails before so much as laying a finger on the keyboard, which she—whose fingernails I always saw clipped excessively short, far below the tips of her fingers—kept locked. Additionally, she kept the black upright piano's soundboard covered, like a southern Spanish widow, in a perfectly aligned black Manila shawl with brightly colored floral embroidery and long fringes spreading over the keyboard's cover.) *Looking up toward the front door's translucent glass pane, I notice it is misaligned with the frame at the top right corner, and a steady flow of water is seeping into*

the house. A kind of deluge is taking place outside, and starting to get in. Yet, strangely, my grandmother smiles and seems calm. She conveys that this is right; it should be happening.

This is no place to give a full analysis of my dream, but two events that prompted it do seem relevant: First, my grandmother died the year when we moved into our current house, and since she left me her beloved instrument, we had the 1895 C. Bechstein, made in Berlin, moved from her house in Mexico City to ours, in Buffalo, New York. So this piano no family member could imagine anywhere but in grandmother's living room, standing still against the wall, wrapped in its silk shawl (and out of tune since she had stopped playing when she lost her hearing and hand dexterity), had, of course, to step out her front door, roll across the courtyard, through the gate, up a ramp into a truck, and get across the border with the United States to then roll onto the driveway and enter through my own front door. This move was still a recent occurrence when I had the dream. And more immediately close to having the dream is the fact that I had just related the story of the piano's unlikely trajectory to a friend. Second, upon analyzing it, I had the sense that this dream had been inspired by a scene from Duras. I soon found it in *L'amant*, which I had read over a decade before having the dream, when I myself lived in Mexico City and was beginning to plan my own departure for graduate school abroad. Duras made a powerful impression on me, but only through this dream did I realize that this scene I had once read, without any active attempt at interpreting it, had transmitted some *Thing* that got entangled with my own experiences of the piano and migration. Here is the passage from *L'amant*:

> All the chairs are on the tables, the whole house drips, *the piano in the small living room has its feet in the water* [*le piano du petit salon a les pieds dans l'eau*]. The water flows down the steps, invades the inner courtyard toward the kitchens. The houseboys are very happy, we are together with the houseboys, we spray each other, then we lather the floor with Marseille soap. Everyone is barefoot, the mother too. *The mother laughs. The mother has nothing to say against anything.* [*La mère rit. La mère n'a rien à dire contre rien.*] The whole house is fragrant, it has the delicious smell of the wet soil after the storm, it's a smell that makes one mad with joy especially when mixed

with the other smell, that of Marseille soap. The water flows down to the paths. The houseboys' families come, their visitors too, the white children of the neighboring houses. *The mother is very happy about this mess,* [*La mère est très heureuse de ce désordre*] the mother can be very very happy sometimes, the time to forget, to wash the house can be right for the mother's happiness. The mother goes into the living room, she sits at the piano, plays the only songs she knows by heart, that she learned at the Normal school. She sings. Sometimes she plays, *she laughs* [*elle rit*]. She gets up and *dances while singing* [*elle danse tout en chantant*]. And each one thinks and the mother too *that one can be happy in this disfigured house that suddenly becomes a pond, a field on the edge of a river, a ford, a beach* [*que l'on peut être heureux dans cette maison défigurée qui devient soudain un étang, un champ au bord d'une rivière, un gué, une plage.*]⁵²

I was surprised to discover various resonances between my dream and this passage, since what had brought me back to the latter was only the image of the wet piano, and the figure of the atypically permissive, maternal pianist. For instance, like my dream's misaligned doorframe, letting the rainwater in, the house in Duras becomes *défigurée* by this overflowing water. The piano, too, Duras reminds me, has feet. They might become wet, and they might also step outside, and even leave behind the *petit salon* or my grandmother's living room to go on a journey, as the outside rainwater flows into the house, seeping through the cracks. These piano feet I hardly noticed or considered, perhaps not until the piano's migration, might also dance, for instance to the waltzes my grandmother and I played on it, just as the mother in *L'amant* could sing to her own playing. And it feels as if the piano's feet had been kept a secret from me as a child and piano student to make sure they didn't inspire unruly play, dancing, or worse, drifting.

Turning back to the passage itself, I now notice "the piano's wet feet" were the seed for the transgression and confusion of usually separate spaces, scents, and groups the whole passage emphasizes, since everyone—homeowners and houseboys, non-whites and locals as well as the French family in the colonial Indochina setting—also goes barefoot and soaks their feet together in this house that becomes something of "a pond, a field by a river, a ford, a beach," to the tune of the mother's played and sung airs. One can hear in Duras's passage the assonance in *mère* and *airs*, and therein an insistent French *r*, which also sounds like "erre," to err, to deviate from correctness and wander, as the house becomes soaked in water, soap, song, and laughter.

Laughter is the uncommon reaction registered by the narrator in her mother, the same bitter woman who built a wall against the Pacific waves that destroyed the rice field. The alliterations in the juxtaposed sentences describing the mother's affect, "mère n'a rien à dire contre rien" and "mère rit," underscore this laughter's disruption of an oppositional, prohibitive function of speaking, and at once make audible "mer-riz," the sea-rice encounter whose consequence is devastating to the mother. It is remarkable to find the tragedy of the rice fields ruined by the sea reemerge as laughter. Indeed, the mother Duras depicts in the Barrage Cycle is an unpredictable, oceanic deadly force that may take over her surroundings, and that can just as shockingly become excessively quiet, almost dead, locked within herself. Or laugh, and sing. The piano, in turn, is again closely linked to this mother, like an amplifier of her volatile force in sonorous, temporal, and spatial terms. But perhaps it is more accurate to say the mother's body is already an instrument for a force to course through it, and through the piano, the living room, down the steps, along the paths, to the inner courtyard and through Duras's sentences into my dream, mixing there with my own melancholic grandmother, her piano, and her house with its own inner courtyard.

In 1980, Duras, by then in her mid-sixties, published a dream about the music Carlos d'Alessio had created for her works. In an analytic cure, approaching the inaccessible real begins with dreams, which under transference give expression to something beyond language in its bind to what was or can be said. In Duras's case, the dream comes not as the sole mode of expression for a repressed desire, but rather only *after* the aesthetic work has been produced:

> *Éden Cinéma* was playing at the Orsay theater. And one night, after the end of the shows, I dreamed that I entered into a house with a row of columns, that there were like interior verandas, deep, facing gardens. Upon entering into this house, I heard the songs of Carlos d'Alessio, the waltz of *Éden Cinéma* and I said to myself: say, Carlos is here, he's playing. And I called him. No one answered. And whence the music came my mother came out. She was already taken by death, she was

> putrefied already, her face was full of holes, greenish already. She smiled very subtly. [*déjà prise par la mort, elle était putréfiée déjà, son visage était plein de trous, verdâtre déjà. Elle souriait très légèrement.*] She said to me: "It was I who was playing." I said to her: "But how is it possible? You were dead." She said to me: "I made you believe that to allow you to write *all that*. [*tout ça*]"[53]

In this dream, Duras's distinctive attention to the location housing an event leads to the mother's return from death, insisting on the intricate weaving I have examined between the musical dimension of Duras's work and the mother figure: "Et de l'endroit d'où venait la musique ma mère est sortie." It is by playing the piano that the mother reveals she has "played dead" so the daughter could "write all that." She is "already taken by death" (she actually died in 1957) yet she speaks all the same, and even plays d'Alessio's compositions for Duras. The mother appears through the music to reveal that the idea of her death in her daughter's mind was a condition for the author to "write all that," in particular the play *L'Éden Cinéma*, given the waltz the dreamer hears. So, the dream thinks about the conditions of creation, of writing that might enable a return of the real beyond parental ideals or prohibitions.

In the introductory remarks of *L'Éden* the mother is to appear, as previously mentioned, "immobile in her chair, without expression, a statue."[54] It is as if this impassible image of the mother had, by way of the music, deformed itself into the dream's gruesome face "full of holes, and greenish," at once lightly smiling (again one hears the tragedy of *riz* "rice" subverted, in her smiling "*souriait*") and speaking. Language seems to privilege clear-cut boundaries between life and death, outside and inside, wet and dry. This facial deformation, like the misaligned frame in my dream, or the house "disfigured" by water in the passage from *L'amant*, expresses the impossible irruption of the real into reality.

At first glance the dream seems to present, as a nightmare, the very problem my essay has been trying to overcome, namely, that of entrapment within a maternal horizon, within her words and world (where the girl's survival depended on being an object of sexual satisfaction for a rich man, for example). I have highlighted the importance of the mother's story in *L'Éden Cinéma*, of her production of an absence on the stage, and of her tight bond with music in the play and elsewhere. I also argued that the composition of a new waltz instead of playing the pieces the mother knew marked a step beyond familial and representational limits, all while keeping the waltz form associated with the mother. The dream seems to test Duras's work of writing *with* the mother and her story "to open onto a future," as I stated earlier in citing Deleuze and Guattari. The mother in the dream seems to cast doubt on the writing and music "belonging" to anyone but her in the end. But the act of writing, staging, and, in a literal translation of the French idiom *donner*, "giving" performances of the play at the theater, has already occurred. From that perspective, the dream just confirms the operation of transmitting something of the drive, of a musical bliss coursing through a space. The subject is in the position of encountering its audible effect from outside, as she advances through an unknown house, guessing it must be d'Alessio's playing she hears. The mother *permits* writing, while the music *emits*, audibly, something of the drive that fuels Duras's writing. The dream's avowal of a matricidal wish, together with the wish for the mother to come back from the dead to play the piano pieces from Duras's works and speak to her, can be read as a confirmation that the unique *mark of the real* her writing bears has come across, into d'Alessio's compositions, for instance. The music performs a material emission, onto another body, of that distinctive thing that remains inaccessible except through writing as the reverberation of a force beyond meaning.

As I have pointed out through the "Valse de l'Éden Cinéma," the waltz is not only "the mother's story," but also the girl's music. Not just "Ramona," symbolizing the situation of the mother left behind by the children and sound film, as well as the adolescents' capture by an illusion of love. Like the dream, in which the mother never totally died, the daughter didn't simply separate herself from the mother's piano or the waltz form. The final pages of *L'amant* show that the piano followed its protagonist across the oceans, in the form of a Chopin waltz that pervades the starry night, on the boat in which she immigrated to Paris from French Indochina, Duras's birthplace and home until the age of eighteen.

> ... during the trip across [*la traversée*] this same ocean, the night again had already begun, in the great salon of the main port the outburst [*l'éclatement*] produced itself of a Chopin waltz she knew in a secret and intimate way because she had tried to learn it for months and she had never managed to play it correctly, never, which then led to her mother's consent to her abandoning the piano. That night, lost among many other

nights, of that she was sure, the young woman had spent it on this boat and she had been there when this thing had produced itself, this outburst of Chopin's music under the sky illuminated with brilliances [*cet éclatement de la musique de Chopin sous le ciel illuminé de brillances*].[55]

The outburst of this unspecified Chopin waltz is an uncanny event, which I will seek to interpret by way of concluding. The waltz returns from the past or has followed her onto the boat from the Indochina she is leaving behind, for the girl had unsuccessfully tried to learn this very waltz, and her failure led her to abandon the piano, with her mother's consent. But from the dream and from the waltz of *L'Éden Cinéma* we have learned these separations never work unambiguously. The invocation of the mother and her permission, again, are no accident. The girl has permission to abandon the piano, but the music she knows most intimately seeps through the borders.

I became curious as to which Chopin waltz this could have been, so I listened to all of them again. There was the *Valse Minute*, op. 64 no. 1, the one my grandmother played so well, which is full of thrilling nervous energy and concludes in a speedy yet languorous descending sequence. The extraordinary minute Chopin invented had moved and made me want to play piano as a child. There was also op. 64 no. 2, a much less *vivace* and rather odd one (subdued in tone except for the slower third section in the tonic major, D flat), which I came to know "in a secret and intimate way." Upon rereading Duras's passage, its insistence on *l'éclatement*, the outburst of this waltz, as well as the environment into which this explosion is released, a boat in the vast ocean under the night whose scintillating stars are called *brillances*, suggested that it would have to be one of the Grandes Valses Brillantes, where there is certainly no shortage of *éclat*, as well as emphatic introductions that abruptly suspend ordinary time and prepare listeners for complete submersion in their enchanted atmospheres.

But what makes this moment of *listening* into a *true event* in the text is the girl's discovery, through the music, of two essential things about life, and these two things, I'm inclined to think, narrow down the possibilities, and point to another waltz. The two essential things for Duras in the melody are, first, a strange, powerful feeling of wanting to die, less related to despair than to the sublime, and second, an ineffable kind of love closely related to music and the sea, to which, one can fairly say, she devotes all of her writing. The description accounts for the unbound drive in its specific musical form. At this point she has narrated the passionate affair between the protagonist and the rich Chinese man who is in love with her but must marry his Chinese fiancée. Only after they have separated does love "hit" her, through the waltz:

> And the young girl had raised herself up as though to go kill herself in turn, to throw herself in turn in the sea [*s'était dressée comme pour aller à son tour se tuer, se jeter à son tour dans la mer*] and afterward she had wept because she had thought of this man from Cholen and she had not been certain all of a sudden of not having loved him with a love she had not seen because it had gotten lost in the story like the water in the sand and she found it only now in this instant of the music thrown across the sea [*perdu dans l'histoire comme l'eau dans le sable et qu'elle le retrouvait seulement maintenant à cet instant de la musique jetée à travers la mer*].[56]

The impulse to "throw herself in turn into the sea"[57] arises from the music's being "thrown across the sea" *jetée à travers la mer*, where one also encounters again music and mother (*mère*), crossing each other and crossing through the girl's body. Bearing in mind the final farewell to the man, love's emergence only after the separation,[58] and the abrupt reaction it provokes in the girl's body, ready to drop from the boat into the sea forever, the appropriate waltz could be the posthumous op. 69. no. 1, known as *Adieu* or *Farewell* since Chopin dedicated the work to the artist María Wodzińska in 1835, when their engagement ended.[59]

The *Adieu* waltz starts with a melancholic but sweet theme that features swift, ascending flourishes whose gesture of "raising themselves up" one might compare to the girl moved by the waltz to the edge of the boat. It then turns to another sweet theme of almost childish sets of skipping intervals to be played *con anima*, followed by a return to the first theme, before continuing to a theme somewhat similar in feeling to the second one, though here the phrase's *dolce* idling gets interrupted twice, by an officious, *poco a poco crescendo* phrase that, unlike the vehement introductions for the Grandes Valses Brillantes, fails to lead to the arrival of some grand ceremony or enchanted universe, and instead returns to *dolce* idling, which now seems less merry and more trivial. The piece concludes with yet another return to the main, gentle melancholia of the beginning, and lets the flourish climb higher this time, so as to drop more dramatically and end in languor. Yet the beauty of indeterminacy as it emerges in literature and dreams has to do with the endless possibilities of condensation they allow. This passage from *L'amant* can make audible all at once, for the reader's inner ear, the *brilliance* and *éclat* of the *brillante* waltzes and the unrealized, languorous, bittersweet finality of the *adieu*, neither one drowning the other out. If the girl discovered this capacity to hold the tension of the unbound drive through her body, in the untimely, sublime feeling of love that invades her through Chopin's music, and if, neither dropping off the stage once and for all, nor returning to her mother's control, she was able to produce from the experience of a jouissance out of limits a writing, of this and other scenes, then an opening onto the forces of the future beyond herself did take place. In which case the repetition, rather than following and referring to a model, is an original act that transmits something unheard-of.

Notes

1. The set of texts referred to as the Barrage Cycle focuses on Duras's childhood and adolescence in Indochina and on a love affair between the girl and a melancholic Chinese billionaire. See Eva Ahlstedt, *Le "cycle du barrage" dans l'oeuvre de Marguerite Duras* (Göteborg: Acta Universitatis Gothoburgensis, 2003).

2. Duras criticism that has examined the functions of music in Duras's oeuvre include Midori Ogawa, *La musique dans l'oeuvre littéraire de Marguerite Duras* (Paris: L'Harmattan, 2003); the work of Wendy Everett; and, recently, Joe Hughes, "Formal Destruction: The Art of the Fugue in Destroy, She Said," S 12 (2019): 42–66.

3. Duras has called this space-time in some of her works "eternity," in the context of a subject revisiting a state of extraordinary solitude. See for instance Marguerite Duras, *Hiroshima mon amour* (Paris: Folio, 1960), 93–94; or Marguerite Duras, *Le ravissement de Lol V. Stein* (Paris: Folio, 1964), 49.

4. In an important essay that inspires my exploration of the real with the piano in Duras, Lucie Cantin defines the function of language of "link[ing] the being to a symbolic space in which the receivable and the possible [. . .] are established"; see Lucie Cantin, "Practices of the Letter: Writing a Space for the Real," *Umbr(a)* s.n. (2010): 13. See also Willy Apollon, "L'intraitable," in Lucie Cantin, gen. ed., *La cure psychanalytique du psychotique. Enjeux et stratégies* (Québec: GIFRIC, 2008), 327–52.

5. Duras, *Ravissement*, 48. Translations throughout this essay are mine unless otherwise noted. I have discussed this oft-quoted passage in more detail

in Fernanda Negrete, "Acts of Love and Unconscious Savoir in Marguerite Duras's Writing," *S* 12 (2019): 15–41.

    6. In fact, Lol V. Stein never speaks directly about the supposed scene that provoked in her a crisis ten years before meeting Jacques Hold. There are only rumors about this, especially from their common friend Tatiana Karl, and a scene where Lol is aware that Jacques is eavesdropping while she and Tatiana reminisce together.

    7. Jacques Lacan, *Le Séminaire XI: les quatre concepts fondamentaux de la psychanalyse* (Paris: Seuil, 1973), 73.

    8. Lacan, *Séminaire XI*, 73.

    9. Lacan, *Séminaire XI*, 73.

    10. Gilles Deleuze and Félix Guattari, *A Thousand Plateaus: Capitalism and Schizophrenia*, trans. Brian Massumi (Minneapolis: Minnesota University Press, 1987), 311.

    11. Hughes points out that in the film Duras directed of her *Détruire, dit-elle*, just before a theme from Bach's *Art of the Fugue* is heard, she produced a gong resonance by slamming the piano lid while pressing on the sustaining pedal "creating a deep, Dionysian noise that resonates across the overtone series, setting the whole sonic spectrum alight." See Hughes, "Formal Destruction," 42.

    12. Renate Günther begins her book on Duras as film director by offering biographical details that justify her "conjecture that the work of Duras expresses a desire to return to her ideal of the early mother/child relationship, where an imaginary sense of union would prevail over separation and conflict. In this respect, Madeleine Borgomano has rightly argued that the cinema of Duras functions both as a substitute for the mother and as a return to her origins." See Renate Günther, *Marguerite Duras* (Manchester: Manchester University Press, 2002), 4. The work Günther cites by Borgomano is *L'écriture filmique de Marguerite Duras* (Paris: Albatros, 1985). See also Madeleine Borgomano, "The Image of Cinema in *The Sea Wall*," in Rosana Maule and Julie Beaulieu, gen. eds., *In the Dark Room: Marguerite Duras and Cinema* (Oxford: Peter Lang, 2009), 65–86.

    13. This return occurs across films and novels from different periods, in the rewritings of the Barrage story and beyond it. For example, there is the reticent child at the piano lesson in the novel *Moderato Cantabile* (1959) or the children in the film *Nathalie Granger* (1972), where the camera travels over scattered scores of Bach's *Fugues* while Czerny's traditional piano exercises are heard.

    14. Suzanne and Joseph first appeared in the 1950 novel *Un barrage contre le Pacifique*, along with their mother and a younger brother, whose early death is mentioned in some of the works considered to be part of the Barrage Cycle.

    15. Marguerite Duras, *L'Éden Cinéma* (Paris: Mércure de France, 1977), 12.

    16. Günther, *Marguerite Duras*, 4.

    17. Duras, *L'Éden Cinéma*, 11.

18. This creativity is spurred by the unbound drive, which Freud qualified as a death drive in *Beyond the Pleasure Principle*, in a distribution of conservative and destructive work, on different sides. Duras's writing is exemplary of the drive as creative and destructive, as deadly and creative at once insofar as its excess responds to a satisfaction of its own and not to the demands or ideals of civilization. On creation and destruction in Duras, see Llewellyn Brown, *Marguerite Duras, écrire et détruire: un paradoxe de la création* (Paris: Lettres Modernes Minard, 2018).

19. Duras, *L'Éden Cinéma*, 12.

20. Duras, *L'Éden Cinéma*, 13.

21. Duras, *L'Éden Cinéma*, 16.

22. Here the reader learns that the music consists, more specifically, of two waltzes and two one-steps (150). The available collection of recordings of d'Alessio's music for film, however, only includes one waltz of the Eden Cinema.

23. D'Alessio speaks of his composition method for Duras in the interview "Entre Marguerite Duras et Carlos d'Alessio, de la musique avant toute chose. . . . Une rencontre rapportée par Dominique de Gasquet," in Anne-Marie Réboul and Esther Sánchez-Pardo, *L'écriture désirante: Marguerite Duras* (Paris: L'Harmattan, 2016), 275–82.

24. Marc Phéline, "Les mélodies de Carlos d'Alessio: D'*India Song* à *L'Éden Cinéma* . . . ," in Dominique Bax, ed., *Marguerite Duras, Alain Robbe-Grillet: 13e festival, 13–29 mars 2002, à Bobigny* (Bobigny: Magic Cinéma, 2002), 71.

25. Phéline, "Mélodies," 71.

26. D'Alessio, "Entre Marguerite," 278.

27. My description corresponds with the interpretation recorded in a compilation of d'Alessio's music for film, which in fact combines sections from two *Éden Cinéma* waltzes he composed. "Valse de l'Éden Cinéma (foutaises)," track 21 in compact disc 1 in Carlos d'Alessio and Marguerite Duras, *India Song et autres musiques de films*, Le Chant du Monde, 2009. See the scores in Carlos d'Alessio, *Musiques de films pour piano* (Paris: Éditions du Chant du Monde, 1992), 21–25.

28. Special thanks to Heidi Arsenault for her instruction in analyzing the waltzes for this essay.

29. From this point on I describe the recorded interpretation, which incorporates part of the score for "L'Éden Cinéma valse II."

30. Duras, *L'Éden Cinéma*, 150.

31. Isée Bernateau has explored the problem of separation in Duras's writing with a specific focus on the Barrage Cycle and highlighting "le ravage maternel" (the maternal ravage) this cycle presents. See "Ravages de la separation chez Marguerite Duras." *Carnet PSY* 7, no. 165 (2012): 32–35.

32. Duras, *L'Éden Cinéma*, 15.

33. Duras, *L'Éden Cinéma*, 37–38.

34. Duras, *Un barrage contre le Pacifique* (Paris: Gallimard, 1950).

35. Duras, *Barrage*, 70–71.

36. Duras, *L'Éden Cinéma*, 42.

37. This is what is at stake in Duras's insistent repetitions of the same love stories in the Barrage and India cycles; the love encounter never satisfies the push to continue writing, as her characters continue pacing aimlessly, dancing, singing, or humming across different works.

38. Phéline, "Mélodies," 71.

39. Julia Kristeva remarks on the painful quality of Duras's speech in Julia Kristeva, *Soleil noir. Dépression et mélancolie* (Paris: Gallimard, 1987), 233–36.

40. Deleuze and Guattari, *Thousand Plateaus*, 312.

41. Deleuze and Guattari, *Thousand Plateaus*, 312.

42. This the most desirable of all functions they present for a *ritournelle* in their discussion, which also include setting up a territory and also imposing fascistic regimes that destroy the territory. Deleuze and Guattari point out "the potential fascism of music," which they develop throughout the plateau "On the refrain"; see Deleuze and Guattari, *Thousand Plateaus*, 348. They develop the characteristics of fascism in the plateau "Micropolitics and Segmentarity"; see Deleuze and Guattari, *Thousand Plateaus*, 208–31.

43. Translation modified from Deleuze and Guattari, *Thousand Plateaus*, 349.

44. Marguerite Duras and Michelle Porte, *Les lieux de Marguerite Duras* (Paris: Minuit, 1977), 28–29; cited in Hughes, "Formal Destruction," 44. Hughes reads a longer portion of the passage, observing that to Duras music points to a remote past, which he refers to in terms of "integrity and wholeness," as well as to the future, which he presents in terms of "redemption." My own proposal to align this statement with the remarks on time and the refrain by Deleuze and Guattari emphasizes the unreceivable and thus radically creative nature of the time music brings for Duras, which is neither about a wholeness lost to the past nor a redeemed future.

45. This is also the logic of making audible unprecedented timbres in the invention of instruments. Jean-Luc Nancy highlights this in citing André Schaeffner's 1968 *Origine des instruments de musique*, which states: "In every case [treatment of the voice or fabrication of instruments by amplification or alteration of sounds] it is less a matter of 'imitating' than of surpassing something—the already-known, the ordinary, the relatively moderate, the natural. From which emerge unlikely inventions, a propensity to acoustic monstrosities that will puzzle physicists (25)." See Jean-Luc Nancy, *L'écoute* (Paris: Galilée, 2002), 23n3.

46. Deleuze and Guattari, *Thousand Plateaus*, 311.

47. Freud, of course, underscored this in his research on Totemic cultures and on the biblical figure of Moses, as well as in clinical studies that posit a primal scene for the analysand (such as the Wolf Man case).

48. On the limits of the signifier and Freud's work with the Wolf Man on the letter of the body of the drive, see Cantin, "Practices."

49. Cantin, "Practices," 14.

50. See the "Proposition du 9 octobre 1967 sur le psychanalyste de l'École," in Jacques Lacan, *Autres écrits* (Paris: Seuil, 2001), 243–59. At the École Freudienne du Québec, the *passant* meets with two people who are far along in their analysis and receive the *pass*, an unconscious transmission from the *passant*, in order to relay it, each in a separate meeting, to a cartel of analysts, who are able to discern whether a new object has actually been transmitted through the bodies of these two *passeurs*.

51. The aesthetic transmission to a reader in a work of art or writing is effective, even if it does not necessarily offer to accompany a subject to the point of living on without the fantasy of the unbarred Other. An analysis is concerned with the discovery that the Other is also lacking and cannot be completed, as well as the dismantling of a specific fantasy about serving this Other's desire that the subject has cultivated in order to cover over this structural lack, at the cost of her own desire.

52. Duras, *L'amant* (Paris: Minuit, 1984), 76–77.

53. Duras, *Les yeux verts* (Paris: Denoël, 1987), 112–13.

54. Duras, *L'Éden Cinéma*, 12.

55. Duras, *L'amant*, 137.

56. Duras, *L'amant*, 137–38.

57. The impulse in the passage to "raise herself up and kill herself" by throwing herself into the sea resonates with the *passage à l'acte* in Freud's "The Psychogenesis of a Case of Homosexuality in a Woman." The young woman in question talks about an impulsive suicide attempt by throwing herself into the railway cutting at a decisive moment. Lacan discusses the case in Jacques Lacan, *Le séminaire X: L'angoisse* (Paris: Seuil, 2004), 136: "The moment of the passage to the act is that of the greatest embarrassment of the subject, with the behavioral addition of emotion as a movement disorder. [. . .] [F]rom there where it is—from the site of the scene where, as a fundamentally historicized subject, it can only keep its status of subject—it precipitates itself and falls out of the scene. This is the very structure of the passage to the act."

58. Duras is profoundly Racinian. This key scene reenacts the unusual ending of the tragedy *Bérénice*, where the queen accepts her exile from Rome and separation from her lover Titus, who will be emperor, without replacing him with Antiochus, a friend to the lovers who has always been in love with her. She embarks alone on a ship that sails back to her Palestinian hometown, Caesarea. I have discussed this important reference for Duras in Fernanda Negrete, "Marguerite Duras's *Césarée* and the Subject of Love," *New Centennial Review* 15.3 (2015): 167–99.

59. See Fryderyk Chopin, *Waltzes*, vol. 9 of *Complete Works: According to the Autographs and Original Editions, with Critical Commentary*, gen. ed. Ignacy Jan Paderewski (Cracow: Instytut Fryderyka Chopina, 1949).

References

Ahlstedt, Eva. *Le "cycle du barrage" dans l'oeuvre de Marguerite Duras*. Göteborg: Acta Universitatis Gothoburgensis, 2003.
Apollon, Willy. "L'intraitable." In *La cure psychanalytique du psychotique. Enjeux et stratégies*, edited by Lucie Cantin, 327–52. Québec: GIFRIC, 2008.
Bernateau, Isée. "Ravages de la séparation chez Marguerite Duras." *Carnet PSY* 7, no. 165 (2012): 32–35.
Borgomano, Madeleine. *L'écriture filmique de Marguerite Duras*. Paris: Albatros, 1985.
Borgomano, Madeleine. "The Image of Cinema in *The Sea Wall*." In *In the Dark Room: Marguerite Duras and Cinema*, edited by Rosana Maule and Julie Beaulieu, 65–86. Oxford: Peter Lang, 2009.
Brown, Llewellyn. *Marguerite Duras, écrire et détruire: Un paradoxe de la création*. Paris: Lettres Modernes Minard, 2018.
Cantin, Lucie. "Practices of the Letter: Writing a Space for the Real." Translated by Michael Stanish. *Umbr(a)* s.n. (2010): 11–32.
Chopin, Fryderyk. *Waltzes*. Vol. 9 of *Complete Works: According to the Autographs and Original Editions, with Critical Commentary*, edited by Ignacy Jan Paderewski. Cracow: Instytut Fryderyka Chopina, 1949.
d'Alessio, Carlos. *Musiques de films pour piano*. Paris: Éditions du Chant du Monde, 1992.
d'Alessio, Carlos, and Marguerite Duras. *India Song et autres musiques de films*. Le Chant du Monde, 2009, compact disc.
Deleuze, Gilles, and Félix Guattari. *A Thousand Plateaus: Capitalism and Schizophrenia*. Translated by Brian Massumi. Minneapolis: Minnesota University Press, 1987.
Duras, Marguerite. *L'amant*. Paris: Minuit, 1984.
Duras, Marguerite. *Un barrage contre le Pacifique*. Paris: Gallimard, 1950.
Duras, Marguerite. *L'Éden Cinéma*. Paris: Mércure de France, 1977.
Duras, Marguerite. *Hiroshima mon amour*. Paris: Folio, 1960.
Duras, Marguerite. *Le ravissement de Lol V. Stein*. Paris: Folio, 1964.
Duras, Marguerite. *Les yeux verts*. Paris: Denoël, 1987.
Duras, Marguerite, and Michelle Porte. *Les lieux de Marguerite Duras*. Paris: Minuit, 1977.
Gasquet, Dominique. "Entre Marguerite Duras et Carlos d'Alessio, de la musique avant toute chose. . . . Une rencontre rapportée par Dominique de Gasquet." In *L'écriture désirante: Marguerite Duras*, edited by Anne-Marie Réboul and Esther Sánchez-Pardo, 275–82. Paris: L'Harmattan, 2016.
Günther, Renate. *Marguerite Duras*. Manchester: Manchester University Press, 2002.
Hughes, Joe. "Formal Destruction: The *Art of the Fugue* in *Destroy, She Said*." *S* 12 (2019): 42–66.

Kristeva, Julia. *Soleil noir. Dépression et mélancolie*. Paris: Gallimard, 1987.
Lacan, Jacques. *Autres écrits*. Paris: Seuil, 2001.
Lacan, Jacques. *Le séminaire X: L'angoisse*. Paris: Seuil, 2004.
Lacan, Jacques. *Le séminaire XI: Les quatre concepts fondamentaux de la psychanalyse*. Paris: Seuil, 1973.
Nancy, Jean-Luc. *L'écoute*. Paris: Galilée, 2002.
Negrete, Fernanda. "Acts of Love and Unconscious Savoir in Marguerite Duras's Writing." *S* 12 (2019): 15–41.
Negrete, Fernanda. "Marguerite Duras's *Césarée* and the Subject of Love." *New Centennial Review* 15.3 (2015): 167–99.
Ogawa, Midori. *La musique dans l'oeuvre littéraire de Marguerite Duras*. Paris: L'Harmattan, 2003.
Phéline, Marc. "Les mélodies de Carlos d'Alessio: D'*India Song* à *L'Éden Cinéma* . . ." In *Marguerite Duras, Alain Robbe-Grillet: 13e festival, 13–29 mars 2002, à Bobigny*, edited by Dominique Bax, 70–71. Bobigny: Magic Cinéma, 2002.

Chapter 7

Outside In

Chorus and Clearing in the Time of Pandemic and Protest

JULIE BETH NAPOLIN

As I am writing on the last day of August 2020, a small but resonant march passes by my window, chants floating down the Sunday main street.[1] Some days I leave my desk and join, marching to the park; today I sit still. The sounds of chanting "I can't breathe" and drumming dissipate, and I return to thinking and writing after having paused to open the window and listen. As the breeze comes in, a stack of papers on my desk flutter into disarray, upset by the air.

In one of the last evenings of June, after an unseasonable torrent of hail in New York City, dozens of string players gathered in Washington Square Park for a violin vigil for Elijah McClain, a twenty-three-year-old Black man murdered by the police in the summer of 2019 in Aurora, Colorado.[2] He once delighted in soothing animals in shelters with the sound of his violin. He had been walking home from a convenience store with his headphones on, moving his arms in time to the sound of music we cannot hear. The gift of headphones is the gift of an inner world that silences for a time signals, invitations, and interpellations. Lost in the music and waving his arms in ways that did not move with the rhythm of the outside, McClain followed the pulse of an inner soundtrack. He was dancing. Wearing a face mask to protect himself, though it was not yet the time of COVID-19 (he was a vulnerable body with anemia), he struck a passerby as "suspicious." The stranger deputized himself to call the police, though he conceded in the call that he doubted McClain was a threat.

When the police arrived on what was suddenly transmuted into a *scene*—a suggested crime, a person recast as a racialized and criminalized body—they attacked McClain for "resisting contact" and injected him with the tranquilizer ketamine, sending him into cardiac arrest until his heart gave out. It took several months for the police to release the body-camera footage that captured only audio. It is an aural document of a violent spectacle. He can be heard reasoning with the police, explaining that he was "stopping [his] music to listen" to them. As they struggle, he says, "I can't breathe. I have my ID right here. . . . I was just going home. I am an introvert. I'm just different. That's all. I'm so sorry. I have no gun."[3]

It took almost a year for the public to hold musical vigils, which happened in more than one city across the US and received global attention.[4] I had never heard Elijah's McClain's name, but I had heard other names in these months of Black Lives Matter protests, perhaps the most powerful social movement in the world at this moment. Protestors are met, time and again, with extreme and gratuitous police brutality, also being held in unventilated conditions without protective masks and at extreme risk for catching and transmitting COVID-19. The protests were galvanized by (though they certainly did not begin in) the police murder of George Floyd on May 25, 2020, in Minneapolis, Minnesota. Among his dying words were "I can't breathe."

That phrase had already been a watchword for Black Lives Matter, chanted in unison in memorial recognition of the last words of Eric Garner, who uttered the phrase eleven times when, in 2014, Daniel Pantaleo, an officer with NYPD, put Garner in a fatal choke hold.[5] Derek Chauvin, an officer with the Minneapolis police, had also asphyxiated George Floyd in a showman-like performance of domination. He thrust his knee into the neck of the supine man for 8 minutes and 46 seconds, which has become a memorial temporality when protestors sit in silence in the middle of city streets.[6] This memorial is marked by a struggle for the right of Black and brown people to breathe amidst pandemic and ongoing environmental catastrophe.

At the same time that the protests are taking place, the pandemic has meant a quieting of the city largely cleared of the noise of activities that define it. In the early days, when the deaths in New York City were rapidly rising, the outside world made a punctuated intrusion into interior spaces in areas closest to hospitals, people often describing the experience of hearing sirens every twenty minutes into the night. Microphones on downtown New York City street corners installed by noise pollution researchers unwittingly captured a change in decibel level, from seventy-six decibels on April 16, 2019, to sixty-nine decibels on April 18, 2020. They were aiming to capture the ebb and flow of city noise, yet the timing meant they captured among the sharpest cessations in sound-emitting activity in the history of the city. The *New York Times* reported, "The coronavirus quieted city noise. Listen to what's left."[7] It was the sound of day becoming the sound of night.

In the American news, we still do not see images of those dying from COVID-19, which ransacks the respiratory and vascular systems. One mark of the virus has been the physical separation of loved ones from those who die alone in the isolation of quarantine or the ICU—it is an unrecorded sound. As the awareness of the scope of the pandemic was dawning in the US, one terrifying image surfaced from around the globe: the satellite image of mass, empty graves in Iran, graves so vast they were visible from space. This and the image of empty streets are "images of absence," a friend of mine observed at the time.[8] In the face of that invisibility, the sense of hearing has become, for me, more acute.

In what follows, I present a piece of writing that is, by necessity, aleatory and an ensemble. It is a collage of sounds, images, and acts of listening that drift in time and space. When I began this essay, it was by writing my way through the anxiety of turning inward during the pandemic and sheltering in place, keeping a sensory journal of observations, a series of notes on the changing conditions of listening to my environment and the mediascape while also contemplating their acoustical possibilities in a moment when being outside, traveling, and moving were severely restricted. The reverberation between moments is such that chronology itself becomes inverted, or its direction reversed, for the meaning-making function goes both backwards and forwards.

I want to begin with two audiovisual documents of protest and pandemic that pair in my memory; to my sensibility, it is as if one resonates with the other, the vibration of one continues to act at a distance or make itself felt within the space-time of the other and long after the event has taken place. On June 13, 2020, the streets of Paris in Place de la République filled with vocal bodies in protest for Black Lives Matter.[9] On March 11, 2020, a video captured the streets of an unknown city in a pandemic-stricken Italy emptied of bodies. A group of young Black men, African immigrants, step through the deserted streets with great freedom ("racism free"), gliding with large strides to Janet Jackson's "The Pleasure Principle."[10] Why present these recollections in reverse, going from June to March? There is something about the second sound-image (chronologically first, but second in my narrative), that prepares the first sound-image (chronologically second, but first in my narrative). A street emptied in one European town has been emptied of the activity that used to define it to make space for another kind of activity and rhythm—a choreography—that is usually prohibited, if not legally, then socially. When I watch this video and hear the sound of joy, even in the midst of such loss, my senses tell me that only through emptying out, a clearing, did mass demonstration and rhythmic gathering and chanting of the people become possible. In the pandemic's clearing away of mundane sounds and encounters, the sidewalks became a site for the perfect amplification of an anthem and, with it, the free expansion of Black vernacular gestures. How can pandemic and protest, quieting and sounding out, be heard together? How does the one sound the depths of the other?

In the spirit of Pauline Oliveros's "Some Sound Observations," written in the late 1960s during the Vietnam War and on the heels of civil rights uprising, I was keeping a journal of these audio-visions, turning outward, toward the acoustics of my ordinary spaces in an effort to quell and contain. I was noting the changing conditions of sound, light, and air and wishing to document an acoustics that I knew bore some index of something outside of me that I cannot see and only touch obliquely.[11] At stake in these sensory observations has been something like the threshold between inside and outside. That is a common and perhaps constitutive stake in listening. But this stake is often muted when the "who" of my listening subjectivity is put on hold, as it were, in order to concentrate on its object.

At first, I was writing of and recording neighborhood streets. On April 20, 2020, unable to go anywhere or see anyone, I simply walked for a mile in a direction I had never walked before, just as the sun was setting. Suddenly, I was confronted with the most profound quiet I had ever heard in the city. There was only the sound my foot falling on the pavement and the closeness of distant sounds that would usually be lost in their reverberation: across the street, a dog's collar and his feet trotting on the pavement, a piano wafting out of an open window, girlfriends giggling on a stoop, evening birds in the magnolia trees, and then two men talking loudly and boisterously, enjoying the echo of their voices on the pavement. Later on, in mid-May, I wrote that I could "sense that the hum of the city was returning," but I didn't yet know to what it was returning—the protests had not yet begun, demanding the shared world.

Sensing this hum, I was reminded of Virginia Woolf's 1929 description of listening to polite lunchtime conversation in postwar England, the way her mind was suddenly pulled "back into the past, before the war indeed," such that she could set the sound of present-day talk "against the background of that other talk," superimposing them:

> Nothing was changed; nothing was different save only—here I listened with all my ears not entirely to what was being said, but to the murmur or current behind it. Yes, that was it—the change was there. Before the war at a luncheon party like this people would have said precisely the same things but they would have sounded different, because in those days they were accompanied by a sort of humming noise, not articulate, but musical, exciting, which changed the value of the words themselves.[12]

She listens to the atmosphere through which words move as their medium. I have always loved this passage but previously had no sensory relationship to the radical transformation it documents. When I got home from the walk, I remembered Woolf and wrote, "beneath all sounds is a bed of quiet." I opened my window to hear the thump of a drum being struck with a mallet; dull, low, and resonant. I didn't yet know what I was listening for.

I only understood later that, in documenting the experience of quieting, I had been unwittingly recording the sound of uprising, a sound about to rise up. To record is a deliberate act: I sense the signal and capture it, in word or with a device. How do we also record what we cannot fully register, hearing coming first and understanding coming later, if at all? Listening itself becomes, in this way, multiple in its temporality and dimension.

It is impossible to present my sonic observations to you in a chronological fashion, in part because the dynamic of this listening has been both a harkening backward and forward, or what, in *The Fact of Resonance*, I describe as a "preaudition" and "retroaudition."[13] These neologisms underscore a divergence from premonition and its Latin root *monere*, or to advise, warn, and remind: premonition never quite loses its ecclesiastical register of a monitoring authority.[14] To monitor is to see and hear from afar, to measure the visual and audible signal for signs of disturbance in order to quell and contain them. Instead, what I want to try to put into words is the current, a calling across the span of my sensibility over time, an antiphonic response and the air in between. As I was hearing, writing, and recording, there were portents, notes of warning. These were the sounds of things to come, both personally and collectively.

Elijah McClain's cry had been over a year ago, and yet it was already an echo of Eric Garner's last words. Both voices—and still more that have gone undocumented—demanded to be heard again when the cry of George Floyd struck the memory of those familiar with McClain. Others had already long been hearing in the pandemic the portents of uprising, but this sound not yet been sensible to me.

∾

During one of the first nights after New York City instituted a curfew (for the first time in multiple generations in an effort to quell rebellion against the racial state), the police arrested a Broadway singer and her husband, a white couple, on their stoop in the Upper West Side. They had come out to cheer for a march that had gathered and mobilized, in an act of civil disobedience, in the street past curfew. While police arrested the couple for violating curfew by standing on the stoop, their neighbors shouted from the threshold of the door. It stood newly erected and politicized, a sounding site between inside and outside. The Fourth Amendment protects American citizens from such violation, which can be construed as unlawful search and seizure. It was the opinion of the Supreme Court in *Florida v. Jardines* that the front porch is the dwelling's "curtilage"—the land immediately surrounding a home and not its "open fields beyond"—rendering the threshold part of its inside.[15]

The boundaries of a curtilage are "imprecise and subject to controversy."[16] So, too, with listening. In listening, the subject moves to a threshold. It has perhaps not yet amounted to any sort of change or action; some additional waiting room is there, not because the inside has expanded but the outside has come in. Oliveros writes: "As I sit here trying to compose an article for *Source*, my mind adheres to the sounds of myself and my environment. In the distance a bulldozer is eating away a hillside while its motor is a cascade of harmonics defining the space between it and the Rock and Roll radio playing in the next room. Sounds of birds, insects, children's voices and the rustling of trees fleck this space."[17] Returning to Oliveros's essay now, I am struck by the way it bears little trace of the radical demands of her moment, one still to be heard in the ongoing sound of uprising. She attuned herself to the meditative practice of listening to "myself and my environment." Where does one end and the other begin, and what are the limitations of each? They are marked by their own beyond, a curtilage, where one is not simply exterior to the other, as if there could be a single dividing line over which sounds tiptoe or rush in. The attention to sonic detail gives rise to questions of where the listener—self and environment—is situated, that is, along what kind of social and political threshold. What sounds do not fleck a room simply because they also cannot pierce it?

For some, listening to the recordings of the quieting of New York City streets collected by researchers in mid-April, six weeks before the city was to break out into massive protest, it was as if "the sound of the pandemic" itself had been captured.[18] Such an observation, made by the scientific researcher with an ear for objectivity, positions the microphone—a mechanical ear—as an objective witness that receives what human ears cannot. In the researchers' recording of and commentary on the city's quieting, there was more than one clamorous and perhaps unrecordable omission. The sense that the recording captures the sound of the pandemic itself fails to recognize what the sensor, sequestered and sheltered-in-place, cannot hear: the unbearable sounds of lost life on the other side of a threshold, the *cordon sanitaire*.

The recordings of the body camera that captured McClain's last words are so horrific precisely in the way that the microphone also crossed a threshold, making his plea public and disseminated. The body-camera recording of McClain captured not only death, but also the authorities' unhearing. Officials believe that the body camera, when necessary, will controvert the police eye and ear before a neutral judiciary. At best these recordings are twisted through description to validate the police narrative. At worst, it does not matter what the camera ear and eye present. Nor can the fall in decibel level recorded on April 18, 2020, in itself, tell us that the quieting of the city, its clearing out, was existential in proportion, a preparation for an astonishing articulation of togetherness.

During the early days of quarantine across American cities, the 7:00 p.m. shout out began, an echo from Italy where, during quarantine in March 2020, people took to terraces to sing and play music.[19] In New York City, people leaned out their windows or went to their stoops and doorways to clap and make noise during the hour that medical workers were leaving their shift and being bussed across town to their hotels. While sheltering in place, I wrote on April 27, 2020:

> Tonight's shout out in the East Village was for the ER doctor who committed suicide. It was cold yet still a good turnout. On Avenue A, one of the churches rings its bells, and tonight was the second night that a horn and a siren played Marco Polo with each other across the neighborhood. As the days go on, it becomes possible to attach faces to sounds, and the young person with a snare drum on a fire escape becomes more skilled at a drum roll.

In listening, my mind came up against these emotionally distant truths, unable to compass them. In my walks, I often took my phone with me, using it as a recorder, but could not capture what I was hearing and feeling, in part because what I was hearing was quiet, or the new resonances of emptied out spaces that only made sense to me when held up to or set against other sonic memories. I felt that if I could write it, I would better remember this sound of quieting that I knew would never be there again. For Woolf, Tennyson had answered the call and "set this humming noise to words."[20]

I will never be able to reproduce the sensation, the overwhelming feeling, of what it was to walk two blocks in late May 2020 in Brooklyn into the center of protest for George Floyd—I tremble, even remembering the sound—and hear hundreds or perhaps thousands of people, after having been separated for two months, gathered and chanting in rhythmic unison, their voices reverberating against Barclays Center. Its threshold space of entryway had suddenly become an amphitheater, its architectural flourish—a metal awning—repurposed for its reverberant potential. For us, the fear of contact had suddenly washed away simply because it was now politically impossible to stay separated.

The heart, its diastole and systole, is the fundamental rhythm of body, emitting from the inside a low sound difficult to hear except through auscultation. According to literary theorist Stephen Best (2004), in "The Right to Privacy" legal scholars Samuel D. Warren and Louis D. Brandeis find grounds in common law for "the right to be let alone," and with it, a right to quiet certain kinds of noise in the outside world understood as a violation of privacy.[21] This common law right, Best has shown, is deeply entangled in American legal code with the poetics of the Fugitive Slave Act (1850), which enforced the capture of runaway slaves and presents a foundational understanding of personhood: it cannot coincide with property (the slave, not being "person," was property). "The violation of personality can be prevented by surrounding the personality with a buffering space of 'solitude and privacy' to insulate emotions and sensations from the world," wrote one legal commentator of the right to privacy.[22] In the moment the passerby questioned McClain's movements, followed by the police attacking this acoustical buffering space or self-curtilage created by headphones, they divested McClain of personhood and privacy insofar as they are contiguous with the right to quiet. Cultural critic Kevin Quashie suggests of the demand for Black publicness that quiet instead originates in "the sovereignty of the interior."[23] As the body cameras of the police attacking McClain went blank, they captured a perverse soundtrack of an authoritarian outside that insisted upon its absolute right to command the rhythm of the world. This command is to be found in one of the probable causes for "Stop and Frisk," or the practice of frisking Black and brown youth in New York City: "furtive movements." If your skin is a certain color and you move in a way that seems strange or "off" to the outside, you must submit to being frisked.

In thinking of this commanding rhythm, recall that a police officer forcibly stopped and yelled at Michael Brown in Ferguson, Missouri, because he was standing in the middle of the street. The police car moved in one rhythm, and Michael Brown walked in another. The officer lethally demanded that Brown move in a different time. But if someone is in the middle of the street, why not wonder if that person needs help? The first question is not "are you okay?" In such a question, outside comes in and it requires a moment of listening. When someone called the police on Elijah McClain, the question was, who is the outsider and why has he come in?

For the Marxist theorist Louis Althusser, the police hail—"Hey, you there!"—and its twin in response, turning around to stop, are a bare quantum tying the legal subject to subjectivation.[24] For Althusser, there is an inventiveness to the moment of the hail; something is created that was not there before. But it is crucial that the scene of call and response also exists, for Althusser, within a structure capable of redress. I can question why you question me, or if I am wrongfully arrested, I can count on the fact that I may demand an explanation and adjudication later. For Frantz Fanon, the postcolonial psychologist who theorized a similar scene in his 1952 *Black Skin, White Masks*, the call brings into being the racialized subject. "Look! A Negro!" has a particular charge of being triangulated. It is not directed at the Black body, who comes into being as the object of the call rather than a subject of listening and response.[25] The police gave McClain no possibility of response (nor to Breonna Taylor, when the police sprayed her home with bullets after a "no knock warning" raid). *You should comply when the police command you*, people often say. But to imagine such a scene is to imagine oneself in a peculiar sort of way, as both the addressee (the compliant object) and the addressor (a reasonable subject).

In the structure that Althusser takes for granted—in some ways imagining a body without skin—response and redress are a priori unavailable to the Black subject, who has been pulled away into some other scene before there can even be a call. For Fanon, this scene is also inventive to the extent that it repeats over and over again, the Black body being historically re-instantiated, one body echoing others that came before it. Fanon wonders how it can become possible to speak in the first person amongst these echoes, and he feuds across his writings with a series of quotations, citations, and vocal addresses that haunt him.

A related refrain across African-American thought and letters is the thought of the chasm between white American's hearing (which is passive) and listening (which is active, but neither neutral nor given). A foundational moment of this thought appears in W. E. B. Du Bois's *The Souls of Black Folk* (1903) when he describes his hope for his book: "And now what I have briefly sketched in large outline let me on coming pages tell again in many ways, with loving emphasis and deeper detail, that men may listen to the striving in the souls of black folk."[26] He concludes his book with a plea (from *appeler*, "to call," but also "to cry out"): "Hear my cry, O God the Reader; vouchsafe that this my book fall not still-born into the world wilderness." He is uncertain that his reader has received the possibility of the first demand, also a hope for the future that wraps itself in the anxiety of being dashed: "that men may listen."[27]

∽

The existence of a selective and hegemonic field of audition is evidenced by the fact that, in February 2018, Donald Trump held a "listening session" at the White House for survivors of a school shooting in Florida. A photo close-up of the notes he held in his hand reveals five reminders, bullet points, to guide his session. Of the five, it was the final note-to-self that was the most intolerable: "I hear you."[28] It was not a reminder to sympathize, but rather a reminder to utter the words used by the sympathetic. *I hear you* is a common phrase whose simple utterance can be healing and bear significant weight in its ability to open a space for speaking. When it happens, there is an opening—one that is nearly physical in dimension—for a vibration between two people. Suddenly, business as usual is suspended, and the sense that what we were meant to do, by some external pressure, must pause in the face of this weight. It can be heavy, almost atmospheric, and if it is passed over, damage to relation is done and may be irreparable. A clearing, this space orients the spatiotemporal sense that something, once there, has left and for how long, we do not know.

Of course, the word *clearing* is highly oxymoronic in the time of pandemic, since we say an infection has "cleared up." The idiomatic expression "all clear" indicates a dissipation of threat and the way opened for safe movement. There are also imperial associations of deforestation and extraction, and still more associations in the history of philosophy and literature, from Martin Heidegger's 1971 *On the Way to Language* to Toni Morrison's 1984 *Beloved*, which I cannot touch on here. But one bears mentioning, and that is the semantic family of the Greek word, *dechomai*, or to admit and let in, also to lend an ear to. Among its semantic family are *chora* and chorus but also *choreo*, from which the English language derives choreography, or "to make room for another by withdrawing."[29]

One can understand this withdrawal in terms of a transformation of hearing into listening, as did the essayist Roland Barthes, who once described the distinction in nearly evolutionary terms. Human beings, he argues, share with other creatures the sense of hearing. Beyond the sense of hearing, human beings also share with animals listening, which Barthes calls a "psychological act," the first order being "alert," listening for prey or for the lover. The second order is a threshold between human animal: "deciphering; what the ear tries to intercept are signs."[30] For Barthes, it is here that the human begins (Barthes does not consider deafness or even a spectrum of hearing that might be nonlocalized in the ears). In a third order of listening, the human becomes modern: "such listening is supposed to develop in an intersubjective space where 'I am listening' also means 'listen to me'; what it seizes upon—in order to transform and restore to the endless interplay of transference—is a general 'signifying' no longer conceivable without the determination of the unconscious."[31]

There is something of this passage from hearing to listening that is delimited by the terms of psychoanalysis, or by the kind of *subject*—anonymous and implicitly universal—that psychoanalysis proposes. One wonders if the intersubjectivity he describes can be achieved (and, indeed, it is positioned as an achievement) beyond the purview of psychoanalysis and the everyday transferences it annotates and organizes. What are the limitations of transference in regard to listening?

The limitations begin to pinch the expression *I hear you*, which idiomatically marks the intersubjective movement of listening. We can think of the expression in terms of "fake it until you make it." Perhaps if you say it enough times, the intersubjective will manifest. When uttered by Trump before the survivors of horrific violence the expression became hollow in the truest sense of the word. It did not even meet the basic requirement for the kind of performativity that poet and critic Denise Riley (2005) attributes to so many of our redundant phrases, which she argues are guided by "impersonal passion."[32] Impersonal passion belongs to a lyric subjectivity where language, through the power of address, animates and brings into existence something that was not there before. These forms of language, particularly idioms, have the power to incarnate what they refer to precisely because the words themselves "are saturated in strong affect."[33] *I hear you* is one such idiom: it clears a space for sympathy and the voice of the other by virtue of being stated. That space can be momentary and may lead to no action, but it has nonetheless been cleared. I do not give a precise reply to what the other says; I just say *I hear you* and make room for the other by withdrawing.

In thinking of this relay space between hearing and listening, but also address and addressee, I am pulled back to the way the body-camera audio of the last words and mortal encounter of Elijah McClain had existed for over a year before being widely heard. The words were laying, as Du Bois might say, stillborn in the world wilderness. To whom were those recordings addressed? Posed differently, who hears? By this second question, I do not mean to ask *what* person can and does press play, but *who*, as in the auditory subject position or addressee. McClain had an addressee in the moments leading up to his death—he spoke to the police—but that address exceeded that space and time by virtue of having been recorded.

In the days following his murder, officials surely listened to the audio, but either they could not hear or wished to suppress the audio's significance, refusing to release the recordings to the public. It sat, in a kind of indisposed state, calling out but unheard, waiting to make contact with the addressee in a time become both elliptical and proleptic: a lyric temporality. In the moments leading up to his death, McClain's physical and auditory self made violent contact with the environment. The contact produced an acoustics that exceeds the audio document that inscribes and testifies to it.

∼

McClain's family has spoken of the gratification of hearing his name chanted now, so many months later, on the heels of mass demonstrations for justice for Floyd. The two names touch along the axis of last words. In the rhythmic chant, *say his name*, an airy thread is drawn out between different places and times, heard within what literary critic Carter Mathes might call an "acoustics of unfreedom."[34] When adequately heard or registered, these acoustics challenge "the presumption of realism in American historical documentation and memory construction." The sounds of names and the chant, which are caught between multiple selves and moments, become a "narrative struggle," that is, a struggle over the meaning of time and to say, this, here, and now cannot be severed from that, then, and there.

This narrative struggle and its forms of recitation exist at the limits of my commitment to a certain kind of subject. When Freud wrote in *Beyond the Pleasure Principle* (1920) of postwar shell shock and the compulsion to repeat traumatic experiences, he described the structure of *Nachträglichkeit*, commonly translated as "afterwardsness" but in this case perhaps better understood more literally as "after-the-eventness."[35] His essential point was that it takes something happening again to elicit the traumatic registers of the first event. But Freud's modernist theory of the subject is autotelic. It is purely developmental and self-reflexive, an inner subject referencing a *fantasy* of the outside. Freud failed to account for the rhythmic structure of a repressive state in its contact with political life. For Freud, there is ultimately the promise of full "remembrance" in the face of repetition. But in political life, it takes another event to ask why there was not justice the last time. And so on. There is not only an interminable waiting for justice, but a structure where the singular, to become itself, must be tied to another singularity just outside of it.

Across the protests, there are shards of names from the past-that-is-not past, shining on handmade signs, names that demand being chanted in the present. "The city is being remade in the image and sound of liberation," I wrote in my journal, the names of the dead painted on the boarded-up windows and shouted out loud, signs posted on the bridges usually closed to feet but now overtaken by them, and the ringing of bicycle bells as they rally in the thousands to take over streets and Times Square.

As the recording of McClain's last words resurfaced against new scrutiny, they gave rise to the sensation of a connective tissue of utterances, of the current or murmur behind them and what it means to rehear Derrick Elliott Ollie Scott's utterance when, on May 20, 2019, he was pinned by officers in Oklahoma City and pleaded, "I can't breathe! Please! Help me! I can't breathe!" Protestors often paint the phrase across their protective face masks, which they wear during direct actions in the midst of the pandemic (the enemy of the breath is not simply the virus, but tear gas and pepper spray.) I once saw a photograph of a police officer wearing a t-shirt: "I can breathe," it said. I wondered to whom the statement was addressed. In some ways, it is a description and statement of fact. He is alive and breathing. But it is also a statement of domination: he never needs to fear his breath might be stolen. The phrase paints a still more perverse scene because it is a response—a retort—to an imagined supine body who once called (perhaps even to him), *I can't breathe*. The t-shirt's imagined dialogue is premised upon a failure in listening. It is not dialogue, for the second statement remakes the first in its image, as if *I can't breathe* were simply a descriptive statement and not a request to live.

In marches, young Black leaders at the bullhorn lead a series of chants, commanding us, across gender and race, to say collectively the names of the departed. *George Floyd. Breonna Taylor*. At times the command turns to "whose streets?" We respond "our streets!" Other times the command turns to reciting "I can't breathe." I have always held myself back with this cry, unable to understand what it would mean for me to chant it when, in fact, I can breathe. The chant *our streets* is plural and desires unity; we share a goal. *I can't breathe* is the singular; its object is identity. I cannot speak for something that only happens to Black people. I have wondered if holding myself back from recitation is part of the problem. Does it stage something irreducible about my subjectivity as it has been culturally constituted? I can consent to the utterance or not. McClain and Floyd were afforded no such right. It is literally not true when I say it. But is it right to say it when I am invited? The re-inscription of the last words is a memorial citation, but it is also a re-injury, particularly when uttered by white people. Why is this injurious speech, no doubt painful and traumatizing to some auditors, worth re-inscribing and by whom?

When I participate in chants and sonically observe, I am being a witness, which is important for white people to do precisely because many of us have no direct knowledge of this kind of loss. In chanting the phrase, I am marking it. But beyond that, it is important to reflect on the meaning of the words and on how these men—and this phrase is largely attributed to Black men—have been killed. I am not sure that I have heard of such a story involving a Black woman being choked to death by the police, though my thoughts turn to Sandra Bland, a Black woman whom the police report hanged herself in jail after she was arrested during a traffic violation. No guards were present during her death and the surveillance cameras cut out: Bland had no witness, her last words unrecorded and inaudible. Through a perverse power of imagination, I can wonder after these last words and shudder at the thought of their addressee. The phrase, as uttered by her, floats in some airy space that is even more indeterminate, more difficult to compass than that of lyric address and its murmurous current. No one can hear it. (It is this forgetting of Black women that first galvanized the chant, *Say her name*.)

I am not in a position to reflect on what it means for Black women or women of color to chant *I can't breathe*, but I can reflect on the significance of the phrase being uttered and then picked up by white people in the street. If I were to say, *I can't breathe*, I am quoting the last words, but also quoting a ubiquity, quoting the very fact of their repetition and iteration. If I were to say it, I would require as a condition (for my own psychological comfort) the kind of distance afforded by the stylistic fact of citation and quotation, or what is known in literary studies as "reported speech" (I am not saying it but quoting someone else).

Perhaps some white people, especially those who never stand to be racialized, do actually feel themselves to be shouting a phrase that *could* come to them where they to be confronted with an authority potent enough. That is a powerful fantasy, and it is one that relates to a situation that historian and philosopher Saidiya Hartman (1997) treats as being at the heart of the psychic economy of white abolition in the nineteenth century. Looking across journals and other historic documents, Hartman found the reiteration of a sentiment of white abolitionists when confronted with the spectacle of the suffering body of the enslaved person. *What if that were me? What if that were my family?* These rhetorical questions, Hartman suggests, rest upon a commodity-form where the enslaved person is "fungible," that is, continually replaceable. In feeling for the other, I have stood in the other's place; I am only feeling for myself and have bypassed the place of the other.[36]

There are still more rhetorical dimensions and transferences of the chant. It is as if I say, *it is not me who says this, but someone else*. It is an instance of language trying to separate the speaker from the violence. It is "hard to state an excluded middle," Riley writes, "difficult to balance inside a pressing thought and not tilt and collapse onto one side or another, either the self-importance of guilt or the insouciance of self-exoneration."[37] This tilting and collapsing are not merely represented in forms of language, she continues, but incarnated by them, for example in the persuasive rhetorical question, "why me?" Such questions do not really seek an answer nor do they have an addressee, and their strength lies in "the ardor of utterance itself," of overhearing ourselves cry out.[38] Riley wonders if the same kind of affective valence of the refused middle—neither guilt nor exoneration—can also be found in the slogan that appeared on protest banners in the wake of the US invasion of Iraq and Afghanistan: *not in my name*, in the singular, or *not in our name*, in the plural. Such a phrase "flourishes" precisely because it incarnates "their askers' dilemmas of wanting to be effective yet also sensing that they are not," being both present and "helpless."[39]

Not in my name censures oneself from the scene of invasion. It is perhaps too easy, carrying too great a sense of what language can actually do. Uttering the phrase does not separate me from the invasion. With *I can't breathe*, the opposite occurs, and I insert myself into a violence from which I was absent and will continue to be absent. Any chant reminds us, but also plays on roles of inclusion/exclusion and the work of fantasy. It is dangerous to cut myself off (*not my president!*) and an equally dangerous fantasy to imagine that I am with the other who was killed. Perhaps the chant is important precisely because it makes a space for this excluded middle, neither guilt nor exoneration. It is also important to the extent that *I can't breathe* is also a citation, a form of memory.

George Floyd uttered his dying words in a moment when breath has become a worrisome and politicized sign of contagion and fear. "Momma, momma," he uttered, calling to his deceased mother. Neither a murmur to himself nor a statement to his murderer, the utterance was a "sacred invocation" caught somewhere between inside and outside, without a stable, worldly addressee.[40] In repeating *I can't breathe*, perhaps what I am saying is, *I am listening*. All of this has to do with the claim, or what it means to claim that I am listening. It does not constitute a subject per se, since the classical grammatical form—subject, verb, object—is undermined and its hermeneutic circle unclosed. I am not identifying, which is to appropriate the subject positions of the ones who are dying.

I am thinking back to the month of April in 2020, when the hospitals in New York City had reached capacity, and a colleague, also a psychoanalyst, responded to a call for a social worker willing to conduct volunteer palliative care in a hospital. Her job was to hold a tablet up to the faces of the dying, those whose loved ones wished to see them and hear their last words. "There has to be someone," she wrote of the experience.[41] Holding the electronic device, she had become a medium for dying words and looks. I wrote in my journal about how the *someone* who will listen is not a first-person subject position, but empty in its waiting.

For me to chant *I can't breathe* is to occupy that space, to listen to people who have said these words. I listen not as a subject, but as "someone," also an echo chamber or clearing. In the echo, the phrase's subject (the first-person singular) and its imputed source (a single person) continue to be re-anonymized by the names and voices of others. The repetition amongst these men is re-politicized the moment it is seized by the chorus. It becomes in that moment a demand by the collective for the right for Black people to live. And it has to be uttered every day until it is true. Unlike other slogans, this form of language does not incarnate: it listens. Are there limitations to this act of listening? In chanting, we are listening to the voices of the dead, but in the moment of encountering the stranger, it demands another form of listening, and something, perhaps, in excess. Do I have more in my power than to record and report?

By the sixteenth day of protest, New York City had become a place where one could simply wander around until finding a demonstration. They were multiple, decentralized, and convergent. Wandering to Washington Square Park, I listened to a group of young organizers speak in an empty fountain, which had not yet been filled (public water seen as a pandemic hazard). Instead, the empty fountain had become a place of amplification. The event was already nearing its end when I arrived, and I do not know whether they had marched or convened there, or a mixture of both. Some people were in the park relaxing, and listening to the organizers and chants could be casual rather than purposive.

In the fountain (since blocked by police gates), the group of young black and Latinx activists each took turns speaking into a bullhorn. The crowd hushed in order to receive a voice of a Black woman, which the device—designed for the male register of the voice—could not strongly carry. She asked if she could please pray over us, which slowly became an act of spoken word. She spoke of the police blaspheming against God in a series of poetic verses that culminated in the cry, *If God had a pistol, he would blast-for-me*, a subtle turning of the sound of the word. The crowd responded uproariously.

The space of the fountain had been cleared for its mundane purpose to make way not for the "Voice," a master signifier that is, in principle, soundless and abstract, but a chorus. It was surrounded by the kind of gathering that is now largely forbidden. A young man took to the bullhorn, educating listeners gathered around him of the fact that the mayor is selling public housing to a private developer and in the midst of an affordable housing crisis. He spoke of his grandmother's daily words to him as she watches him walk out of the apartment to the elevator, *Be safe*. He receives those words in a curtilage, their echo wrapping arms around him. "When I see a police car . . . my heart starts beating faster," he shouted. "I'm going to say that again. My heart starts beating faster!"

They were each speaking from a radical tradition demanding that we listen. They were some of the most clarifying voices I have heard in a long time. Another young man addressed still more concretely the vulnerable threshold between inside and outside:

> Little by little they're talking about, "oh, we're going to reopen." They're talking about Phase 1, Phase 2. . . . But we can't allow that to happen. Because we know the people united will never be defeated! [the phrase then folded into a collective chant]. . . . The brain and the nervous system wants to hold on to the past. It doesn't want to go into the unknown. It's afraid to change because it doesn't know what's going to happen. Right now, we are in the unknown. We got to embrace the unknown and reprogram our minds, because they try to control our minds, but they can never control our spirits [applause and a police helicopter hovering over the scene]. Right now, our spirits are speaking loud. That's our intuition. We had an opportunity to go within, with this COVID situation happening. It allowed us to really face that

mirror, whether we're looking at a mirror or looking at a mirror from the inside. We are realizing who we truly are, and we are meant to be sharing resources. We are meant to be together as a community. That's right, momma. You feel the energy and I feel it, too! [applause and cheering]. . . . So right now, what I would like everyone to do, we can just close our eyes for a few moments and take a few collective breaths for those that cannot breathe anymore, to be grateful to our planet as a source of life that connects us all.

Notes

1. This essay was originally published in different form in Julie Beth Napolin, "Outside In: Choreography and Chorus in the Time of Pandemic and Protest," *Sociologica* 14, no. 2 (2020): 41–45. Thanks to the editors, Ester Cois, Naomi Waltham-Smith, and Jessica Feldman. This essay owes a great debt to David Copenhafer, whose sensitive responses were central to revising and developing it.

2. See Claire Lampen, "What We Know about the Killing of Elijah McClain," *Cut*, August 11, 2020, accessed May 8, 2022, https://www.thecut.com/2020/08/the-killing-of-elijah-mcclain-everything-we-know.html.

3. "Death of Elijah McClain," *Wikipedia*, revision from February 10, 2021, accessed May 8, 2022, https://en.wikipedia.org/w/index.php?title=Death_of_Elijah_McClain&oldid=1005940768.

4. TRT World Now, "Protesters in Aurora Play Violin for Elijah McClain." *YouTube*, June 28, 2020, https://www.youtube.com/watch?v=BVKTDpRmBt4.

5. In 2013, three Black women (Alicia Garza, Patrisse Cullors, and Opal Tometi) founded Black Lives Matter.

6. During the trial of Chauvin in 2021, video analysis showed the time to be nine and a half minutes.

7. Quoctrung Bul and Emily Badger, "The Coronavirus Quieted City Noise," *New York Times*, May 22, 2020, accessed May 8, 2022, https://www.nytimes.com/interactive/2020/05/22/upshot/coronavirus-quiet-city-noise.html.

8. Thank you to Todd Barnes.

9. Diallo Oumy (@DialloOumy4), "Paris, Place de la République le 13/06/2020 [. . .]," *Twitter*, June 13, 2020, accessed May 8, 2022, https://twitter.com/DialloOumy4/status/1271831489915879428?s=20.

10. Nkem (@Vincredible_), "Africans Walking through the Deserted Streets of Italy, Racism Free," *Twitter*, March 11, 2020, accessed May 8, 2022, https://twitter.com/Vincredible__/status/1237832993806393344?s=20.

11. When I first published a version of this essay, I still had no direct experience of COVID-19. Later, I contracted it and recovered. I maintain the original tense here because, as aleatory, the essay is caught between temporalities, both retrospective and anticipatory.

12. Virginia Woolf, *A Room of One's Own*, annotated ed. (New York: Harcourt, 2005), 12.

13. Julie Beth Napolin, *The Fact of Resonance: Modernist Acoustics and Narrative Form* (New York: Fordham University Press, 2020), 195.

14. Napolin, *Fact*, 83 and 264n45.

15. For the common law definition of curtilage, see "Curtilage Law and Legal Definition," *USLegal*, accessed February 19, 2021, https://definitions.uslegal.com/c/curtilage. In *Florida v. Jardines*, the court held that the warrantless search of the front porch of the Jardines's home "was a 'search' within the meaning of the Fourth Amendment," the porch also defined as a curtilage and therefore part of the home. See Florida v. Jardines, 569 U.S. 1 (2013), https://www.law.cornell.edu/supct/pdf/11-564.pdf. Watching and listening to the arrest unfold on Twitter, an incorrect but related word rang in my ears before locating the verbatim opinion: codicil. Thinking about it now (in revision), "codicil" suggests the act of writing (we add a codicil to a legal document, such as an addendum to a will).

16. See "Curtilage Law."

17. Pauline Oliveros, "Some Sound Observations," in Christoph Cox and Daniel Warner, eds., *Audio Culture: Readings in Modern Music* (New York: Continuum, 2004), 102.

18. Bul and Badger, "Coronavirus."

19. Pamela Z (@pamelazed), "Someone started circulating a message yesterday calling for everyone in Italy to take instruments to their windows at 6 PM and play music. This is me singing Vissi d'arte from my terrace [. . .]," *Instagram*, March 14, 2020, accessed May 8, 2022, https://www.instagram.com/p/B9tn94sIbin/?igshid=1xj15tg5pe5c0.

20. Woolf, *A Room of One's Own*, 12.

21. Cited in Stephen Best, *The Fugitive's Properties: Law and the Poetics of Possession* (Chicago: University of Chicago Press, 2004), 47.

22. Best, *Fugitive's Properties*, 51

23. Kevin Quashie, *The Sovereignty of Quiet: Beyond Resistance in Black Culture* (New Brunswick: Rutgers University Press, 2012), 11–26.

24. Louis Althusser, "Ideology and Ideological State Apparatuses," in Julie Rivkin and Michael Ryan, ed., *Literary Theory: An Anthology*, 2nd ed. (Malden: Blackwell, 2004), 693–702.

25. I describe the acoustics of this scene as the "echo of the object" in Napolin, *Fact*, 67–102. As I argue there, Fanon is a disavowed source of Althusser's theory.

26. W. E. B. Du Bois, *The Souls of Black Folk*, Project Gutenberg, 2008, accessed May 8, 2022, https://www.gutenberg.org/files/408/408-h/408-h.htm.

27. Du Bois, *The Souls of Black Folk*.

28. For Kaster's photo, see Kyle Griffin (@kylegriffin1), "This AP photo shows more of what's on Trump's notes," *Twitter*, February 21, 2018, accessed May 8, 2022, https://twitter.com/kylegriffin1/status/966482719692685312.

29. John Llewelyn, as cited in Napolin, *Fact*, 4. For a discussion of *dechomai*, see Napolin, *Fact*, 4, 154–55 and 240n3. For a discussion of *chora*, see Julia Kristeva *Revolution in Poetic Language*, trans. Margaret Walker (New York: Columbia University Press, 1984).

30. Roland Barthes, *The Responsibility of Forms*, trans. Richard Howard (Berkeley: University of California Press, 1991), 245.

31. Barthes, *The Responsibility of Forms*, 246.

32. Denise Riley, *Impersonal Passion* (Durham: Duke University Press, 2005).

33. Riley, *Impersonal Passion*, 69.

34. Carter Mathes, *Imagine the Sound: Experimental African American Literature after Civil Rights* (Minneapolis: University of Minnesota Press, 2015), 10.

35. Sigmund Freud, *Beyond the Pleasure Principle*, trans. James Strachey, ed. Peter Gay. New York: Norton, 1961.

36. Saidiya Hartman, *Scenes of Subjection: Terror, Slavery, and Self-Making in Nineteenth-Century America* (New York: Oxford University Press, 1997).

37. Denise Riley, *Words of Selves: Identification, Irony, Solidarity* (Stanford: Stanford University Press, 2000), 69.

38. Riley, *Words of Selves*, 70.

39. John Llewelyn, as cited in Napolin, *Fact*, 4.

40. Lonnae O'Neal, "George Floyd's Mother Was Not There, but He Used Her as a Sacred Invocation," *Undefeated*, May 28, 2020, accessed May 8, 2022, https://theundefeated.com/features/george-floyds-death-mother-was-not-there-but-he-used-her-as-a-sacred-invocation.

41. Jamieson Webster, "End Notes: What Palliative Care Looks Like in a Pandemic," *New York Review of Books*, April 24, 2020, accessed May 8, 2022, https://www.nybooks.com/daily/2020/04/24/end-notes-what-palliative-care-looks-like-in-a-pandemic.

References

Althusser, Louis. "Ideology and Ideological State Apparatuses." In *Literary Theory: An Anthology*, 2nd ed., edited by Julie Rivkin and Michael Ryan, 693–702. Malden: Blackwell, 2004.

Barthes, Roland. *The Responsibility of Forms*. Translated by Richard Howard. Berkeley: University of California Press, 1991.

Best, Stephen. *The Fugitive's Properties: Law and the Poetics of Possession*. Chicago: University of Chicago Press, 2004.

Bul, Quoctrung, and Emily Badger. "The Coronavirus Quieted City Noise," *New York Times*, May 22, 2020. Accessed May 8, 2022, https://www.nytimes.com/interactive/2020/05/22/upshot/coronavirus-quiet-city-noise.html.

"Curtilage Law and Legal Definition." *USLegal*. Accessed February 19, 2021, https://definitions.uslegal.com/c/curtilage.

"Death of Elijah McClain." *Wikipedia*, revision from February 10, 2021. Accessed May 8, 2022, https://en.wikipedia.org/w/index.php?title=Death_of_Elijah_McClain&oldid=1005940768.

Du Bois, W. E. B. *The Souls of Black Folk*. Project Gutenberg, 2008. Accessed May 8, 2022. https://www.gutenberg.org/files/408/408-h/408-h.htm.

Florida v. Jardines, 569 U.S. 1 (2013), https://www.law.cornell.edu/supct/pdf/11-564.pdf.

Freud, Sigmund. *Beyond the Pleasure Principle*. Translated by James Strachey. Edited by Peter Gay. New York: Norton, 1961.

Griffin, Kyle (@kylegriffin1). "This AP photo shows more of what's on Trump's notes," *Twitter*, February 21, 2018. Accessed May 8, 2022. https://twitter.com/kylegriffin1/status/966482719692685312.

Hartman, Saidiya. *Scenes of Subjection: Terror, Slavery, and Self-Making in Nineteenth-Century America*. New York: Oxford University Press, 1997.

Kristeva, Julia. *Revolution in Poetic Language*. Translated by Margaret Walker. New York: Columbia University Press, 1984.

Lampen, Claire. "What We Know about the Killing of Elijah McClain." *Cut*, August 11, 2020. Accessed May 8, 2022. https://www.thecut.com/2020/08/the-killing-of-elijah-mcclain-everything-we-know.html.

Mathes, Carter. *Imagine the Sound: Experimental African American Literature after Civil Rights*. Minneapolis: University of Minnesota Press, 2015.

Napolin, Julie Beth. *The Fact of Resonance: Modernist Acoustics and Narrative Form*. New York: Fordham University Press, 2020.

Napolin, Julie Beth. "Outside In: Choreography and Chorus in the Time of Pandemic and Protest." *Sociologica* 14, no. 2 (2020): 41–45.

Nkem (@Vincredible_). "Africans Walking through the Deserted Streets of Italy, Racism Free." *Twitter*, March 11, 2020. Accessed May 8, 2022. https://twitter.com/Vincredible__/status/1237832993806393344?s=20.

Oliveros, Pauline. "Some Sound Observations." In *Audio Culture: Readings in Modern Music*, edited by Christoph Cox and Daniel Warner, 102–6. New York: Continuum, 2004.

O'Neal, Lonnae. "George Floyd's Mother Was Not There, but He Used Her as a Sacred Invocation." *Undefeated*, May 28, 2020. Accessed May 8, 2022. https://theundefeated.com/features/george-floyds-death-mother-was-not-there-but-he-used-her-as-a-sacred-invocation.

Oumy, Diallo (@DialloOumy4). "Paris, Place de la République le 13/06/2020 [. . .]." *Twitter*, June 13, 2020, accessed May 8, 2022, https://twitter.com/DialloOumy4/status/1271831499915879428?s=20.

Pamela Z (@pamelazed). "Someone started circulating a message yesterday calling for everyone in Italy to take instruments to their windows at 6 PM and play music. This is me singing Vissi d'arte from my terrace [. . .]." *Instagram*, March 14, 2020. Accessed May 8, 2022. https://www.instagram.com/p/B9tn94sIbin/?igshid=1xj15tg5pe5c0.

Quashie, Kevin. *The Sovereignty of Quiet: Beyond Resistance in Black Culture*. New Brunswick: Rutgers University Press, 2012.

Riley, Denise. *Impersonal Passion*. Durham: Duke University Press, 2005.

Riley, Denise. *Words of Selves: Identification, Irony, Solidarity*. Stanford: Stanford University Press, 2000.

TRT World Now. "Protesters in Aurora Play Violin for Elijah McClain." *YouTube*, June 28, 2020. https://www.youtube.com/watch?v=BVKTDpRmBt4.

Webster, Jamieson. "End Notes: What Palliative Care Looks Like in a Pandemic." *New York Review of Books*, April 24, 2020, accessed May 8, 2022, https://www.nybooks.com/daily/2020/04/24/end-notes-what-palliative-care-looks-like-in-a-pandemic.

Woolf, Virginia. *A Room of One's Own*, annotated ed. New York: Harcourt Inc., 2005. First published in 1929.

Afterword

Sounding Silence, Sounding Thought

KRZYSZTOF ZIAREK

It is October 14, 2022, and I take a short break from sessions at the 2022 Society for Phenomenology and Existential Philosophy meeting in College Station, TX, to try to listen to the announced premiere of Clara Iannotta's[1] new work "where the dark earth bends," which is to open the livestream of the SWR Symphonieorchester's concert at the 2022 Donaueschingen Musiktage. In my hotel room, I open my old MacBook Air and navigate to the SWR Donaueschingen web page only to find out, through a note added on the page, that there has been a last-minute program change. Soon the announcer appears on the stage and tells the audience that both Iannotta and the live electronics performer have become mildly ill with COVID-19 and that Weston Olencki and Mattie Barber, the two trombonists performing as RAGE Thormbones, who were to take part in the premiere of Iannotta's composition, will instead present their own work "zero said in a low voice." She also adds that, unlike in Iannotta's composition announced on the program, all the sounds in this piece will be produced by the instruments, with no live electronics. Even if little disappointed, I am intrigued by the title of the "replacement" work: "zero said in a low voice." Is zero here equivalent to "nothing being said?" The "low voice" of the muted trombones, held extremely close to the microphones, emerges from silence to produce a rumbling sound-noise, intermittently submerged again in silence.[2] The very low voice, even if amplified by mics, gets overlaid with frequent coughing from the audience, often louder than the music itself. Silence-sound threshold extended, with further timely and aleatoric, "spontaneously" timed, reminders that the pandemic is still with us, even if more subdued. Like the echoes of involuntary bodily responses to viruses and to violence, resonant through parts of this collection, and of less immediately audible responses to the viral violence of what Bernard Stiegler labels contemporary "digital technical system."[3]

I remember reading Iannotta describing her composition as coming from her need to "sound" what her bodily experience cannot render directly into words, state in language. The composition that was to be premiered at the 2022 Donaueschingen Musiktage festival is the second composition that reflects Iannotta's recent experience with illness, a lengthy process of various forms of radiation and convalescence. In the program note to "where the dark earth bends," Iannotta explains:

> My music has always been an intimate investigation of the self. Sound has the power to reach depths which words cannot; it taught me who I was; and who I was becoming.
>
> In 2020, I got sick, and I was forced to change. Instead of composition feeling like a sometimes difficult, but focused, process of investigation, I felt lost. I know that I cannot write the same music I used to, but I don't know who I am yet or what my music will be. where the dark earth bends is about everything and nothing. It gathers scraps from somewhere in my future, beyond the curve of what I know. Reaching out of sight, I've collected possibilities that might be mine, or might be someone else's, digging for a harvest that makes no sense.[4]

As the Radio France concert host indicated before the September 2022 premier of Iannotta's previous orchestral work, "darker stems," that piece resonates the noises and sounds of radiation machines in response to what Iannotta describes as irrevocably altered circumstances of life and composition.[5]

Does music ever "say" anything, or as in the RAGE Thormbones' composition, there is "zero said"? Yet the voice is there, whether instrumental, electronic, harmonious or dissonant, low or high. The voice of music, never simply human nor nonhuman. Yet how does this voice, and more broadly sound, come to be heard, and what is heard in it, apart from literally vocal parts, if they contain sequences of linguistically meaningful expressions? Zero said: no information, no meaningful utterance, no interpretable signs, just low rumbling voice? So low that sometimes it seems to be below the threshold of human hearing. And yet it registers and resonates, and it notes something that is not directly inscribed through musical notation and which nonetheless allows the music to "speak," even if there is "zero said." My preferred way of naming this complex node briefly outlined above is the German term *Stimmung*, specifically in the resonance this word is given by Heidegger to transform our sense of language and the role it takes in opening the possibility of what, adapting Hölderlin, Heidegger calls "poetic dwelling." *Stimmung* comes from *Stimme* (voice), with the verb *stimmen* meaning "to tune, to attune, to pitch, to vote," but also "to be right or correct." *Stimmung* can refer to mood, sentiment, atmosphere, tuning, pitch, tendency, and trend. In Heidegger's inflection, it carries primarily the sense of tonality and attuning, with the emphasis given to the manner in which such toning disposes, inclines, and emplaces, lending or giving voice in the process. *Stimmung* thus names the disposition and the attuning of a complex relatedness, which enfolds silence and sound, voice and noise, meaning and melody, bodily and mental resonances. *Stimmung* is always more than "human," while calling for hearing and molding the listening it allows and the thinking it entails.

As Heidegger playfully suggests through the title of his published 1951 lecture course *Was heisst Denken*?: it is not only "what is called thinking" but also rather "what calls thinking," already calling it forth while calling for it. Calling forth thinking for it to be in tune, to let itself be disposed and attuned, so that it not only can listen but also hear. Hear even, or perhaps above all, what transpires when there is "zero said." For *while* zero is being said, this "saying" puts being/beings in the tune, beyond the purported division between the sensible and the intelligible, body and mind, place and time, etc. The spatio-temporal "site" indicated by *while* is pivotal here. It marks the patient openness to how this while unfolds, what it actuates, and how it disposes, even beyond the threshold of direct influence or perception, what kind of resonance or response it calls forth. In its oscillation between the adverbial and the nominal, *while* frees from the conceptual comfort of artificial divisions into nouns and verbs and the corresponding distinctions between entities and their temporal being, between things or objects and their "histories," between what "is" and what "becomes." *Stimmung* describes this complex traversal, underscoring the fact that what matters most is not the call nor the outcome but the undergoing itself. Heidegger calls attention to this undergoing by using the adverb *unterwegs* (under way, on the way, on the go). It is never merely "the way"—its figuration, understanding, or grasp—that is at stake but instead the whole thinking response in its irreducibly singular "under way." Not losing sight of any of its elements or dimensions, its silences, sounds, or noises, while staying attentive to its spatio-temporal singular, i.e., its "while," and while knowing that what remains, what resonates later does not quite repeat or retain what took place. Zero said yet so much heard, while listening. And open to the possibility of having misheard. The complex jointures of such tonality (*Stimmung*) are poetic, or more properly, poietic, that is, having inceptual force. They are thin, membrane-like paths, irreducible to the calculus of understanding or the expression of meaning. They call for a poetic thinking, attentive to their resonance, withstanding the temptation to arrest or grasp, to cede priority to understanding over bodying experience, to collapse the inceptual momentum of the while into an image or a figure, muting it. They require a "poetic" ear, sensitive to the molding of language: not only its signification or conveyed meaning, let alone information, but also sound, rhythm, melody, what Heidegger names the *melos* of language's saying: "The saying is the mode in which the propriative event [*Ereignis*] speaks. Yet mode is meant here not so much in the sense of modus or 'kind'; it is meant in the musical sense of the *melos*, the song that says by singing."[6] At stake is attentiveness not only to how people speak language but also to how language speaks and what comes to be said beyond intention or information. No doubt Heidegger's interest in "poetic dwelling" has to do centrally with art, language, and poetry in particular, but the sense of dwelling is holistic, pertaining to how the world unfolds, in what tonality it comes to resonate, mean, arrange, empower or disempower. The *Stimmung*, the tonality conveyed musically as composition, has the force of attuning the audience specifically to the threshold, the resonant membrane between silence and sound. The membrane resonates silently into sound. Still, sound and silence are not contraries or even opposites. Inflecting Yuk Hui's account of the Daoist recursive logic of *xuan* as "oppositional continuity,"[7] one can perhaps say that silence/sound unfold a non-disjunctive, while contrastive, continuity.

Coming from the discipline of philosophy, Heidegger discerns the necessity to transform thinking, especially in the wake of calculative thought and cybernetics, which now has developed into a full-fledged informational, digital technical system. He characterizes the type of thinking that has come to dominate and regulate the world through the spread of Western techno-scientific civilization as *rechnendes Denken*: calculative thought, understood in the broad sense of counting, accounting, and reckoning, which achieves particular salience in the computational, digital makeup of contemporary reality. One might say that the tonality of the contemporary global world can be characterized as digital (ac)counting. What is given voice, what sounds loud, even if the algorithmic processing remains firmly and proprietarily "black boxed," is only what can be calculated, processed computationally, counted and accounted for, and thus, eventually profited from. Silence does not count, and yet, all the more importantly, how can we account for it without mis-translating it into pieces of information, let alone sound bites? Heidegger's answer, though in some ways already dated, especially with regard to rapidly advancing digital processing technologies, remains noteworthy.

Thinking (*Denken*) is always at issue, always *unterwegs*, in Heidegger's voluminous writings. In their course, it is given various modifiers, including: phenomenological, metaphysical, (fundamental) ontological, poetic, and meditative (*besinnliches Denken*). I want to draw attention to this last designation, which Heidegger foregrounds in the title of one of his manuscripts, *Besinnung*. The contours of such thinking are intimated by the term *Sinn*, cognate with the English "sense." What is crucial in outlining its scope but especially its tonality is that "sense" resonates both as sensible and as intelligible. *Besinnung* indicates a thinking whose path vibrates the membrane joining sense and senses, silence and sound. It is "musically" poetic, oscillating between silence and sound, meaning and rhythm, invention and repetition, shadowing the entire tonality of its while. *Besinnung* marks a counter to thought as abstraction, calculation, or de-sensed, de-sensitized, computation, which, although located in a world, sheds or mutes many aspects of worldly existence in a bid to assert, through the dominant value and the apparent "objectivity" of scientifically correct calculus, manipulative control. Eschewing the ease of abstraction, *Besinnung* "senses" and tropes in words the way that the human sensorium is underway and at work in thinking and its language. Its rigor is more difficult than scientific precision, as it is not a matter of calculation or proof but of lengthy and often improvisatory apprenticeship, always open to unsuspected openings, unmarked paths, blind or blocked—intentionally or accidentally, historically or politically—alleyways, trails, or shortcuts. Never certain, incalculable, integrally open to and endeavoring to be in tune with what remains beyond calculation. Unlike computation, its logic and rigor are not based on what is recursively known, or on established measuring standards, but instead on morphing openness and attentiveness to the unknown and the incalculable, to the ways in which such incalculability modulates the tone of thinking, giving it unexpected sense(s). Musically speaking, the rigor of such thinking is to keep in tune with the resonant membrane of silence releasing into sound, in a difficult attempt not to mute this release in words or drown it in the din of meaning. For those open to listening, its "musicality" is unmistakable, continually reverberating poetically, calling on us to re-tune our language and thought.

How can such thin line of thinking on the hinge of silence and sound matter in the political uproar of the world in the grip of various pandemics and endemics: from medical emergencies, racialized inequalities, and violence to continuing and new forms of economic exploitation, and the suffering of forced migrations, whether political, religious, or climate related? There is no facile or easy movement between artwork and politics, perhaps even less so from "zero said" to political activity, protest, or resistance. And perhaps there should not be one. Does politics—ideas and ideologies, resistance, protests, revolutions—need to be overtly or implicitly present in art, be it thematically or symbolically, or as is often the case in oppressive regimes or cultures, by way of subtle allusions, almost unspoken, as it were, hidden in plain view between the lines. Or can politics be—perhaps even has to be—resonant otherwise in art? What is the sound (or silence) of the political in art? Is this other(wise) resonance not the strongest dis-articulation of politics, and thus more political than oppositional or contestatory articulations of politics? Can attentiveness to the silence resonating into sound, while being obviously pre-political in some sense, not be the "most" political? And be so because any understanding, response, or action should remain in tune with what is calling for it? Language comes from and remains enveloped by silence; action stirs from thinking that listens, even if in many cases it appears to remain deaf instead and acts accordingly. Perhaps music provides the best literacy of silence, "poetic" and "thoughtful" in its sensing of sound and noise (think of Cage's 4'33"), keeping flexible the joint of sense to sensing. A *Besinnung* "*avant la lettre*," literally before letters, before words written or spoken.

I am writing this "afterword" almost after the pandemic, when it has likely already become endemic, the thin film separating them casting its shadow-light on this entire collection of essays. After the outburst(s) of protests have seemingly subsided, echoing in its ever-spreading wake the endemic character of racialized violence in our contemporary culture, and not allowing, one hopes, to forget or to mute their echoing. Yet the "after-word" cannot be merely posterior, simply taking place post-factum or following occurrences in a temporal sequence. "After" also marks the foreshadowing and presaging as it "takes after" the word(s)/sounds. It needs to remain in tune with the sounding words, keeping their resonance in its own words. The afterword, if genuine, does not simply get the last word but instead keeps its word, that is, keeps to words it has listened to and noted, attuning its answer. The afterword needs to be an "after-word," the hyphen marking the echoing of words in the after-words. No response without listening resonance; no sound without attentive silence. Otherwise, the silence from which any sound, word, or action issues gets no resonance, the originatively critical, decisioning and decisive membrane between silence and sound forgotten or drowned out.

The tracing of the spatio-temporal projection opening out of the artwork, of the moment/while in its momentum remains crucial. The artwork's projection opens the future instead of foreclosing it through a calculated prediction. Its resonance needs to keep being amplified in the age increasingly ruled and shaped by predictive analytics. What is called for is not the fabricated muteness of black boxing but the loud echo of silence on the verge of sound, saying zero in its low, "poetic" voice. Cueing and attuning to this morphing "momentousness" of art may be what opens us most deeply and radically onto the (possible) response. "Opening" here is projected in the sense of transformation and inception. Heidegger calls this transformative release the highest acting before any deed or effect. "Thinking does not become action [*Aktion*] because some effect issues from it or because it is applied. Thinking acts [*handelt*] insofar as it thinks. Such action [*Handeln*] is presumably the highest, because it concerns the relation of Being to man."[8] Before any action or doing, thinking "handles" the world; it stewards and protects it while enacting its openness. The stewardship-like "handling" actions the world before taking any action within it. Clearly such actions need to follow, not least because they are called for, but one should not forget that whether or how they will ensue, or what shapes they might take, all these re-soundings come to be released by way of the tonality "actioned" in the encounter. If art is committed, it is to this attuning, which fore-words the listening, the reception, and thus also the responses coming in its aftermath, in decisions, actions, or words. In this manner, art is engaged in fore-tuning the world, disclosing it and giving it momentum through the resonant holding of all soundings to silence. Any other demands or calls, whether for commitment or critique, however timely or just, may all too easily risk becoming ideological impositions.

Notes

1. www.claraiannotta.com.
2. https://www.swr.de/swrclassic/donaueschinger-musiktage/livestream-swr-symphonieorchester-donaueschinger-musiktage-14-10-2022-100.html.
3. Stiegler, *The Age of Disruption*, 18.
4. http://claraiannotta.com/works/orchestra/where-the-dark-earth-bends-2022/
5. https://www.radiofrance.fr/francemusique/podcasts/le-concert-du-soir/festival-musica-2022-orchestre-national-de-metz-grand-est-david-reiland-et-xavier-de-maistre-7006178

Here is the part of the French review of that concert, describing Iannotta's composition, its context, and the use of electronic sounds and recorded voice (English translation follows the French):

> Clara Iannotta avait entamé pour la saison 2019–2020 une résidence de deux ans à la Cité musicale de Metz vite rattrapée par la pandémie qui en a annulé beaucoup de concerts, et la compositrice est elle-même tombée malade d'un cancer qui a conduit à d'autres annulations. C'est cette expérience de la maladie et du traitement qu'elle impose qui a inspiré cette œuvre d'une vingtaine de minutes il n'est pas étonnant que cette œuvre éminemment autobiographique ajoute au grand orchestre qu'elle convoque une partie électronique. C'est cette dernière qui commence, comme il se doit, puis l'orchestre vient comme en écho de cette introduction. L'étrange paysage sonore des machines d'abord, son écho intérieur ensuite, non sans étrangeté (l'usage abondant de modes de jeu inhabituels et d'instruments supplémentaires, des harmonicas pour les cuivres par exemple, n'y est pas pour rien). / On pourrait trouver dans son écriture orchestrale une froideur qui ne serait que l'écho du monde électronique en les mains duquel son destin s'est trouvé un moment, mais ce mimétisme ne masque pas tout ce que cette situation a d'humain, comme si la conscience douloureuse trouvait sa paix en aspirant en elle tout cet attirail technique. Un court épisode, à la fin de la pièce, fait entendre par l'électronique des fragments de voix réduits à des phonèmes, premier retour à un contact avec le monde extérieur des humains. Une telle pièce, pleine d'une sourde émotion mais sans complaisance sur

ses moyens musicaux, ne peut que faire regretter les circonstances adverses qui ont réduit la résidence messine de Clara Iannotta à presque rien.

Clara Iannotta had begun a two-year residency at the Cité musicale de Metz for the 2019–2020 season, quickly overtaken by the pandemic which canceled many concerts, and the composer herself fell ill with cancer which led to further cancellations. It is this experience of the disease and the treatment it imposes that inspired this twenty-minute work. It is not surprising that this eminently autobiographical work adds an electronic part to the large orchestra that it calls for. It is the latter which begins the work, as it should, then the orchestra comes as an echo of the introduction. The strange soundscape of the machines first, then its inner echo, not without strangeness (the abundant use of unusual playing modes and additional instruments, harmonicas for the brass for example, is not there for nothing). / One could find in her orchestral writing a coldness which would only be the echo of the electronic world in whose hands her destiny one moment found itself, but this mimicry does not hide all the human aspects of this situation, as if a consciousness in pain found its peace by taking into itself all the technical paraphernalia. A short episode, at the end of the piece, makes heard through the electronics fragments of voices reduced to phonemes, the first return of contact with the outside world of humans. A piece like this, full of muted emotion but without complacency about its musical means, can only make us regret the adverse circumstances that reduced Clara Iannotta's Metz residence to almost nothing.

(https://www.resmusica.com/2022/09/21/darker-stems-de-clara-iannotta-en-ouverture-de-saison-a-larsenal-de-metz/).

    6. Heidegger, *Basic Writings*, 424.

    7. Drawing on *Daodejing*, *Zhuangzi*, and Chinese landscape painting (*shanshui*), Hui sketches out the *xuan* logic of "oppositional continuity," whereby re-cursivity operates as oppositional unity without separation or inclusion/exclusion. See *Art and Cosmotechnics*, 154–90.

    8. *Basic Writings*, 217.

References

Adrian, Dominique. "Darker Stems de Clara Iannotta en ouverture de saison à l'Arsenal de Metz." ResMusica. September 21, 2022. https://www.resmusica.

com/2022/09/21/darker-stems-de-clara-iannotta-en-ouverture-de-saison-a-larsenal-de-metz/.
Heidegger, Martin. *Basic Writings*. David Farrell Krell, ed. and intro. New York: HarperCollins Publishers, 1977, 1993.
Heidegger, Martin. *Besinnung (1938/39)*. *Gesamtausgabe* 66. Frankfurt am Main: Vittorio Klostermann, 1997.
"Home." Clara Iannotta: Composer, accessed January 25, 2023. http://www.clara-iannotta.com.
"Home." ResMusica, accessed January 25, 2023. http://www.resmusica.com.
Hui, Yuk. *Art and Cosmotechnics*. e-flux, 2021.
Stiegler, Bernard. *The Age of Disruption: Technology and Madness in Computational Capitalism*. Translated by Daniel Ross. Cambridge: Polity Press, 2019.

Contributors

Laura Chiesa is associate professor in the Department of Romance Languages and Literatures at the University at Buffalo. She is the author of *Space as Storyteller: Spatial Jumps in Architecture, Critical Theory, and Literature* (Northwestern University Press), she coedited the special issue of the journal *Formules* 14: *Formes urbaines de la création contemporaine*, and she has published articles and chapters on the avant-gardes, neo-avant-gardes, critical theory, and the interarts.

James Currie is a multi-arts practitioner and associate professor in the Department of Music at the University at Buffalo. Author amongst other things of *Music and the Politics of Negation*, his written work takes place at the intersection of music history, philosophy, politics, and creative writing.

Kim H. Kowalke is professor emeritus of musicology at the Eastman School of Music and the Turner professor emeritus in humanities at the University of Rochester. He is the author of many articles and four books on twentieth-century music and theater, including *Speak Low: The Letters of Kurt Weill and Lotte Lenya*, which inspired the Broadway musical *LoveMusik*, directed by Hal Prince, and *Lenya-Story*, which premiered in Vienna in 2017. He is a five-time winner of ASCAP's Deems Taylor Award for excellence in writing about music and two Irving Lowens Awards for the best articles on American music. Since Lotte Lenya's death in 1981, Kowalke has served as president of the Kurt Weill Foundation, founding both the Kurt Weill Edition and the Lotte Lenya Singing Competition. He has conducted dozens of musical theater productions and received the 2020 Erwin Piscator Honorary Award for his contributions to international musical theater.

Jacques Lezra is distinguished professor of English and Hispanic studies, University of California—Riverside, and 2022 Chaire Internationale de Philosophie Contemporaine, Université de Paris-8. His most recent books are *República salvaje: De la naturaleza de las cosas* (2020); *On the Nature of Marx's Things: Translation as Necrophilology* (2018); *Untranslating Machines: A Genealogy for the Ends of Global Thought* (2017); "Contra todos los fueros de la muerte": *El suceso cervantino* (2016); and *Wild Materialism: The Ethic of Terror and the Modern Republic* (2010; Spanish translation 2012; Chinese translation 2013). He is the coeditor of *Dictionary of Untranslatables: A Philosophical Lexicon* (2014). His translations include Paul de Man's *Visión y ceguera*; Etienne Balibar's *Universales*; and (forthcoming) Alain Badiou's *The One*.

Julie Beth Napolin is an associate professor of digital humanities at the New School. She is the author of *The Fact of Resonance: Modernist Acoustics and Narrative Form* (Fordham UP, 2020), shortlisted for the 2021 Memory Studies Associate First Book Award. She is a member of the editorial board of *Sound Studies: An Interdisciplinary Journal* and copresident of the William Faulkner Society. She has published a number of essays on sound, race, modernism, and listening.

Fernanda Negrete is the author of *The Aesthetic Clinic: Feminine Sublimation in Contemporary Writing, Psychoanalysis, and Art* (SUNY Press 2020), and of several essays engaging modern literature in French and Portuguese, contemporary art, and theory, published in various scholarly journals volumes. She is the editor of *Angelaki*'s special issue *Philosophy with Clarice Lispector* (28.2) and coeditor of *Beckett beyond Words*, a special issue of *Samuel Beckett Today/aujourd'hui* (30.2). She is associate professor of French at the University at Buffalo, where she also directs the Center for the Study for Psychoanalysis and Culture. For the Center she hosts *Penumbr(a)cast—The Other Scene*, a podcast on psychoanalysis today, and coedits the online open-access journal *Penumbr(a): A Journal of Psychoanalysis and Modernity* (penumbrajournal.org).

William Solomon is professor and chair of the English department at the University at Buffalo. He is the author of *Literature, Amusement and Technology in the Great Depression* (Cambridge, 2002) and *Slapstick Modernism* (University of Illinois, 2016), and editor of *The Cambridge Companion to American Literature of the 1930s* (Cambridge University Press, September 2018).

Peter Szendy is David Herlihy professor of humanities and comparative literature and musicological advisor for the book series published by the Paris Philharmony. His work has focused on the archaeology of listening (*Listen: A History of Our Ears* [2001], *All Ears: The Aesthetics of Espionage* [2007]), on the politics of reading (*Prophecies of Leviathan: Reading Past Melville* [2004], *Of Stigmatology: Punctuation as Experience* [2013], *Pouvoirs de la lecture: de Platon au livre électronique* [2022]), and on the economies or ecologies of visuality (*Apocalypse-Cinema: 2012 and Other Ends of the World* [2012], *The Supermarket of the Visible: Toward a General Economy of Images* [2017], *Pour une écologie des images* [2021]). He has curated the exhibition *The Supermarket of Images* at the museum of the Jeu de Paume in Paris (February–June 2020).

Krzysztof Ziarek is professor of comparative literature at the State University of New York at Buffalo. He is the author of *Inflected Language: Toward a Hermeneutics of Nearness* (SUNY), *The Historicity of Experience: Modernity, the Avant-Garde, and the Event* (Northwestern UP), *The Force of Art* (Stanford UP), and *Language after Heidegger* (Indiana UP). He coedited two collections of essays, *Future Crossings: Literature between Philosophy and Cultural Studies* (Northwestern UP) and *Adorno and Heidegger: Philosophical Questions* (Stanford UP). He has published essays on Heidegger and the intersections of poetry and philosophy and edited two special issues of the online journal *Humanities* (MDPI) devoted to "Encounters between Philosophy and Literature."

Index

abjection, 43–47
Abu Ghraib, 6–7, 51–52
academia: BDS and, 37–38; fascism and, 15–18; relevance of, 16–17; slowness of, 16–17
accounting, 35–39, 43–47, 170–71
acoustics, 12n8, 145–46, 154–55; of unfreedom, 155. *See also* sound, soundscape
action: communal, 16–17; inaction, 1–2, 22–23, 154; labor of, 18–19, 31; music and, 172; political, 16–22, 30–31, 172–73; shaming and, 21–22; temporality of, 18–21; thinking and, 16–18, 173–74
activism, 18–19, 159–60, 172. *See also* Black Lives Matter
address, 29–30, 47, 117–19, 124, 151–52, 154–59
Adorno, Theodor W., 23–25, 68–69, 73, 77–78
aesthete, 39–40
aesthetics: audience and, 23–29; class and, 40; communism and, 39–40; comparative, 4–6; digital technical systems and, 10–11; fascism and, 39–40; formalism and, 40–41; future and, 173–74; history and, 45–47; labor and, 19–20; Marxism and, 20–21; material conditions of, 25–28, 37, 40–41, 45–47; outrage and, 4–6, 35–47; piracy and (piraesthetics), 4–6, 35–37, 41–47; politics of, 4–6, 10–11, 18–32, 37–43, 45–47, 76–77, 172–74; as public pedagogy, 20–21; self-contemplation and, 39–40; sovereign function of, 44–46; torture and, 52; of translation, 45–47; of transmission, 127–30, 132–33, 140n51; world and, 38–39
affect: common, 40–41; detachment and, 87–88; history and, 35–37; language and, 154, 158; laughter and, 131; outrage and, 41; reflexive, 40; shaming and, 21–22; shock and, 21–22; theatricality and, 101–102
Afghanistan, 158
Althusser, Louis, 151–52
Anderson, Maxwell, 6–7, 67, 75–76
Anthropocene, 21–22
apartheid, 6–7, 37–38, 67, 76–77
appropriation, 35–39, 89–90, 99–100, 158–59
Arendt, Hannah, 16–17, 40–43; on *The Threepenny Opera*, 41–43
Armstrong, Louis, 35–37, 68
Atkinson, Brooks, 67–68
avant-garde: African American performance practice and, 4–6,

avant-garde *(continued)*
  25–26, 28–29; of interwar period, 4–6; music and, 4–6; obsolescence of, 41–43; politics and, 18, 20–21, 25–26, 28–29; theater and, 4–6. *See also* modernism

Bach, J. S., 31–32
ballad, 4–6, 35–36, 43–47, 75–76, 92–93, 102n3
Barber, Mattie, 167–68. *See also* RAGE Thormbones
Barthes, Roland, 153–54
BDS (Boycott, Divestment and Sanctions), 37–38
bebop, 4–6, 25–29
Becher, Johannes, 74
Beckert, Hans, 98–99
beggar (figure), 35–37, 44–45
Benjamin, Walter, 4–6, 39–41
Bentley, Eric, 73
Bergson, Henri, 22–23
Berio, Luciano, 4–6
Berlin Wall, 6–7, 70–71
Berliner Tageblatt (newspaper), 23
Berman, Russell, 41–43
Besinnung, 171–72
Best, Stephen, 150–51
big band music, 25–28. *See also* race, racism
Bigelow, Kathryn, *Zero Dark Thirty*, 6–7, 57–58
Billy the Kid, 94–95
Black Lives Matter, 9–10, 39, 143–46, 148, 150, 155–57, 159–61, 172–73
Black radical tradition, 2–3
Blake, Peter, 90–91
Bland, Sandra, 157
Blind Lemon Jefferson, 91–92
Blitzstein, Marc, 35–38, 43–44, 46–47, 68
Bloch, Ernst, 23–25

blues, 7–8, 89–93, 98–99, 101–102, 103n12, 104n15
body: aesthetics and, 40; mother's, 118–22, 131; music and, 120–22, 132–36; racialized, 143–44, 150–52, 156–58; sound and, 167–70; torture and, 52–56; witnessing and, 114–15
Bowie, David, 86–88, 101–102; "Alabama Song," 86–87; *Baal*, 86–87; *Images 1966-1967*, 86–87; *The Rise and Fall of Ziggy Stardust and the Spiders from Mars*, 7–8, 86–87
Brandeis, Louis D., 150–51
breath, breathing, 9–10, 46–47; police violence and, 143–44, 156–59
Brecht, Bertold, 4–8, 18, 20–26, 30–31, 35–39, 41–47, 70, 72, 75–76, 92–95, 98–99. *See also* Weill, Kurt
Broadway, 66–69, 72–73, 76, 96–98, 105n19
Brown, James, 101–102
Brown, Michael, 151
Buarque, Chico, 4–6, 43–47
Buffalo (New York), 10
Bull, Michael, 3
Burroughs, William, 86
Butler, Judith, 2–3

Cale, John, 97–98
Canetti, Elias, 23–25
Cantata, 6–7, 51
Capalbo, Carmine, 95–96
capitalism, 23–25, 40–41, 47; racial, 40–41
Carewe, Edwin, 123
Carmen (Bizet Georges), 77
Chakrabarty, Dipesh, 25
chanting, 9–10, 143–46, 150, 155–61
Chopin, Frédéric, 133–34; *Adieu waltz*, 134–36
choreography, 101–102, 153

Christgau, Robert, 85–86, 95–96
circulation, 10, 25–26, 35–37, 55–57
civil rights, 4–6, 18, 25, 29–30, 146
Clapton, Eric, 7–8, 90–91
Clash, The, 85–86
class, 12n8; aesthetics and, 40, 86–88; revolution and, 43–44
clearing, 152–53
Clurman, Harold, 73
Cocteau, Jean, 75
Cold War, 6–7, 35–37, 70–71
collage, 145
collectivity, 38–39, 47, 87–88, 93–94, 159
Collins, Judy, 47
commodity, commodification, 22, 27–28, 35–37; enslaved person as, 157–58
communality. See under action
communism, 39–40
composing, 6–7, 67, 74–75, 77–79, 88, 100–101, 126, 138n23, 168–69, 170, 174n5
Conference of Nyon, 43–44
confession, 6–7, 53
consumerism, 4–5, 38–39
contrafact, 27–29
Costello, Elvis, 7–8, 86
counterculture, 87–88
counterfactual, 37–38, 43–44
COVID-19 pandemic, 9–11, 143–50, 153, 158–61, 167–68, 172–73
creativity, 77, 115–18, 124–28, 138n18, 139n44
Currier, Kevin, 98
curtilage, 148–51, 160–61, 162n15
Cusick, Suzanne, 12n8, 52

d'Alessio, Carlos, 120–26, 131–33
Dallapiccola, Luigi, 59
dandy, 39–40
Darin, Bobby, 35–37, 68

Davis, Angela Y., 18–19
decadence, 22–23
defamiliarization. *See* distancing effect
Deleuze, Gilles, and Félix Guattari, 8–9, 116, 124–26, 132–34, 139n42
democracy, 1–3; fight for, 18–19; listening to, 10; as postulate, 11n3
desire: aesthetics and, 25; death and, 89; political labor and, 18–19; to rest, 23–25; romantic love and, 123. *See also* pleasure
dignity, 19–20, 26–27, 31–32
disarmament, 76–77
disorientation, 21–23
distancing effect (*Verfremdungseffekt*), 22–23, 25, 89–90
Dixon, Willie, 89–90
Dolphy, Eric, 88–89
Donaueschingen Musiktage, 167–68
Doors, The, 88–90
Dorfman, Ariel, 54
Dostoyevsky, Fyodor, 71
dramatic monologue, 99
dream, dreaming, 43–44, 128–33
Drew, David, 65–66
Du Bois, W. E. B., 152, 154
Duncan, Todd, 67
Duras, Marguerite: *L'amant*, 128–31, 133–36; *Le barrage contre le Pacifique*, 117–18, 123, 137nn13–14; Barrage Cycle, 113–14, 123, 131, 136n1, 137n14, 138n31, 139n37; *L'Éden Cinéma*, 8–9, 113–14, 117–26, 131–34; *India Song*, 117–18, 124; mother, 116–18, 120–23, 131–36; music and, 113–14, 120–26, 128–36, 136n2, 139n44; *Le ravissement de Lol V. Stein*, 114–16
Dylan, Bob, 7–8, 91–94

Edison, Thomas, 6–7
Eliot, T. S., 88

Ellington, Duke, 27–28
encounter, 92–93, 114–16, 118, 123–24, 132–35, 139n37, 145–46, 159, 173–74
engagement, 4–5, 17–18, 31, 76–79, 125–26, 173–74. *See also* withdrawal
Erlmann, Veit, 3
escapism, 16–17, 88
eugenics, 22–23
Evers, Megdar, 25
exhaustion, 6–7, 30–31
exploitation, 43–45, 89–90, 172
expressionism, 28, 67–68

Faithfull, Marianne, 7–8, 85–86
Famous Flames, 101–102
Fanon, Frantz, 151–52
fascism, fascistic, 1–6, 11n3, 15–16, 139n42; in academic thought, 15–18; aesthetics of, 39–40; decentering, 8–9; post-fascism, 2–3
"*fiat ars-pereat mundus*," 4–6, 39–41
film, 6–7, 49n10, 97; ad hoc filmography, 53; as frequentative, 59–61; mother and, 117–18, 137n12; music and, 59–60, 113–14, 137n11, 137n13, 138n22, 138n27; silent film, 116–17, 122–23; sound film, 123, 133–34; torture and, 57–59, 63n10
Fitzgerald, Ella, 35–37, 68
Florida v. Jardines, 148
Floyd, George, 144, 148, 155–59
Frankfurter Rundschau (newspaper), 68–69
Freud, Sigmund, 115–16, 127, 138n18, 155
Fugitive Slave Act, 150–51

Garner, Eric, 144, 148

Gay, John, *The Beggar's Opera*, 23–25, 35–37, 43–44
gender: masculinity, 62n4, 89–90, 95; race and, 89–90, 95, 157; sound studies and, 12n8
Gershwin, Ira, 72, 76
Gerswhin, George, 27–29
Gilbert, W. S., and Arthur Sullivan, 76
glam rock, 86, 88
Glimmerglass Opera Festival, 65–66
Godard, Jean-Luc, 6–7, 53, 59–60
Goldovsky, Boris, 78–79
Goll, Iwan, 6–7, 51
Gordy, Berry, 95–96
Great American Songbook, 27–28
Great Depression, 35–37
Green, Paul, 75
Groth, Helen, 3
Group Theatre, 72
Guantánamo, 6–7, 51–52
Günther, Renate, 117–18
Guthrie, Woody, 92–93

hailing, 151–52
Hale, Grace Elizabeth, 93
Hamilton, John, 52
Hammond, John, 91–92
Hart, Moss, 72, 75
Hartman, Saidiya, 157–58
Harvey, P. J., 7–8, 86
Hauptmann, Elizabeth, 46–47
hearing, 1–2; alternate positions of, 4–6, 28–29; COVID-19 pandemic and, 144–46, 149–50; listening and, 152–54; *Stimmung* and, 168–70; temporality of, 147; voice and, 168–69; whiteness and, 152. *See also* listening
Heidegger, Martin, 16–17, 38–39, 153, 169–71, 173–74; on *Besinnung*, 171–72

Hinton, Stephen, 7–8, 74, 85–86
history: aesthetics and, 45–46; as present, 17–18; moment and, 35–36, 45–47; nature and, 21–22, 25–26; outrage and, 35–37, 45–46
Hitchcock, Alfred, 6–7, 57–58
Hoffman, Abbie, 87–88
Hoffmann, E. T. A., 22
Hölderlin, Friedrich, 168–69
Hone, Penelope, 3
hope, 37–38, 152
Howlin' Wolf, 7–8, 89–90
Hughes, Langston, 75–76
Hui, Yuk, 169–70, 175n7
humanism, 19, 39–40

Iannotta, Clara, "darker stems," 168; "where the dark earth bends," 10–11, 167–68
identity, identification, 6–7, 71–73, 78–79, 158–59; artifice and, 87–88, 93–95, 99; collectivity and, 93–94; dis-identification, 99
illness, 168
immediacy, 11n3, 16–17, 22, 28, 37–38, 77
Impressions, 93
improvisation, 27–28, 95, 125–26, 171–72
insomnia, 18–19
intertextuality, 77, 81n31, 107n43
Iraq, 158
irony, 30–31, 42–43, 71–72, 75–76, 87–88, 99–101
Israel, 37–38. See also apartheid; BDS
itinerary, 4–7, 71–72

Jackson, Andrew, 21–22
Jackson, Janet, 145–46
James, Jesse, 94–95
January 6 insurrection, 1–3, 10

jazz, 27–28, 36–37, 57–58, 88–89
Jim Crow, 25, 89–90
Johansen, David, 85–86
Johnson, Robert, 91–93

Kaiser, Georg, 67–68, 75
Kaye, Lenny, 94–95
Kirchner, Ernst Ludwig, 28
Kotschenreuther, Hellmut, 70
Kowalke, Kim, 4–7, 96–97
Krieger, Robby, 89–90
Kundera, Milan, 6–7, 71–73
Kurt Weill Festival (Buffalo, NY), 2–3

labor, 4–6; aesthetics and, 19–20; desire for, 18–20; performance and, 31; race and, 26–27, 31
Lacan, Jacques, 8–9, 114–16, 127–28; on *fort-da* game, 115–17
Lang, Fritz, 98–99
language: being and, 38–39; *Besinnung* and, 171–72; boundaries and, 132; everyday, 154; fascism and, 39–40; poetry and, 22–23; real and, 113–14, 118–19, 123–32, 136n4; saying and, 169–70; silence and, 172; violence and, 158
Lee, Peggy, 100–101
Lee, Robert, 21–22
Lehár, Franz, 23–25
Leiber, Jerry, 100–101
Lenya, Lotte, 7–8, 35–37, 47, 68, 75, 78–79, 88–89, 93–94
Lerner, Alan Jay, 66, 75–76
lethargy, 22–23
Lewis, John, 88–89
Lewis, Joseph H., 6–7, 53–54
listening, 1–2; as casual, 159–60; as event, 134–35; *Besinnung* and, 171–72; failure in, 156; hearing and, 152–54; politics of, 9–10, 12n8, 145;

listening *(continued)*
　reading and, 8–9; resonance and, 172–73; subjectivity and, 146–50, 153–54, 158–59; temporality of, 147–48; threshold between inside and outside, 146, 148–49, 151–53, 158–61; torture and, 6–7; whiteness and, 152. *See also* hearing
Lorre, Peter, 98–99
Lost in the Stars (album), 7–8, 85–86
Lott, Eric, 89–91
Louie Ellison Orchestra, 101–102
Loewe, Frederick, 76
Lowe, Fisher, 98

Mamoulian, Rouben, 67
Manheim, Ralph, 37–38, 46–47
Mann, Thomas, 100–101
Manzarek, Ray, 88–89
Marcus, Greil, 98–100
Marcuse, Herbert, 19–20
Marx, Karl, 21–23
Marxism: aesthetics and, 20–21; disorientation and, 22–23, 25–29; theater and, 21; vanguardist, 41–43
Mathes, Carter, 155
Maurrant, Frank, 73–74
Mayfield, Curtis, 93
McClain, Elijah, 143–44, 148–52, 154–57
McCoy, Alfred, 52
media, mediascape, 3, 9–10, 22, 39, 74, 145
mediation, 3, 38, 97–98, 103n12, 114
melodrama, 21, 39–40
melody, 23, 44–47, 73–74, 121–22, 124, 168–70
meme, 39
memory, 54, 76–77, 117–18, 121–22, 145–46, 148–50, 155–58
metonymy, 6–7, 51, 54–57, 59–61
Metropolitan Opera, 78–79

Modern Language Association, 37–38
modernism: avant-garde and, 4–6; critique of spontaneous art, 41–43; expectations of artistic development, 65–66, 70–71, 96–97; global, 25, 28–29; hybridity and, 6–7; identity and, 71–72; Marxism and, 22–23; musical, 68–71; performance and, 88; politics and, 18, 20–21, 25–26, 28–29; populism and, 38, 47, 96–97; resonance and, 9–10; rock music and, 7–8, 88; subject and, 155; transhistorical practices of, 4–6, 8–9. *See also* avant-garde
modernist studies, 2–3, 6–7
monotony, 53, 60
Monterey Pop Festival, 87–88
morality, 18–19, 23–25, 40–41
Moreau, Jeanne, 124
Morrison, Jim, 7–8, 88–90
Morrison, Toni, 19, 153
mother (figure), 115–26, 131–35. *See also under* Duras, Marguerite
Mothers of Invention, 98
motif, 54, 77, 94–95, 101–102, 121–22
Mozart, Wolfgang Amadeus, 77
Murphet, Julian, 3
music, 1–2, 6–7; African American practices of self-fashioning in, 25–32; *Besinnung* and, 171–72; body as, 131; disenchantment and, 28–29; economics and, 27–28, 96–97; Eurocentrism and, 25, 28–29; film and, 59–60; genre and, 52; intoxication and, 23; mechanized reproduction of, 51, 55–56; memory and, 120; after modernism, 70–71; poietic thinking and, 10–11, 169–70; politics and, 4–7; race and, 25–29; real and, 113–14, 116, 118–19,

124–26, 132–33; self and, 168; silence and, 116–17, 172; text and, 72–73, 75–76; in theater, 120–23; temporality of, 8–9, 59–61, 113–16, 119–20, 122–26, 239n44; torture and, 6–7, 51–61; vocabulary and syntax of, 73–74, 121–22; voice of, 168–69; writing and, 132–33. *See also* sound, soundscape
Music Survey, 69–70
musical theater, 4–8, 72–74, 76–77; "concept musical," 6–7, 66, 72–73
musicology, 12n8, 52

Nancy, Jean-Luc, 2–3, 11n3, 139n45
narrativity, 9–10
Nash, Ogden, 75
National Liberation Front, 60
nature, 21–22, 25–26. *See also* history
Nazism, 4–6. *See also* fascism, fascistic
Neher, Caspar, 75–76
Nelson, Oliver, 101–102
neoliberalism, 40–41
New Music, 96–97
new wave, 86
New York Dolls, 86
New York Herald Tribune, 69–70
New York Times, 1–2, 67–68, 86–87, 144–45
Newman, Randy, 98–101
Nicolas, Bernard, 43–44
Nietzsche, Friedrich, 22–23
noir (film), 6–7, 53
nostalgia, 121–26

O'Neill, Eugene, 75
Obama, Barack, 37–38
Oklahoma! (Rodgers and Hammerstein), 67–68, 72–73
Olencki, Weston, 167–68. *See also* RAGE Thormbones

Oliveros, Pauline, 146, 148–49
opera, 4–8, 44–47, 67–68, 77, 96–97; as consolation, 23–25; as revolutionary, 4–6
ordeal, 6–7, 53, 56–61; oral (*orale Ordal*), 53–56
outrage, 4–6, 35–47

Paddison, Max, 98
Parker, Charlie, 27–28; and Dizzy Gillespie, *Anthropology*, 27–28
Parks, Van Dyke, 85–86
Paton, Alan, 6–7, 67
pedagogy, 20–21
"*pereat ars-fiat mundus*," 4–6, 39–41
Perelman, S. J., 75
performance, performativity: affect and, 87–88; audience and, 29–31, 47, 87–88; as confessional, 88; of impersonal passion, 154; as labor, 31; race and, 25–27, 29–31; technology and, 12n8. *See also* theater, theatricality
personhood, 150–51
Phalaris's bull, 52, 58. *See also* torture
Phéline, Marc, 120–21
philosophy: action and, 16–17, 20–21; Greek, 39–40; music and, 46–47; outrage and, 41–43; thinking and, 21–22, 170–71
phonography, 58–59, 61
photography, 58–60
pirate, piracy, pirating, 4–6, 35–39, 41–47
Plato, 16–17
pleasure, 19–20, 115–16; aesthetics of, 25, 39–47
Polanski, Roman, 6–7, 54–57
politics: academic thought and, 16–18; action and, 30–31; of aesthetic, 4–6, 10–11, 18–32, 37–43, 45–47, 76–77, 172–74; digital

politics *(continued)*
  technical systems and, 10–11; dignity and, 19–20; labor of, 18–19; of reconceptualization, 21–22; shaming and, 21–22; of theater, 23–29. *See also* aesthetics
populism, 38, 47, 96–97
Porgy and Bess (George Gerswhin), 77
Porter, Cole, 68–69
postpunk, 86
Pound, Ezra, 88
pragmatism, 18–19
primitivism, 89–90
privacy, 43–44, 88, 150–51
property: enslaved as, 150–51; intellectual, 43–44; private, 22
prosopopoeia, 56
psychoanalysis, 76–77, 115–16, 127–30, 154
Puccini, Giacomo, 65–66, 77–79

Quashie, Kevin, 150–51
quiet, quieting, 9–10, 144–47, 149–51

race, racism, 19, 47; apartheid and, 67; Black revolution, 25; commodity form and, 157–58; critique of popular music, 25–31; freedom and, 145–46, 155; gender and, 89–90, 157; identification and, 88–92; interracial interplay, 7–8, 90–91; labor and, 26–27; listening and, 152; minstrelsy and, 90–91, 93, 99–100; personhood and, 150–51; police violence and, 156–57, 159–61; quiet and, 150–51; racial capitalism, 40–41; racial violence, 9–10, 35–37, 144, 172–73; racialized subject, 151–52, 155–58; romantic racialism, 89–90; in rock music, 89–92, 95, 99–100; self-fashioning and, 25–32; in sound studies, 128n8; whiteness and, 152, 156–58
rage, 29–31. *See also* outrage
RAGE Thormbones, "zero said in a low voice," 10–11, 167–69
real, realism, 113–16; in American historical documentation, 155; culture and, 126–27; music and, 116, 124–26, 132–33; return of, 8–9, 127–32; structural void of, 118–19; time and, 124–27; word-hole (*mot-trou*), 113–15, 118–19, 123
recording, 6–7, 9–10, 29–31, 56, 88–89, 95, 101–102, 123, 144–50, 154–57, 159
Redding, Otis, 87–88
Redlich, Hans, 69–70
Reed, Lou, 7–8, 85–86, 95–98, 101–102
refrain (*ritournelle*), 8–9, 124–26, 139n42
Reik, Theodor, 53–55
relationality, 9–10, 152–54, 168–69
repetition, 8–9, 113–17, 135–36, 155, 157
reproduction, reproducibility, 6–9, 51, 54–56, 59. *See also* real, realism
resistance, 2–3, 37–39
resonance, 2–3, 13n14, 128–30; as atmospheric, 16; listening and, 10–11, 172–73; politics and, 172–74; of real, 8–9; relationality and, 9–10; sound and, 168–70
revolution, revolutionary, 4–6, 43–47
Rice, Elmer, 75
Ridgway, Stanard, 85–86
Riley, Denise, 154, 158
Rilke, Rainer Maria, 74
rock (music), 7–8, 85–88, 92–93, 95–99; artificiality and, 87–88,

93–95, 99–101; modernism and, 88; race and, 88–92, 95, 99–100; theatricality and, 101–102
Rockwell, John, 86–87, 95–96
Rodgers, Richard, and Oscar Hammerstein, 76
Rolling Stone, 93–94
Ross, Diana, 95–96
Ross, Lanny, 66
Rotolo, Suze, 92–93
Rundgren, Todd, 85–86
Russian formalism, 22–23

Schiller, Friedrich, 19–20, 33n10, 43–44
Schmitt, Carl, 43–44
Schubert, Franz, 54–55
Scott, Derrick Elliott Ollie, 156
self: embodiment and, 101–102; listening and, 148–49; making, 25–32, 36–37, 39–40, 88, 93, 155
senses, sensing, 39–40, 145–47, 149–50, 153–54, 171–72
September Songs (album), 7–8, 86
shame, shaming, 21–22, 30–31
Shepp, Archie, 43–44
shock, 21–22, 28, 40–41, 155
Show Boat, 72–73
show tune, 28–31. *See also* musical theater
silence, 1–2, 116–19, 167–74
Simone, Nina, 4–6, 18, 31–32, 45–47; "Mississippi Goddam," 25–26, 29–31; "Pirate Jenny," 25, 35–37, 41–44, 46–47
Sinatra, Frank, 35–37, 68
Sixteenth Street Baptist Church bombing (Birmingham, Alabama), 25
Smith, Patti, 7–8, 93–95
solidarity, 25

Sondheim, Stephen, 75
sound, soundscape, 1–6, 9–10; body and, 150–51, 167–70; everyday, 145–46; hearing and, 168–69; noise and, 167–68; politics and, 9–10, 148–49, 172; quieting and, 145–51; recording, 145–51, 154–55, 157; repetition and, 114–16; silence and, 169–74; technology and, 6–7, 12n8; thresholds of, 145–46, 48; time and, 147–48, 155–56; torture and, 6–7, 51–61; of urban life, 27–28, 144–47, 149–50. *See also* music
sovereignty, 44–47
space, spatiality, 117–20
Spedding, Chris, 85–86
Steeleye Span, 92–93
Steinbeck, John, 75
Stiegler, Bernard, 167–68
Stimmung, 10–11, 168–71
Sting, 7–8, 85–86
Stoller, Mike, 100–101
Stravinsky, Igor, 71–73
subject, subjectivity: aesthetic, 38; anti-modernist, 38; collective, 39, 47, 93–94; egoless, 7–8; embodied, 87–88; insurrectional, 43–44; intersubjectivity, 153–54; listening and, 146–49, 153–54, 158–59; lyric, 154; modernist, 155; political, 47; racialized, 151–52, 155–58; revolutionary, 47; repetition and, 115–16; subjectivation, 151–52
Swift Show, The, 66
SWR Symphonieorchester, 167–68
symposium, 4–6

Taruskin, Richard, 70–71
Taylor, Breonna, 151–52, 156–57
Taylor, James, 99
technology: calculative thought and, 170–71; digital, 167–68, 170–71,

technology *(continued)*
  173–74; reproducibility and, 55–56, 59; sound and, 12n8
tempo, 8–9, 16–17, 25–26, 46–47, 116, 119, 125–26
theater, theatricality: disorientation and, 22–23; music and, 118–23; politics and, 23–25, 76–77; as public pedagogy, 21; staging and, 117–20. *See also* performance, performativity
Theater de Lys, 92–93
thinking: action and, 16–18, 173–74; *Besinnung* and, 171–72; calculative thought, 170–72; as dwelling, 16–17, 168–70; poetic (poietic), 10–11, 169–71
Thomson, Virgil, 69–70
threshold: of home, 148; between inside and outside, 145–46, 148, 150–53, 160–61; of perception, 169–70; social and political, 148–50
Tik Tok, 39
timbre, 8–9, 116, 126, 139n45
time, temporality, 124–26; aesthetic and, 47, 173–74; after, 172–73; chronology and, 8–9, 145–48, 155–56; dignity and, 26–27, 31–32; fabrication of, 8–9; future and, 124–26, 173–74; listening and, 147–48; lyric, 154–55; music and, 59–61, 113–16, 119–20, 122–26, 139n44; past and, 17–18; politics and, 18–21, 31–32; real and, 114, 116, 126–27; slow, 16–17; theft of, 19; trauma and, 155; waltz and, 8–9, 116, 122–26; wasting, 18–19. *See also* refrain
Tolstoy, Leo, 71
tone, tonality, 168–71. See also *Stimmung*

torture, 51–61; extraction and, 53; interrogation and, 6–7; no-touch, 52–53
Toscano, Alberto, 2–3
transference, 127–28, 131–32
translation, 39–43, 45–46; untranslatability, 4–6, 46–47
trauma, 54, 127, 155–57
Traverso, Enzo, 2–3
Trump, Donald, 9–10, 15–16, 37–38, 152–53; connection to January 6 insurrection, 1–2
TSE, *Luxe*, 120–21

universalism, 39–40

Van Ronk, Dave, 91–92
Velvet Underground, 95–98
Verri, Pietro, 56–57, 60
Vietnam War, 146
Village Voice, 85–86, 95–96
Villiers de l'Isle-Adam, Auguste, 6–7, 58–59
Villon, François, 94–95
violence: nonviolence, 2–3; police, 143–44, 148, 150–52, 154–56, 159–61, 172; productive, 39; torture and, 53–54, 61; white supremacist, 1–2, 10
vitalism, 22–23
voice, 9–11, 54–55, 61, 154, 159–61, 167–71
Wagner, Richard, 23
Waits, Tom, 7–8, 85–86, 98–99
Walton, India, 10
waltz, 8–9, 116, 121–26, 128–36. See also *under* time, temporality
war, 22–23, 39–40, 52. *See also* torture
Warhol, Andy, 97–98
Warren, Samuel D., 150–51
Weill, Kurt, 6–8, 18, 20–23, 25–26; on accessibility, 96–97; biography,

74–75; collaborations, 75–76; death, 67–70; as revolutionary, 4–6; rock music and, 7–8, 85–88, 92–102; two Weills (identity and), 65–66, 68–74, 77–79, 96–97; on Wagner, 23; *Zeittheater* (topical theater), 76–77

Weill, Kurt, works by: *Die Bürgschaft*, 77–78; Cello Sonata, 73–74; *Down in the Valley*, 6–7, 67–68, 77–78; "The Drowned Girl," 86–87; *Fantasia, Passacaglia, und Hymnus*, 74; *The Firebrand of Florence*, 75; *Frauentanz*, 73–74; "The Future of Opera in America," 77; *Happy End*, 77–78; *Der Jasager*, 77–78; *Johnny Johnson*, 70; *Knickerbocker Holiday*, 101–102; *Lady in the Dark*, 6–7, 67–68, 72–73; "Let Things Be Like They Always Was," 73–74; "Lonely House," 73–74; *Lost in the Stars* (with Maxwell Anderson), 6–7, 67, 73–74, 77–78; *Love Life* (with Alan Jay Lerner), 6–7, 66, 77–78; "Mack the Knife," 36–37, 68, 85–86, 89–90, 94–95, 106n29, 106n32; "Moritat vom Mackie Messer," 73–74; "My Ship," 73–74; *The New Orpheus*, 6–7, 51; *One Touch of Venus*, 67–68; *Der Protagonist*, 67–68, 75; "Pirate Jenny" (*Seeräuber Jenny*), 25, 35–37, 43–47, 92–93; *The Rise and Fall of the City of Mahagonny* (Aufstieg und Fall der Stadt Mahagonny, with Brecht), 7–8, 70, 77, 86–87, 95–96; "The Saga of Jenny," 73–74; "Das schöne Kind," 73–74; "September Song," 101–102; *Seven Deadly Sins* (Die Sieben Todsünden, with Brecht), 70, 75–76; *Der Silbersee*, 77–78; "Die stille Stadt," 73–74; *Street Scene*, 73–78; String Quartet in B Minor, 73–74; *The Threepenny Opera* (Die Dreigroschenoper, with Brecht), 6–7, 23–25, 30–31, 35–37, 41–47, 68, 70, 72–73, 75–76, 92–93; *Tsar Has Himself Photographed*, 67–68; "What Good Would the Moon Be?," 73–74

Weinstein, Larry, 86
Wenner, Jann, 93–94
Wess, Richard, 35–37
Whisky A Go Go, 88–89
white supremacy, 1–2, 10
Who, The, 101–102
Wilder, Billy, 6–7, 57–58
Willet, John, 37–38, 46–47
withdrawal, 9–10, 16–18, 153–54. See also engagement
witnessing, 114–15, 149, 157
Wizard of Oz, 72–73
Woodstock, 87–88
Woolf, Virginia, 9–10, 147, 149–50
world, world-making, 20–21, 38–40
Woulk, Herman, 75
Wright, Martha, 66
writing, 17–18, 113–15, 124–27, 132–33, 135–36, 138n18, 139n37, 143–45

xuan (oppositional continuity), 169–70, 175n7

Zappa, Frank, 98

www.ingramcontent.com/pod-product-compliance
Lightning Source LLC
Chambersburg PA
CBHW022028240426
43667CB00042B/1406